THE FRENCH
FOREIGN LEGION

ALSO BY JEAN-DENIS G.G. LEPAGE
AND FROM McFARLAND

*German Military Vehicles of World War II:
An Illustrated Guide to Cars, Trucks, Half-Tracks,
Motorcycles, Amphibious Vehicles and Others* (2007)

The Fortifications of Paris: An Illustrated History (2006)

*Medieval Armies and Weapons in Western Europe:
An Illustrated History* (2005)

*Castles and Fortified Cities of Medieval Europe:
An Illustrated History* (2002)

The French Foreign Legion

An Illustrated History

Jean-Denis G.G. Lepage

McFarland & Company, Inc., Publishers
Jefferson, North Carolina, and London

Acknowledgments

The author wishes to thank Jeannette à Stuling, John Beauval, Anne Chauvel, Michèle Clermont Eltjo de Lang, Ben Marcato and Simone and Bernard Lepage.

LIBRARY OF CONGRESS CATALOGUING-IN-PUBLICATION DATA

Lepage, Jean-Denis.
The French Foreign Legion : an illustrated history /
Jean-Denis G.G. Lepage
p.   cm.
Includes bibliographical references and index.

ISBN-13: 978-0-7864-3239-4
softcover : 50# alkaline paper ∞

1. France. Armée. Légion étrangère—History. I. Title.
UA703.L5L46   2008   355.3'590944—dc22   2007044730

British Library cataloguing data are available

©2008 Jean-Denis G.G. Lepage. All rights reserved

No part of this book may be reproduced or transmitted in any form or by any means, electronic or mechanical, including photocopying or recording, or by any information storage and retrieval system, without permission in writing from the publisher.

Cover photographs: (foreground) Honor guard from the French army's 6th Battalion during Operation Desert Shield, 1992 (United States Army); (background) The Erg Chebbi sand dunes in the Sahara Desert (Shutterstock)

Manufactured in the United States of America

McFarland & Company, Inc., Publishers
Box 611, Jefferson, North Carolina 28640
www.mcfarlandpub.com

Contents

Acknowledgments iv
Introduction 1

1. CREATION AND EARLY CAMPAIGNS OF THE FRENCH FOREIGN LEGION, 1831–1852
   The Conquest of Algeria 5
   Spain, 1835–1838 16
   A New Legion in Algeria, 1835–1857 20

2. THE FOREIGN LEGION AT THE TIME OF NAPOLÉON III, 1852–1871
   Napoléon III 31
   Crimean War, 1854–1856 31
   Kabylia, 1857 37
   Italy, 1859 39
   Mexico, 1862–1867 44
   The Legion, 1867–1870 54
   The Franco-Prussian War, 1870 56

3. COLONIAL CONQUESTS, 1872–1914
   French Expansion 61
   The Legion in Algeria, 1872–1884 62
   Indochina, 1883–1918 67
   Dahomey and Sudan, 1892–1894 76
   Madagascar, 1895 80
   The Legion at the Turn of the 20th Century 85

4. THE FOREIGN LEGION IN WORLD WAR I, 1914–1918
   Historical Background 89
   Composition of the Foreign Legion in 1914 99
   First Battles, 1914–1915 102
   Battles of the RMLE, 1916–1918 104
   The Foreign Legion on Other World War I Fronts 111

5. THE FOREIGN LEGION BETWEEN WORLD WAR I AND
   WORLD WAR II, 1918–1939
   France in the Interwar Period 114
   Morocco 115
   The Legion at the Time of Lyautey 118
   The Rif War, 1925–1926 125
   Syria, 1925 130
   The Legion, 1926–1939 133

6. THE FOREIGN LEGION IN WORLD WAR II, 1939–1945
   The Foreign Legion in 1939 137
   The Norwegian Campaign 140
   The Battle of France 142
   The Foreign Legion and the Vichy Regime 144
   The 13th DBLE in East Africa 145
   Syria 146
   Bir Hakeim 147
   Tunisia 154
   Italy 159
   The End of the War 160
   French Indochina in World War II 163

7. THE FOREIGN LEGION IN INDOCHINA, 1945–1954
   Historical Background 164
   Warfare in Indochina 165
   The Foreign Legion in the Indochina War 170
   Main Legion Battles in Indochina 174
   De Lattre's Pacification 185
   Dien Bien Phu 187
   Aftermath 193

8. THE FOREIGN LEGION IN THE ALGERIAN WAR, 1954–1962
   Historical and Political Background 194
   Military Aspects of the Algerian War 197
   The Legion in Algeria 200
   The Suez Crisis, 1956 202
   The Battle of Algiers, 1957 204
   Operations in the Sahara 206
   The Battle of the Frontier, 1957–1958 207
   Challe's Plan 209
   The Putsch of April 1961 211
   The End of the Algerian War 216

9. THE FRENCH FOREIGN LEGION FROM 1962 UNTIL TODAY
   The Legion After the War in Algeria 218
   Legion Interventions 221
   The Legion Today 225

Appendix 1. Ranks and Units 235

Appendix 2. The Legion's Song:
"Le Boudin" 237

Appendix 3. The Code of Honor 240

Appendix 4. If You Want to Join the
French Foreign Legion 242

Bibliography 243

Index 245

Introduction

Today we are accustomed to national armies composed of drafted men who fight by national compulsion or volunteers whose main motives are to defend their fatherland's freedom or extend the power of their own country. In both cases a feeling of duty and patriotism plays a central role, but this has not always been so. Mercenaries were combatants who joined an army for pay. They were hired to reinforce a regular army or to replace citizens who had little or no inclination for war. The great advantage of hiring such warriors was, of course, that they were experienced soldiers accustomed to the highly dangerous business of war, effective professionals who knew how to use their weapons and how to fight in formation. A French minister even claimed that each foreign mercenary was worth three men: one more for the French army; one less for the enemy's force; and a Frenchman left home who worked and paid taxes. The great disadvantage of mercenaries was that they were always very expensive and they could prove unreliable at critical moments, refusing to fight—or even turning coat—if their pay fell into arrears.

Mercenaries were already used in ancient Egypt, and in Carthage, Greece and Rome, particularly those with special weapons and skills to obtain a greater diversity in effective long-range missile weapons such as Aegean bowmen and Balearic slingers. In the fourth and fifth centuries the declining Western Roman Empire made use of barbarian mercenary light cavalrymen to an ever-increasing degree to defend its borders. Mercenaries were also a common answer to obtaining soldiers during the Middle Ages. To palliate the shortage of combatants during the Hundred Years' War (1337–1453), mercenary activities reached an appalling peak, and this conflict produced the greatest concentration yet seen of professional troops raised with royal commissions.

The 15th and 16th centuries marked the heyday of mercenary service, and wars were fought largely by mercenary troops and all armies were of mixed nationalities. The 17th century saw the appearance of national armies, notably that of Sweden whose King Gustavus Adolphus based his military organization essentially on national conscription yet still supplemented by mercenary units. This example was soon followed by all the major European kingdoms (notably the French armies of Louis XIV).

In the 18th century use of mercenaries fell into disarray, and national armies became permanent institutions. Due to various factors such as the growing feelings of nationalism and patriotism, mercenaries were gradually replaced by national conscription as instituted by the French Revolution of 1789. Foreign soldiers in particular came to be associated with the French king's bodyguards, a practice which began in the ninth century, developed and remained a tradition until 1830. For centuries French kings had Scottish and Swiss mercenaries as private guardsmen. So when French king Louis-Philippe ordered the creation of the Légion étrangère in March 1831, it marked the continuation of a traditional ancient practice.

The French Foreign Legion is not a simple affair. It involves the often dramatic lives of men gathered from all over the world, their feelings, their outward foes and inner demons, their upholding of and withdrawal of loyalty to and from leaders and principles. Since 1831, the French Foreign Legion has attracted romantic youth, malcontents of all kind, adventurers, social drop-outs and petty criminals, but also many genuine professional soldiers, all of whom have contributed to the establishment of the Legion's own traditions, a remarkable fighting reputation and a justly deserved glory. From the earliest days as virtually an armed rabble of despised mercenaries, the Légion étrangère gradually established itself as a tough, thoroughly reliable and respected fighting force. Successive regimes and governments have used the Legion for their colonial ventures all over the world but also when France itself was in danger—notably in 1870, 1914 and 1940.

The Foreign Legion has attracted more than its fair share of myth and legend. Few military institutions have aroused more conflicting opinions than the fascinating French Légion étrangère, which has been extravagantly praised by its patriotic supporters and dismissed with hatred and contempt by its opponents. The very name French Foreign Legion has always carried some mysterious and exotic magic and elusive glamour. Its severe discipline is as celebrated as its reputation for self-sacrifice. The romantic aspect of the Legion has been the inspiration for countless novels, films and songs. Memoirs of former legionaries have aroused the interest of the public to an unusual degree. Rumors of brutality, ill treatment, callous neglect and suffering mingle with those of heroism, endurance, devotion to duty in adverse circumstances and glorious victories. Over the years fact and fiction have become hopelessly confused. This publicity and interest has always embarrassed the French authorities, who were never keen to advertise their corps of foreign mercenaries; their reluctance to answer any questions about the Legion or the legionaries has given impetus to lurid fiction, and many assumed that the French had much to hide. Where then is the truth, what is fact and what is fiction?

The men of the French Foreign Legion were, and still are today, *volunteers who freely join the Corps*, often but not necessarily to escape from their past. Motivations were and still are numerous, ranging from personal or family crises to upheaval in social or political situations. For many others, men who were or are unable to deal with the limitations of every day civilian life, the Legion might offer adventure and excitement—at least they expect that it will. Having broken with their past and their family, coming from all over the world, with different origins, languages, ideals, expectations and personal backgrounds, it would seem that legionaries had or still have nothing to share. But the Legion worked and still works as a true melting pot, quickly teaching its members, with harsh methods, to refuse to be mediocre and to reject easy solutions. But first and foremost the Legion made, and still makes of them men of action, brave in combat, eager for change, with a profound disdain for idleness and routine.

Having lost their roots, or a part of their past, legionaries had, and still have, no option but to give themselves entirely to the Corps, something most of them do without the slightest reluctance. This state of mind binds them together and explains their unrivalled cohesion, sealed with discipline, solidarity and respect for traditions. That accounts for the French Foreign Legion's motto: *Legio patria nostra* (the Legion, our Fatherland).

The author's aim, of course, is not to glorify, denigrate or judge individuals or a military institution but rather to narrate its complicated history and the equally complex forces that impelled this small professional army. This book thus strives simply to furnish the general reader with a straightforward and complete survey of the history of the French Foreign Legion. By outlining the Legion's vicissitudes, victorious campaigns, epic marches, heroic and sometimes hopeless stands, dirtiest battles and dramatic defeats, but also by briefly placing the Legion in the historical background of France, and by describing its development, organization, uniforms, equipment and weapons, the author hopes to dispel myths, and try to give—as far as this is possible—a true and accurate picture of what the French Foreign Legion has been from 1831 until today.

This book tells the legionnaires' story in chronological order; any other approach would prove illogical and confusing. It has no pretension to originality, and, of course, a survey of this kind is largely based upon the work of others, notably Georges Blond's *Histoire de la Légion étrangère* (Paris: Plon, 1981) and *Le Livre d'or de la Légion étrangère* by Jean Brunon, Georges Manue and Pierre Carles (Paris: Charles-Lavauzelles, 1981). My debts to many other historians of the Legion (notably Paul Bonnecarrère, Pierre Sergent, Edgar O'Ballance, Martin Woodrow and several others) will be obvious to those who know their works.

As for the illustrations, they were made by the author. Their inspirations are numerous ranging from Lavauzelles's *Livre d'Or* to the excellent *Gazette des Uniformes*, the official Legion magazine *Képi Blanc*, and the well-known Osprey publications.

Jean-Denis Gilbert Georges Lepage,
Groningen, The Netherlands

1

Creation and Early Campaigns of the French Foreign Legion, 1831–1852

The Conquest of Algeria

French expansion in the early 19th century

At the beginning of the 19th century France was starting to build a colonial empire. By that time, the most important developments took place in North Africa, for centuries a pirate lair from which Arab privateers made the western Mediterranean Sea a very unsafe area for European shipping.

At the time of King Charles X (reign from 1824 to 1830) the French connection with Algeria was established. In an attempt to increase his prestige, and to plunder the Dey's wealth, the king decided to invade Algeria. The pretext was found when the Dey of Algiers insulted and struck the French consul with his fan. An apology was not forthcoming, the port of Algiers was blockaded by the French navy, and soon an expeditionary force was mustered. On June 14, 1830, some 37,000 French soldiers commanded by General de Bourmont landed at Sidi-Ferruch (west of Algiers). The French conquest of North Africa began. Charles X's regime was overthrown by the July 1830 revolution at the precise moment when the expeditionary force was landing, and the conquest was continued by his successor, King Louis-Philippe (reign from 1830 to 1848). The coastal cities of Algiers, Oran, Bône and Bougie were taken in the summer of 1830. The Dey was overthrown and his immense wealth was seized—or better said looted—by the top military authority, the French crown, various speculators and more particularly by the private company which had shipped the armed forces over the Mediterranean Sea. After this successful and fruitful beginning the campaign bogged down, and the number of casualties in this mismanaged venture caused much criticism in France. Louis-Philippe's policy toward Algeria was undefined. At first the invasion had no long-term objective, only the pillaging of the Dey's territory. A decision to occupy North Africa permanently still lay in the future, and for the time being there was no longer a proper local ruler to negotiate with, only independent tribes of raiders to defeat. Military operations were therefore reduced to short-term local battles and costly skirmishes.

In 1834 a Gouvernement général des Possessions françaises de l'Afrique du Nord (General Government of French Possessions in Northern Africa) was established at Algiers. This state of affairs was confirmed by treaty in 1837 with local Arab rulers, among whom emerged the emir of Mascara, Abd-El-Kader (1808–1883), who became the dominant native leader of resistance to the French. Kader was young, clever, brave, ambitious and unscrupulous; having an attractive personality, and being a good orator and a skilled man-of-war, he developed into an able commander who rallied many tribes under his leadership. The general situation was confused and the French position became increasingly insecure, until Constantine was captured by General Valée. Soon French troops marched in pursuit of Abd-El-Kader, whose *smala* (retinue) they captured. After another defeat at the battle of Isly, Abd-El-Kader took refuge with the sultan of Morocco. In 1839 General Bugeaud was placed at the head of the French army in Algeria. Kader proved a formidable opponent for the French but, in the long run his Algerian insurgency proved to be a fragile coalition of tribes and subchiefs, which a clever European commander might split with a combination of force and incentives. In subsequent operations, the French pressed on with the conquest, and Abd-El-Kader surrendered in 1847.

In 1848, after the fall of King Louis-Philippe, the Second Republic (1848–1852) continued the conquest and favored a policy of indirect rule, appointing *caïds* (local chiefs) willing to do their bidding, although as the century progressed the French tightened their administrative grip on their colonial possession. This was a policy forced on the invaders by necessity as they seldom had the capacity to occupy, police and administer the entire country. Although this policy was applied inconsistently and with little effect in the mountainous heartland, administrators worked to organize Algeria into three *départements* (Oran, Algiers and Constantine) similar to the administrative districts of France, inaugurating a permanent establishment. Later, as the conquest was achieved, the huge and largely unpopulated southern desert was administratively named Sahara français (French Sahara).

Under General Bugeaud the pacification proceeded with vigor. After many vicissitudes, what looked like a conquest was achieved in 1857. Algeria remained an integral part of France until July 3, 1962. In 1850 a Ministry for Algerian Affairs was created and soon towns were founded or enlarged, and villages, rural settlements, ranches and agricultural demesnes appeared in large numbers. Railways, roads, bridges and other public and administrative edifices were built for a growing European population. Algeria, with its pleasant climate, its exotic landscapes and its virgin lands, was seen by many poor but audacious and enterprising settlers as a place where they could start a new and better life—something comparable perhaps to the attraction exercised by the Far West for Americans. Some Frenchmen volunteered to settle in Algeria; others were criminals and political opponents condemned to exile. By 1860 Algeria was populated by about 200,000 European inhabitants.

French colonial army

The conquest of Algeria gave the French army an opportunity for exotic adventures, increased responsibilities, pride and glory. It opened up a field for eventual colonization and a base for the later development of a vast new continental territory, but its immediate significance was mainly military. It gave rise to the creation of a virtually separate African colonial army. This was instigated by General Christophe Louis Lamoricière (1806–1865) who fought in Algeria

1. Creation and Early Campaigns of the French Foreign Legion, 1831–1852　　　7

Zouave, c. 1859. Zouaves wore a typical uniform including a chechia (soft red hat), a short dark blue jacket decorated with red or yellow "arabesques" (curved patterns), red baggy Turkish trousers and white gaiters covering marching boots. Equipment and weapons were the same as those of the ordinary French infantry.

Spahi. The Spahis were light cavalrymen recruited from the native population of the French North African colony of Algeria.

and was minister of war in 1848. Special colonial troops were created, and North Africa was for a long time to be the main theater in which French troops could gain direct combat experience. Colonial warfare was highly specialized and difficult for white Europeans. It demanded modifications in uniforms and equipment, and the adoption of logistics and tactics necessarily very different from those required by the army of the metropolis. It also demanded a new spirit, new attitudes and new behaviors. An efficient colonial army had to show endurance in mountain, hot tropical and desert climates. It had therefore to be ready to accept exceptional hardships, be self-supporting, be able to improvise, and learn the practice of antiguerrilla tactics. New units, some quite picturesque, were created for colonial purposes.

Zouaves were light infantrymen formed in 1831 by General Bertrand Clausel as part of the colonial troops; they were originally recruited from a Berber tribe from the Jurjura Mountains called *Zwawa* (whence their name), and soon they were joined by volunteers from the European population of North Africa. They wore an exotic Moorish uniform, which reintroduced an Arab motif into Western military dress. *Chasseurs d'Afrique* were light cavalry squadrons. Although French white settlers opposed any arming of the Arabs (for obvious security reasons), native units were also raised. *Tirailleurs* were infantry riflemen raised from among natives from Algeria, from Black Africa (mostly Senegal), and (later) from Madagascar and Indochina. *Spahis* were light horsemen created in 1831, and they were recruited from the native populations of North Africa, particularly Algeria. Later, Moroccan *goumiers* (native infantry auxiliaries) were raised.

There gradually developed a French Armée de terre (ground force) divided into two distinct main branches with different terms of enlistment, different military units and different tours of duty. The Armée métropolitaine ("Metro") was the metropolitan army for home defense provided by conscripted French national draftees. The Armée coloniale ("Colo") was the colonial army for oversea duties recruited from volunteers and draftees; when France was in danger (e.g., in 1870, 1914 and 1940), the colonial army was also widely engaged in the defense of the homeland.

In addition the Marine nationale (navy) developed its own Infanterie de marine (navy infantry created in 1831), a ground force comprising *bigors* (Navy artillerymen) and *marsouins* (Marines).

As early as 1833, the army played a central role in administering the new territories. Bureaux arabes (Arabian Offices), later Bureaux des Affaires indigènes (Indigenous Affairs Offices), were created, headed by Arab-speaking officers specially trained to deal with the local population and given a wide scope of function. The first role of the colonial army was, of course, police, peacekeeping and occupation duties. But, as the French intended to settle in Algeria permanently, and as they saw themselves as superior cultured people bringing their civilization to "primitive and backward" natives, the army was also to play a role in the development of the economy, public health, education, public works and the establishment of civilian and administrative institutions.

Creation of the French Foreign Legion

Another corps was created for supporting the French colonial expansion: the Foreign Legion.

The direct ancestor of the French Foreign Legion was a regiment of foreign volunteers raised by Napoléon during the "Hundred Days." After the fall of the emperor in 1815, this unit—mostly composed of German and Swiss volunteers—remained in existence under the restored Bourbon king Louis XVIII. It became known as Légion royale étrangère, then designated Régiment Hohenlohe after its commanding officer, Col-

Grenadier, Regiment Hohenlohe, 1816. The shako and the tunic were dark blue. The trousers were red. The rucksack straps and the large cross strap holding the bayonet scabbard and ammunition pouch were white. The weapon was a flintlock musket with bayonet.

onel-Prince von Hohenlohe-Bartenstein. The existence of this well-paid (and thus loyal to the king) mercenary force was eyed with suspicion by a large section of French opinion and perceived by the opposition as a serious threat; indeed, in case of political trouble the foreign mercenaries could be used to crush a popular uprising. Under pressure from the opposition the Regiment Hohenlohe was reluctantly disbanded by Louis-Philippe on January 5, 1831.

The idea of creating a "Foreign Legion" was conceived by the old Napoleonic veteran, Marshal and Duke of Dalmatia Nicolas-Jean-de-Dieu Soult (1769–1851) who, by that time, held the post of minister of war in the newly established July Monarchy. Soult probably had two main reasons for raising such a military force.

First there were a certain number of foreign ex-soldiers in France such as the Germans of the Régiment Hohenlohe, just disbanded in January 1831. There were also countless survivors of the Napoleonic Wars, including Poles, Swedes, Germans, Hungarians and many other nationalities, many of whom were embittered military professionals and mercenaries. Many of these discharged soldiers had remained passionately faithful to the defeated emperor Napoléon I. Many were often in needy circumstances, and open to suggestion. Hot-headed and enthusiastic ex-servicemen were trained to the use of arms, and should they become tools of the politically ambitious or malcontented they would present a distinct threat to the new regime, not yet firmly established. The revolution of 1830 had also left many activists idle, openly looking for troubles and ready to take part in any disturbance. To these must be added the growing number of discontented workers and unemployed proletariat created by the development of industrialization. It was feared that those "unreliable people" could be ready for armed political troubles against the regime.

Second, the conquest of Algeria was unpopular among the French population. After a successful start in 1830, the operation became bogged down in indecisive and costly skirmishes. The Algerian venture was viewed with mixed feelings in a politically divided France. Politicians and common people were not unanimously in favor of it, and many thought the campaign should be terminated at once. The formation of a foreign unit seemed therefore to be an ideal method of killing two birds with one stone: it offered the double advantage of removing potentially dangerous political elements from France and sending them overseas. There they could provide a convenient mercenary cannon fodder: if their casualties were heavy or their conditions not best, there would be no embarrassing reaction and agitation in France on behalf of such foreign legionaries. Clearly, it was both expedient and desirable to remove these potential dangers as far away from France as possible. On March 10, 1831, King Louis-Philippe signed an ordinance permitting the enlistment of foreigners and natives both inside France and in the overseas territories for service outside France. The Légion étrangère was born.

Early organization of the Legion

From the start the Foreign Legion was designed to constitute a small professional corps specifically for oversea duties. Algeria was not specifically mentioned but there was no doubt as to the meaning of the phrase "service outside France." The Legion was to be part of the French army and placed under control of the war minister. Candidates had to be European volunteers, aged between 18 and 40. They enlisted for at least three years, and at most five years. They had to be in good health and at least 1.50 m (five feet) tall. They should present a certificate of birth, and a certificate of good conduct. Married men were not allowed to join without special authorization. Apart from good health and duration of enlistment, all these conditions were not mandatory. In the anx-

Legion infantryman about 1831. When the Legion was created in 1831 it was uniformed like the rest of the French infantry. This uniform was less than practical especially for troops destined to fight in hot regions such as North Africa. Little or no thought was given to adapting the uniform to military necessities or to suitability for wear in battle. It was smart and eye-catching for parade but neither comfortable nor safe to wear on the battlefield.

iety to quickly get dubious, restless characters out of the country no questions were asked as to nationality, previous record, background or history. In fact recruits were not obliged to reveal their real identity. The name and particulars given by the recruits were accepted at face value and many gave false names, or *noms de guerre* (pseudonyms), for understandable reasons. Thus the practice began—and the tradition started—of "asking no questions." Recruits were protected by anonymity regarding their past as long as they served in the Legion.

During the spring of 1831, recruiting started and a large number of unemployed mercenaries and troublesome undesirables, including French thieves and criminals wanted by the police, were enlisted into the new body, so a special decree was hastily issued forbidding Frenchmen to enlist. Many did, however, simply by declaring themselves to be either French-speaking Swiss or Belgian Walloons.

The early Legion was organized into a regiment divided into seven battalions of the same size and composition as those of the regular French infantry of line; each battalion was composed of eight companies of 112 legionaries each. At the start the Foreign Legion was rather inefficient. Because the conditions of enlistment were relaxed, it attracted would-be colonists (who were determined to desert as soon as they arrived in Algeria), criminals and petty thieves on the run, romantic or ruthless adventurers, drunkards, social drop-outs and drifters of all kind. Another weakness was the fact that the seven battalions were divided according to nationalities or composed of men who spoke a common language. They included the 1st Battalion (Swiss and Hohenlohe German veterans); the 2nd and 3rd Battalions (Swiss and German volunteers); the 4th Battalion (Spaniards); the 5th Battalion (mixed but mainly Sardinians and Italians); the 6th Battalion (Belgians and Dutch); and the 7th Battalion (Poles). This arrangement created many problems concerning language and particularly discipline and cohesion as quarrels and prejudices of their native countries were carried on by the legionaries inside the Corps.

The first depot was established at Langres (*département* of Haute-Marne) in 1831, and the first commanding officer of the Legion was Chief of Battalion (Major) Sicco, a veteran of the Napoleonic Wars. Other depots were soon formed at Bar-le-Duc (Marne) for nationals from Central Europe, Auxerre (Yonne) for Italians and Sardinians, Agen (Lot-et-Garonne) for Spaniards, and Chaumont (Haute-Marne) for Belgians and Dutch. During 1831 and 1832, in several batches the Legion was shipped to Algeria, where the French army held a narrow coastal strip. The confusion was total and the legionaries were dumped on the quays of Algiers without proper leadership and equipment until a tough Swiss veteran, Colonel Stoffel, was appointed to lead them. Christoph Anton von Stoffel, born on April 19, 1780, served since 1807 in the French army and had taken part to the conquest of Algeria in 1831. It was not an easy task for the colonel and his few cadres of officers and NCOs to tame this heterogeneous rabble. At first, the despised Legion was not considered reliable and trained enough to be engaged as a combat force. The military authorities were not only unimpressed but also frankly disgusted and sceptical of their military value. The language question made control difficult as officers and NCOs were frequently unable to make their orders understood and a pattern of chaos and disorder was the rule rather than the exception. Drink added to the confusion, causing insubordination, quarrels and brawls. Strong detachments of military police had to deal with those who were drunk and insubordinate among the motley groups of legionaries arriving in Algeria. Colonel Stoffel energetically tackled this wild tangle and, by the end of 1831, had brought it to a semblance of order. The 4th Spanish battalion was shipped off to Oran, the Dutch and Belgian

6th battalion was deployed to Bône, and the remainder of the Legion units were posted in camps and bivouacs in and around Algiers. Discipline, however, remained a problem and, in the early years, the Foreign Legion gained a reputation for being a brawling, undisciplined corps. Another problem which caused much worry was the high desertion rate. The native Algerians offered rewards to tempt Europeans to desert and go over and fight for them against the French. There were at times several small European units of mercenaries and ex–Legion men fighting against the French. For a while the military authorities had good reasons to view the Legion doubtfully and they hesitated to commit them to battle. Before handling muskets and bayonets, the legionaries were given shovels and picks and treated as a pioneer corps employed in the construction of military posts, entrenched positions, blockhouses and other defenses against the Algerian rebels. They also sank wells and built roads—notably between Douala and Boufarik. The men worked 10 hours a day in the blazing sun under the supervision of NCOs who resorted to harsh disciplinary methods, using the point of their boots and musket butts to tame them. A famous personality serving in the Legion in the late 1830s was Alexandre-Joseph Count Colonna-Walewski (1810–1858), the son of Emperor Napoléon I and his mistress Marie Walewski.

Gradually the initial confusion was sorted out, and, under Colonel Stoffel's firm leadership, the Legion took form. Training was carried out, the battalions were brought up to a reasonable pitch of efficiency and then engaged as a fighting force.

First campaigns in Algeria

In the period 1832–1833, the French held only a narrow coastal strip in Algeria, the fringes of which were frequently attacked by uncontrolled local Arab raiders. Military operations consisted of escort and protection duties and searches of the raiders' bases in attempting to destroy them.

The Legion had its baptism of fire on April 27, 1832, when the Swiss and German 3rd Battalion distinguished themselves in stiff fighting by successfully capturing the outpost of Maison Carrée and resisting a fierce counterattack. For the remainder of the year 1832 the Legion units continued to be employed in constructing defensive works.

In June 1832 Colonel Stoffel—who had worked wonders in transforming the Legion into a fighting force—was replaced by Colonel Combe. Combe was soon followed by Colonel Bernelle, a good organizer and a strict disciplinarian who continued the taming and training of the rough legionaries. Gradually the Legion took its place in the fighting line and began to be employed on patrols, sorties and escort missions. Other engagements followed in 1832 at Blida, Bône and Sidi-Chabal, in which the legionaries figured creditably. The port of Arzew and the city of Mostaganem were seized in June and July 1833 by a force including units of the 4th Spanish and 5th Italian battalions. The Legion learned fast to wage a type of warfare they knew little about. As the Legion improved its performance, it was allowed to form elite companies of grenadiers and *voltigeurs* (skirmishers), and the Corps was granted its first flag in the name of the king in August 1834: this bore the legend *Le Roi des Français à la Légion étrangère* (The King of the French to the Foreign Legion).

In 1834–1835, offensive military operations of any importance were not launched as the French attempted to negotiate. Abd-El-Kader temporarily acknowledged their supremacy, and General Desmichels signed a treaty of peace and friendship with the young emir. By that time the Legion was, again, employed in construction works with only occasional sorties. The 4th Spanish Battalion was disbanded and many volunteers went back to Spain to fight in the Carlist civil war.

1. Creation and Early Campaigns of the French Foreign Legion, 1831–1852 15

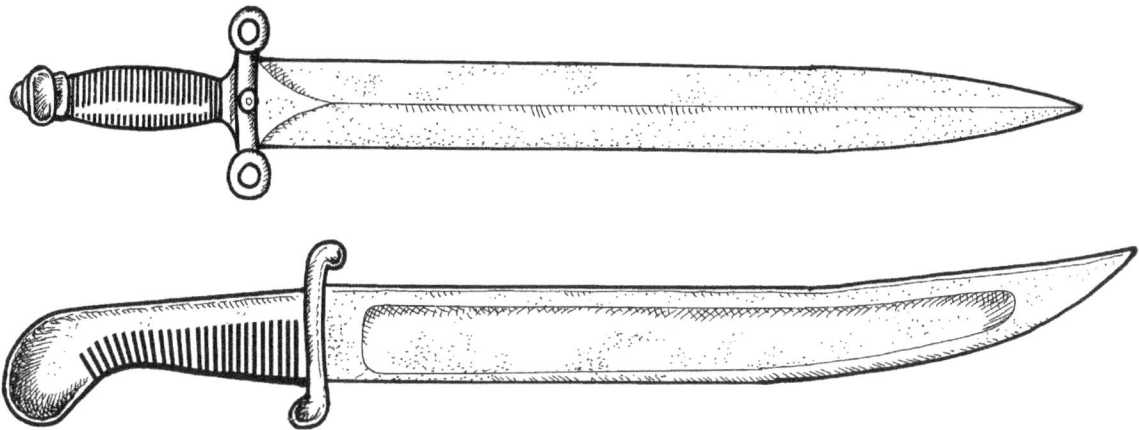

Infantry swords, c. 1835. Top: Neoclassic form derived from the Roman gladius. Bottom: Falchion shape. Both swords, about 60 cm in length, were popularly named **coupe-choux** *("cabbage cutter") by the troops.*

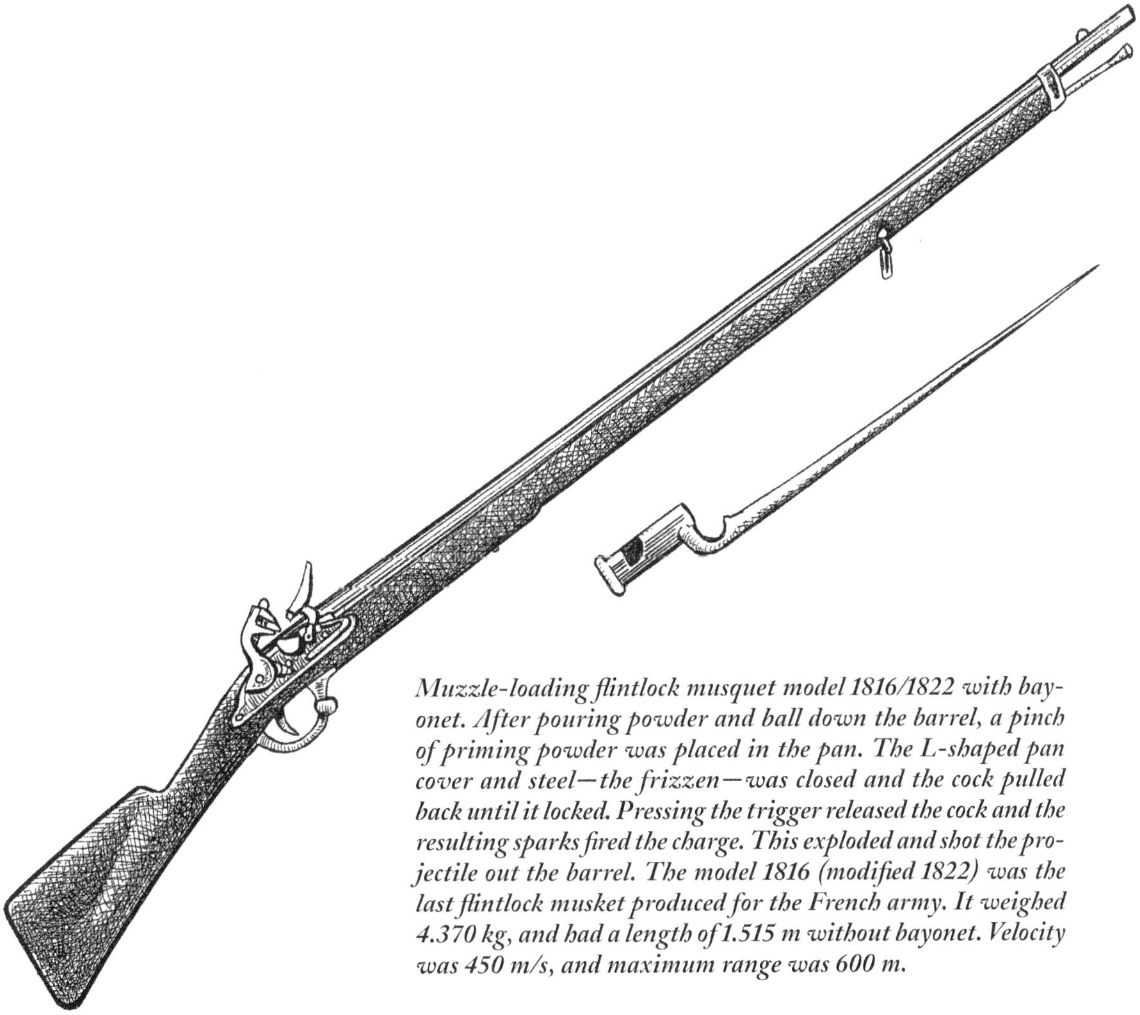

Muzzle-loading flintlock musket model 1816/1822 with bayonet. After pouring powder and ball down the barrel, a pinch of priming powder was placed in the pan. The L-shaped pan cover and steel—the frizzen—was closed and the cock pulled back until it locked. Pressing the trigger released the cock and the resulting sparks fired the charge. This exploded and shot the projectile out the barrel. The model 1816 (modified 1822) was the last flintlock musket produced for the French army. It weighed 4.370 kg, and had a length of 1.515 m without bayonet. Velocity was 450 m/s, and maximum range was 600 m.

Peace in Algeria was, however, fragile. Abd-El-Kader had profited from the truce to consolidate his own political power, and to increase his military force by engaging European mercenary technicians to set up his own arsenals. In 1835 he felt strong enough to attack the French in the region of Tlemcen. He took the towns of Miliana and Medea, and a composite French force was assembled to stop him, in which the Legion was represented by several units. On June 26, 1835, a supply column escorted by companies of the 5th Italian Battalion and the 7th Polish Battalion was ambushed at the Moulay Ishmael Pass. The battalions repulsed the main attack and retreated in the direction of Oran; two days later the column was ambushed again in a salt marsh near La Macta. The Arabs managed to break the column into several groups, and, in confused fighting, separated units were butchered or fled in panic. Fortunately the Polish Legion battalion, headed by their chief Horain, held firm. They contained some 10,000 Berber cavalrymen, thus helping to cover the eventual confused retreat. The battles of Moulay Ishmael and Mecta were disasters for the French, both in fact and in prestige, but they put the Legion on the map. The legionaries had fought with distinction—two officers had been killed and the number of casualties among the soldiers was high. In spite of a still high rate of desertion (some of whom took service in Kader's force), the Legion had proved that it could fight as well as brawl.

Early Legion headgear. The less than practical 1831 shako was soon replaced by a number of homemade hats, generally peaked caps made by stiffening the blue **bonnet de police** *(forage cap) issued as off-duty wear. Soon a properly made cap was issued, named* **casquette d'Afrique**.

Spain, 1835–1838

Historical background

In 1829 the heirless King Ferdinand VII married Princess Maria-Christina in the hope that she would bear him a son to succeed him. Unfortunately she gave birth to a daughter named Isabella. Maria-Christina persuaded the king to abolish the existing law, which prohibited female succession, in order that Isabella could succeed him. In this way Ferdinand excluded his brother, Don Carlos, from the throne. Carlos, denying the legality of his brother's action, proclaimed himself king of Spain right after Ferdinand's death in 1833. Abroad, the autocratic monarchs of Austria, Prussia and Russia gave him moral support by refusing

Casquette d'Afrique. *Right: with black oilcloth cover. Left: with white neck cloth. The African cap later evolved into the Foreign Legion képi, the typical French flat-topped cap with straight peak.*

to recognize the regency of the widow Maria-Christina, who was supported by Great Britain and France.

For six years civil war raged intermittently. The conflict ended in 1839 when Don Carlos renounced the throne and Maria-Christina reigned as regent on behalf of her daughter Isabella II until 1840.

When the Carlist crisis broke out in 1833, France was once one among the European monarchies, and Louis-Philippe—who had a commitment to support Maria-Christana and her daughter Isabella—could openly intervene. The king decided to send a contingent, and he and his military advisers selected the Foreign Legion.

The Legion in Spain

King Louis-Philippe knew that sending French national draftees in the Spanish venture would be unpopular, and he came cynically to the conclusion that the Foreign Legion rabble was the most easily spared troop for that unrewarding job. The agreement with Regent-Queen Maria-Christina was signed in January 1835. The legionaries and their officers were not consulted on the matter. In the following spring, Colonel Bernelle was officially informed that the Foreign Legion was to be handed over in its entirety to Maria-Christina's force (named *Christinos*) to fight against the supporters of Don Carlos (named Carlists). Before leaving, Colonel Bernelle made an important reform. The Legion was reorganized: the division into national battalions was abandoned, and all nationalities merged within the units, giving the corps more coherence and homogeneity.

The Legion (123 officers and 4,021 men strong, less those who died of disease on the transports) arrived at Tarragona on August 19, 1835. The Legion was enthusiastically received as it paraded through the streets of Tarragona; its bearing, marching and discipline impressed observers, which shows that it had much improved since its birth only four years earlier. Colonel Bernelle was immediately granted the sonorous rank of Marshal of the Royal Armies of Her Majesty Isabella II. But Her Majesty's armies were not an impressive lot. The ill-disciplined and badly trained Christinos force lacked everything. The campaign did not begin under favorable auspices as inadequate precautions had been taken to see that the Legion would be properly supplied. As for the Carlist opponents (about 18,000 strong), they were equally ill-disciplined and badly trained, impecunious, ragged and deprived of military equipment, but, owing to wide popular support, they could live off the country as guerrilla fighters. The Spaniards called the French legionaries *Argelinos* ("Algerians"), who were rapidly moved to the scene of operations. The Carlist War soon proved to be as brutal a conflict as any civil war in history, as the Spaniards of both camps made a habit of shooting wounded and prisoners.

During the winter of 1835-1836, Marshal/Colonel Bernelle organized the Foreign Legion into a small autonomous army by adding to his infantry battalions three squadrons of Polish mounted lancers, a mobile battery of howitzer, an engineering company and a medical company. This force was split up, and dispersed units engaged in guerrilla warfare and patrol work against Carlists in Catalonia for some months. General and long-term strategy was practically nonexistent and reduced to a rough and vague plan. The intention was that the Christinos forces should advance northward and defeat the Carlists against the wall of the Pyrenees Mountains. A general move northward was made with the Legion (actually the only organized force ready to march) in the vanguard. One of the first of the Legion's battles was at Arlaban on January 17, 1836. This was followed by a period of bad weather which interrupted the operations. Gradually the initiative seemed to pass to the Carlists, as the ill-organized, poorly commanded and inadequately supplied Christinos concentrated and moved out to attack in January 1836. The recent experience of Algerian fighting proved to be invaluable and the legionaries did very well. At Tirapegui on April 26, 1836, about 6,000 Carlists defeated the Christinos, and about 1,000 soldiers of the 5th French Legion battalion were deployed to cover their withdrawal. They held the 5,000 strong enemy off at a cost of 300 dead and wounded. Another engagement, on August 1, 1836, again proved the worth of the Legion. Two battalions deployed on the right wing of the Spanish army attacked a fortified line near a village called Zubiri. The Polish mounted lancers especially distinguished themselves and the Carlists were driven from their positions. They were forced to withdraw leaving 1,500 men on the field, either dead or taken prisoner.

In spite of these prestigious feats, the morale of the legionaries grew lower and lower as their material and living conditions worsened. There was great ambiguity about responsibility for supply and payment of troops, pensions for the disabled and ransoms of the prisoners—areas in which the Spanish authorities had a bad record. After Zuribi, more skirmishes, patrol work and guerrilla activity took place during the autumn of 1836. At the end of 1836, the Legion had shrunk to three small battalions of ragged, hungry and disheartened men. Casualties, sickness and desertion made inroads into the ranks and the force dwindled significantly. Colonel Bernelle, who for some time had repeatedly complained about the neglect of his legionaries, became involved in a dispute with French ministers. He was dismissed and replaced by Major Lebeau. In November 1836 the German colonel Fritz Conrad took over the leadership of the Foreign Legion.

During the winter of 1836-1837, the situation grew even worse. The neglected, unpaid, badly fed and inadequately clothed Foreign Legion was deployed in the sparse mountain region north of Pamplona. Stationed on the windy, cold and snow-swept plateaus, the legionaries' condition was appalling; they could not even resort to pillaging the countryside. For miles around all villages, hamlets, ranches and farms were empty of provisions as they had already been looted by the Carlists. The sickness rate shot up alarmingly and many legionaries died of cold. There was little fighting; instead, the enemy encouraged defection, and tried to win them over to their cause by promising money, good food and comfortable quarters. In spite of arrears in payment, hunger and cold, amazingly only a few legionaries deserted. Later, in 1840, their action was rewarded by granting the Legion a device displayed on its flag: *Honneur et Patrie* (Honor and Fatherland), later changed to *Valeur et Discipline* (Valor and Discipline) which was again replaced in November 1920 by *Honneur et Fidélité* (Honor and Fidelity).

At the beginning of 1837, due to sickness, exposure, cold and malnutrition, the Legion was reduced to two battalions and a rump of a mounted squadron.

In March 1837 active operations were resumed. The neglected Legion operated in the province of Aragon, where Don Carlos had launched a large offensive at Huesca. At the end of this attack the French Legion had shrunk to one battalion.

On June 2, 1837, the Legion fought its last combat at Barbastro. The unit was marching in barren and hot Aragon when it was attacked by a strong party of Carlist infantry and cavalry. The column was rapidly broken up and encircled. The episode has remained famous in the history of the Legion as the Carlist unit opposite the French Legion was, by an odd coincidence, a foreign volunteer force as well; through the smoke of battle, many legionaries recognized old friends and ex-colleagues (notably the men of the 4th Spanish Battalion which had been disbanded in 1834). The popular Colonel Conrad, "Old Fritz" (as he was called by his men), was the first to charge.

Mounted on his white horse, he was killed immediately, the first of many Legion commanding officers to be killed in battle at the head of his troops. He was immediately replaced by Captain Bazaine. In the confused combat which followed among the olive groves near the village, no quarter was given. After hours of deadly combat, the Carlists won the day, and the French Legion was virtually wiped out.

In 1837, some 500 survivors, starving, sick, neglected and ignored, were left to rot at Pamplona. In a town which had rebelled against both Carlists and Christinos, the abandoned legionaries roamed like specters, and many deserters filtered over the Pyrenees into France. Finally, someone in a remote military administrative office might have remembered that the French Foreign Legion still existed. The rump of the Legion was officially disbanded on December 6, 1838, and the forgotten men were allowed to return to France. In all, the Spanish venture had cost the Foreign Legion 23 officers and 3,600 men killed in battle or dead of wounds or sickness. Amazingly, 159 survivors of the terrible campaign in Spain marched to Pau, where they reenlisted in a new Foreign Legion that, in the meantime, had been re-formed in Algeria. Thus one of the most depressing episodes of the French Foreign Legion history sadly closed.

Legion infantryman in Spain, 1835–1838. When the French Foreign Legion arrived in Spain in 1835, the legionaries wore the same uniform as in Algeria, including a dark blue coat and red pants. As the campaign proceeded the Legion was neglected and improvisations developed resulting in varied uniforms and equipment. The depicted legionary wears a local Basque beret with pompon and espadrille (typical Spanish rope-soled sandal). The large Napoleonic white cross-belts were already discarded. Equipment included a central belly cartridge pouch supported by a black waistbelt and neckstrap, and a local drinking bottle. The weapon was a flintlock musket with bayonet.

A New Legion in Algeria, 1835–1857

Creation of a new Foreign Legion

After the "old" Foreign Legion had been signed over to Spain, there was a gap in the French army fighting in Algeria. On December 16, 1835, King Louis-Philippe issued another royal ordinance for the creation of a New Foreign Legion. At first volunteers were sent off to Spain to fill the gaps left by casualties, sickness and desertion in the former "Old" Legion. When it became obvious that the Carlist War was leading nowhere, volunteers were kept and trained in France. Captain Bernelle's reform had been maintained in the New Legion: all nationalities were merged within the units. The first battalion of 800 legionaries headed by Major Bedeau was shipped to Algeria in January 1837. The "New" Legion took part in an expedition into the Isser Valley, and they escorted several of the columns that went into the countryside. Recruiting in France revived again and the ranks swelled so much that in July 1837 a second battalion was created. Both battalions formed a regiment placed under the command of Colonel de Hulsen, and this unit was posted in the

French Foreign Legion infantryman, c. 1840. The unsuited tall shako had been replaced by a so-called **casquette d'Afrique** *(African cap) often covered with a black oilcloth. The coat was dark grey with red badge at the front edges of the collar. The red trousers were worn loose over white gaiters and black marching shoes. A black waistbelt and neckstrap supported a central belly cartridge pouch. White straps supported the natural cowhide backpack with rolled greatcoat. Additional equipment included a musette (bread bag), a short falchion-shape sword, a tin canteen, and a bayonet generally worn on the left side of the belt. The weapon was still a flintlock musket.*

region of Algiers. A *bataillon de marche* ("marching" or task battalion) was assembled from men from various units in September 1837 and sent to participate in the siege of Constantine.

Constantine

By 1837, the tribesmen of the eastern mountainous region of Constantine posed a grave threat to the French army. The rebels grew bolder in their raids and so it was decided to seize the city. An expedition had first been launched in November 1836, demonstrating France's intention to penetrate farther into the Algerian hinterland. This resulted in a failure, and a year later another attempt was made, which, too, ended in a disaster. In October 1837 a third expeditionary force was formed with General Damremont at its head; it included French army line units, Zouaves and the Foreign Legion *bataillon de marche* (500 men strong headed by Commandant Bedeau). The column suffered great hardship during the advance from Bône through heavy rain and constant harassing attacks by the tribesmen. Constantine was built on a high ridge surrounded by deep ravines, the only weak point being a plateau named Koudiat-Aty. The city was defended by formidable fortifications bristling with 63 guns manned by 500 skilled artillerymen and numerous other Turkish and Kabyle infantry troops armed with various weapons. The city was well supplied and the garrison's morale, strengthened by the French failure of 1836, was high. After having overcome extreme difficulties, the French began the siege of Constantine. Siege batteries were placed on the Koudiat-Aty plateau, and bombardment of the city started on October 9. The defenders made unsuccessful sorties on October 7 and 11. On October 12 General Damremont was killed, and was replaced by General Valée. Siege guns were sited with difficulty on the rocky slopes, and, for four days, the French artillery pounded the city walls. Eventually they made two breaches in the walls and these were assaulted on the morning of October 13, 1837, by a force of about 600 soldiers, including about 100 men from the "New" Foreign Legion—reports vary as to the precise number. The storming party was led by Colonel Combe, who had briefly commanded the old Legion in 1832. The assault was followed by costly, fierce house-to-house combat through the maze of narrow streets and alleys across the town. The Algerian resistance was fierce, but after hours of combat, including storming the barricades and bayonet, charges the defenders capitulated. By nightfall the French were in complete possession of the town. They had, however, suffered a rate of casualties particularly high among men, NCOs and officers, Colonel Combe among those killed. The capture of Constantine was viewed as a great victory for both the French colonial army and the Legion.

After the fall of the city the Legion *bataillon de marche* remained in Constantine on garrison duty. In honor of the part it played in the victory the new Legion was permitted to form *compagnies d'élite*: a *grenadier* (grenadier) company, and a *voltigeur* (riflemen/skirmishers) company in each of the two battalions.

The Legion was growing again. In December 1837 a third battalion was created and the new Foreign Legion's strength totaled by then about 3,000 legionaries who were stationed at Algiers, Bône and Constantine. In 1839, the war against Abd-El-Kader was resumed, and a fourth Legion battalion was formed. Ironically, these new units counted Spanish mercenaries and veterans from both the Carlists and Christinos.

War against Abd-El-Kader

The period 1839–1840 was terrible for the infant French colony of Algeria. The leader Abd-El-Kader had proclaimed jihad (Muslim holy war) against the French invaders, and he had gathered a large force of 6,000

Legion **voltigeur** *in the 1840s. The depicted elite skirmisher wears the red* **casquette d'Afrique** *with dark blue band, a tricolor cockade at the front and white neck-cloth. The short dark blue tunic had a standing collar and yellow epaulettes (shoulder straps). The linen trousers were white and tucked into white leather gaiter. Equipment included a service waist belt holding a bayonet scabbard and a leather belly ammunition pouch, a tin canteen, and a white horseshoe rolled blanket. The weapon was a flintlock musket with bayonet.*

soldiers and some 150 trained gunners. Determined to push the unbelieving intruders back to the sea, the Arabs launched aggressive raids in the coastal plains, murdering all in their path, and they soon threatened the capital Algiers. The French concentrated on strengthening defenses, building forts and fortified posts. These were often cut off and surrounded and some were overrun. The 1st and 4th Legion Battalions were engaged in the region of Medea where they were ambushed. The 4th Battalion more particularly was surrounded and besieged at Milianah; between June and October 1839 the legionaries fought off almost daily attacks. In addition to combat casualties, heatstroke, fever and dysentery struck the garrison. Again the troops distinguished themselves and suffered heavy losses, some 460 out of 750 legionaries were killed in action.

The two other Legion battalions were also engaged and suffered heavy casualties from both combat and disease, notably at Fondouk, where they lost nine officers, 207 dead and 240 incapacitated. The 1st Battalion, deployed in the eastern part of Algeria in the region of Bône, took part in several expeditions. The most noteworthy was the attack to reduce the rocky stronghold of Djidjelli in May 1839. The Polish companies led the assault and they lost their commander in a fierce combat, but they overran the position. After taking the small fort the legionaries were encircled and had to fight their way clear again. The 1st Battalion later took part with distinction in several operations against Kabyle rebels in and around Bougie.

Until 1840 French policy in Algeria remained fluid and French occupation was confined mainly to the defense of the coast. In the dramatic context faced in 1839, the French government adopted a clearly defined policy of total conquest and permanent occupation. Both the French army and the "new" Legion were greatly strengthened. By December 1840 the Foreign Corps numbered two regiments. The 1st Regiment de la Légion étrangère (1st RLE, three battalions strong) was quartered at Algiers and Oran. The 2nd Regiment de la Légion étrangère (2nd RLE with two battalions) operated in the region of Bône, with its base at Setif. With the appointment of General Bugeaud, matters changed, new tactics were introduced and large-scale offensive expeditions inland began.

General Bugeaud

In February 1840 General Thomas Robert Bugeaud, marquis de la Piconerie (1784–1849), was appointed governor-general and commander-in-chief of the French army in Algeria. The new commander brought good experience in antiguerrilla warfare and he was particularly concerned with colonial operations. He immediately instituted new strategy and tactics against the rebellious Algerians. Instead of spreading his forces ineffectually over a vast number of small, vulnerable garrisons, Bugeaud concentrated on a few powerful strategic strongholds. From these firmly held bases he directed a constant series of *colonnes volantes* (flying columns) through the enemy territories. Bugeaud also increased firepower by introducing the use of small mountain guns carried by mules. Each flying *colonne* was generally composed of three battalions of infantry, several squadrons of *Chasseurs d'Afrique* (light cavalry), units of the Foreign Legion, and several light mountain guns. This deployment of course, could vary according to the nature of the mission. To strike with certainty, Bugeaud gathered intelligence from paid infiltrants, spies, turncoat rebels and, exceptionally, from recaptured deserters such as a certain Glockner. This legionary had deserted in the hope of being welcomed as a prince in the rebel force; however, instead of women, riches and honor Glockner was made a slave by Abd-El-Kader. He managed to escape and served marabout Tedjini, a rival chieftain; for unknown reasons he again entered Kader's service in 1840. He was pardoned, but unfortunately was recaptured by General Cavaignac's soldiers. Cunningly Glockner bargained for his life in providing vital information, and he was even permitted to serve again in the Foreign Legion under the new name of Joussef. Garrisoned at Mascara, Glockner-Joussef deserted again, and fled to Morocco where he was arrested by the French authorities. Again he was saved from the firing squad by a certain General Bedlau to whom he probably gave important intelligence; incredibly he was then again pardoned and even allowed to enlist as a spahi (light cavalryman). Glockner—the man who knew too many secrets, talked too much and deserted too often—was finally assassinated by an Arab on Abd-El-Kader's order.

Once intelligence had been gathered General Bugeaud launched deadly *razzias*—swift, ruthless surprise destruction and punishment raids against proven dissident areas. Frustrated by the enemy's understandable reluctance to stand and fight in a pitch battle, his aim was to eradicate the rebels by cutting them off from their supplies and livehoods. Bugeaud elevated the unconventional *razzia* and scorched-earth tactics to the level of total war by burning the rebels' villages and bases and by destroying their agricultural potential in driving off their cattles, burning crops and cutting down trees. It was argued that the rebel was "a

Baggage mule. Mules were an important asset in Bugeaud's flying columns operating in Algeria in the 1840s.

plant that only grows in particular soil" and the most certain way of eradicating him was "to alter the soil." For this reason Bugeaud waged war against grain silos and cattle which fed and clothed the rebels. These scorched-earth tactics—extremely ruthless and brutal—resulted in widespread destruction and in death and misery for countless innocent rural civilians, but they proved extremely effective in the end as the hunters, who first held the initiative, became a hungry and unsupported hunted. By the end of 1842, western Algeria was practically cleared.

The destructive scheme was, however, not a mindless one; it was accompanied by a program of reconstruction in the pacified areas so as to establish a stable, secure, long-term, efficient and productive colonial regime. Once they were victors, the French established fortified posts to control the conquered territories. They showed a comparatively merciful attitude toward the vanquished rebels—at least toward those who put down their arms and fully accepted French rule. New villages were created or rebuilt with Arab-speaking officers overseeing colonization, rendering justice, and administering the conquered population with a firm hand. After conquest, occupation and pacification, the true role of the colonial officer was intended to be an administrator, an overseer, a doctor, a workshop manager, and a teacher of gardening and farming. The local inhabitants, upon whom the rebels relied, were to be persuaded of the material—and presumably also moral—benefit of French

Algerian tribesman, c. 1840

rule, which brought not only safety but also new markets, civil public works and roads.

Abd-El-Kader's defeat

The hard-hitting "flying columns" operated in the 1840s, alternating with occasional large-scale operations aiming at trapping the elusive Emir Abd-El-Kader. In 1843 a major rising inspired by the great Algerian leader was cut up by Bugeaud, and Abd-El-Kader's *smala* (retinue, a large camp) was taken by Louis-Philippe's

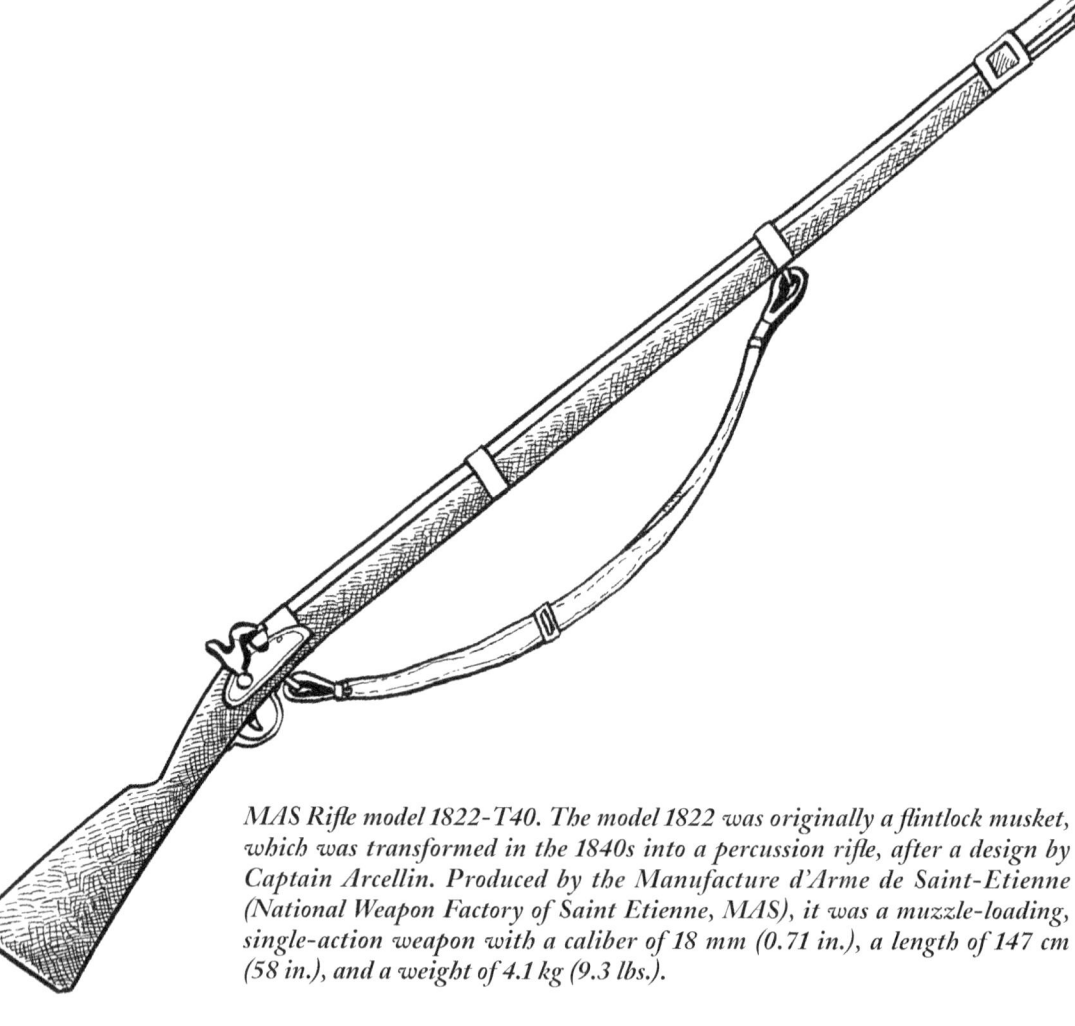

MAS Rifle model 1822-T40. The model 1822 was originally a flintlock musket, which was transformed in the 1840s into a percussion rifle, after a design by Captain Arcellin. Produced by the Manufacture d'Arme de Saint-Etienne (National Weapon Factory of Saint Etienne, MAS), it was a muzzle-loading, single-action weapon with a caliber of 18 mm (0.71 in.), a length of 147 cm (58 in.), and a weight of 4.1 kg (9.3 lbs.).

fourth son, Henri Eugène Philippe d'Orléans, duke of Aumale (1822–1897). The defeated emir was forced to take refuge in Morocco. Bugeaud pursued him, crossed the border and occupied the city of Oudja; he would have marched on the Moroccan sultan's capital but, for political reasons, King Louis-Philippe ordered him to retreat in 1844. The sultan—interpreting this as a sign of weakness—brought his own forces to the Algerian border. On August 13, 1844, General Bugeaud, after a forced march by 8,000 French troops including the 1st Regiment of the French Foreign Legion, defeated the Moroccan army near Oued Isly. At the same time the French navy bombarded Tangier.

For his victory Bugeaud was elevated to the rank of duke of Isly.

At the beginning of 1844, the region around Constantine was subdued and rebellious tribesmen were temporary expelled from the Nememchas and Aures mountains, with several important battles fought, including that of M'chounech in March 1844.

The year 1845 saw the continuation of the conquest with French victories at Mehab-Gharboussa and Ain-Temouchent. The subsequent treaty signed with the sultan of Morocco gave Bugeaud the right of hot pursuit of Algerian rebels over the mountainous frontier. This considerably reduced

Abd-El-Kader's chances of evading him indefinitely. The hunted Abd-El-Kader surrendered on December 23, 1847. He was imprisoned at Amboise (France) until 1852, and later lived a life of religious meditation in exile at Damascus (Syria) until his death in 1883. Deprived of its charismatic leader the Algerian rebellion soon collapsed.

Sidi-Bel-Abbes

A special mention must be made about a small post established by the Legion during Bugeaud's time. To supply the numerous flying columns, Bugeaud set up small fortified supply depots (known as *biscuitvilles*, literally "cookie-towns") at suitable points. In late 1843, the 3rd Battalion of the 1st Regiment of the Foreign Legion was ordered to establish one such depot in a shallow plain about 60 miles south of Oran. The Legion selected a suitable small hill known as Sidi-Bel-Abbes (named after a holy marabout), near the Mekera River. The *biscuitville* Sidi-Bel-Abbes was originally only a small supply depot with men housed in tents and supplies stored in sheds defended by primitive field fortifications. The camp was attacked several times, notably in January 1845, but the Arabs were always beaten off. As it was well sited, the temporary supply camp became a permanent, strongly fortified position designed by engineer Captain Prudhon. Adopting the tradition of the ancient legions of Rome of fighting as well as building, the foreign legionaries went to work and skilled craftsmen, even architects, were produced from their ranks. Permanent well-designed and well-built barracks, stores, buildings, facilities, a church, a school, a police station, streets planted with trees, squares, gardens and place-of-arms were constructed. The legionnaires' industry and skills caused a small town to spring into existence. Within a few years Sidi-Bel-Abbes developed into a city which became the Legion's home in Algeria until 1962. Many discharged legionaries, having no-where else to go, settled in the town and helped to swell the population. In 1849 General Pelissier congratulated the legionaries who had proved themselves as adept with pick and shovel as with rifle and bayonet: He declared, "Out of an encampment you have made a flourishing city, from desolation a fertile township, an image of France!" Even today the Legion does not need a barrack maintenance service, it does all its own repairs and servicing.

Zaatcha

During this period the Foreign Legion was very busy, marching, patrolling and escorting supply columns; they kept on constructing roads, boring wells, and building camps, forts and *biscuitvilles*. They, of course, participated in many operations in actions by General Bugeaud's flying columns in Algeria and at the border with Morocco. They had become efficient and steady, hard-hitting and tough fighters, they knew the country, and they had adapted themselves to the hard Arabian guerrilla warfare. The Legion gradually became synonymous with Algeria, and, together with the Zouaves, the blue-coated legionaries provided the core and backbone of French conquest. The legionaries distinguished themselves on numerous occasions in French expansion southward. They reduced dissidents at Kolea and Mehab-Barboussen, smoked out rebels in mountain grottoes, hunted Ab-El-Kader's men at Biskra (February 1844), assaulted and subdued the Kabyle stronghold of M'Chounech, took part in the battle of Isly in December 1847 (losing one captain and 24 men) and routed besieging rebels at Temouchent. As the French were determined to penetrate through the Sahara Desert several operations were launched. The Legion fought at Ain Sefra, on the edge of the Sahara, opening a path to the great desert.

One of the last large-scale operations in Algeria was the capture of the Zaatcha oasis in the summer and autumn of 1849. The strongly fortified and well-supplied Zaatcha oasis—situated 30 km south of Biskra—was the bastion of the fanatical marabout and rebellious leader Bou Ziane who had taken Kader's place at the head of the rebellion. Revolt suddenly flared up there and a force of 4,000 soldiers commanded by General Herbillon (including the 43th Infantry Regiment and the 2nd Foreign Legion Regiment) was ordered to move against Bou Ziane. The oasis was besieged and bombarded for six weeks. A first assault was repulsed on July 16, 1849. Bou Ziane led a sortie that succeeded in destroying several French guns, but the sally party was soon repulsed. In early October more troops, engineers and heavier guns were brought up. Palm trees were cut down and space cleared so that artillery could be brought into action for firing at the enemy and making breaches in the thick walls. The ground prepared, the French were ready for another assault. On October 20, 1849, using powder bags to breach the walls, Colonel Canrobert's 2nd Foreign Legion Regiment managed to break through, and two columns attacked the city. As each and every house in the oasis, each garden wall and each criss-crossing irrigation canal had been transformed into a stronghold or a hindrance, these fiercely defended obstacles had to be taken one by one with the liberal use of explosive charges and costly infantry assaults. As the attacking columns slowly

Legion officer in the 1850s. This second lieutenant from a **Voltigeur** *company wears the parade dress with full-skirted single-breasted dark blue tunic, and red trousers. The képi is red with a dark blue band and squared black peak. Officers were armed with swords (occasionally a cane or a walking stick on duty), and revolvers or pistols of various models on the battlefield. Note the metal half moon-shaped duty hausse-col (gorget) around the neck suspended by a small chain.*

and painfully converged on the center of Zaatcha, womenfolk fought alongside the men, and no quarter was given. When Bou Ziane was shot by the Zouaves, organized resistance, deprived of leadership, fell apart. Zaatcha was finally taken on November 26, 1849, after fighting equalling in fierceness and savagery that of Constantine. The battle cost the French force some 1,500 casualties and many men became incapacitated by an outburst of cholera. With the reduction of Zaatcha oasis, French occupation of the area was undisputed. In spite of hardship, sickness and hard fighting, the two battalions of the 2nd Legion Regiment had performed well.

Aftermath

Sporadic skirmishes and local resistance continued for a few years, but these did not prevent the French from consolidating their gains and confirming the occupation. In 1851 Berber tribesmen revolted and the French army and Legion went into action against them. General MacMahon's force managed to quell the revolt. In 1852, two battalions of the 1st Regiment of the Foreign Legion were engaged against the Beni Sassen rebellious tribe near the border with Morocco. A year later another expedition was launched against the Berber of greater Kabylia; it had little success as the French were unable to fully

Legion flying columns infantryman in the 1850s. The depicted Legion private of Bugeaud's flying columns wears a red cap with a dark blue band and piping, blue loop to the brass button and front tricolor cockade. This **casquette d'Afrique** *was lower than the shako, and foreshadowed the later képi; it was often fitted with a cloth neck-cover. The man wears a long dark blue coat with red epaulettes. The baggy red linen trousers are worn tucked into white canvas gaiters buttoning up the outside. Ammunition for his weapon is contained in the central black leather belly pouch. Additional equipment includes a tin canteen (a gourd, an essential item for men fighting in a subtropical climate) and a black scabbard for the bayonet. Armament consisted of old 1822 flintlock muskets, but about 1845 new percussion rifles appeared.*

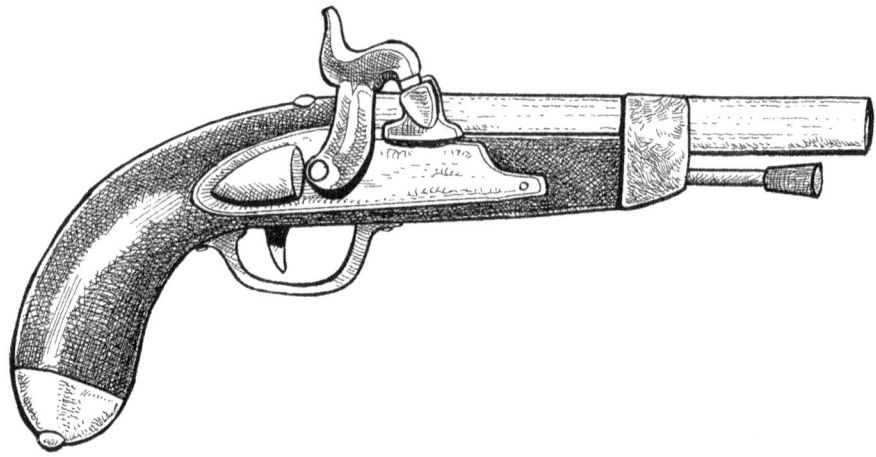

MAS Pistol model 1850. The percussion, single-shot, muzzle-loading pistol model 1850 was issued to officers. It had a caliber of 17.8 mm (0.7 in.), a length of 350 mm (13.8 in.) and a weight of 1,270 grams (45 oz.).

occupy and totally pacify the Berber-populated high plateaus and mountains of Kabylia, Aures and Hodna. These hostile mountains with their proud inhabitants remained inviolate, and, for the time being, the French could do nothing but leave them alone.

By 1857, the harsh conquest of Algeria was achieved. The French firmly held most of the northern part of the country, and they had already begun to penetrate and explore the huge Sahara Desert. In April and May 1853, a detachment of the Legion (about 200 strong), mounted on camels, participated in an expedition to conquer the oasis of Ouargla.

Algeria proved to be a great school for French military authorities. The Foreign Legion was now confident, battle-tried and consolidating. The story of the conquest of Algeria is almost the story of the French Foreign Legion. The 1st Regiment, based at Sidi-Bel-Abbes, and the 2nd Regiment, stationed at Sétif, continued their construction work and now and then went on operations in the central mountains for peacekeeping and maintenance of order duties. With Algeria officially made a French metropolitan *département* in 1848, new colonists came from among the unemployed of France, and also including adventurers and settlers from Spain, Italy and other lands. They formed a new social class whose interests and fate were closely bound up with the land until 1962.

2

The Foreign Legion at the Time of Napoléon III, 1852–1871

Napoléon III

Charles-Louis-Napoléon Bonaparte was born in Paris in 1808. After the fall of his uncle Napoléon I in 1815 Charles-Louis lived in exile. When the duke of Reichstadt and son of Napoléon I (officially Napoléon II) died in 1832, he assumed the leadership of the Bonapartist party. Ambitious and unscrupulous, humanitarian and idealistic, he was a strange combination of visionary and cynic. Owing to the popularity attached to his prestigious name, and playing on social fears, he was elected a member of the French parliament. Conservatives, anxious to defend social order in the face of the socialist "red peril," supported the candidate. The "uncle's nephew" was elected president of the Second Republic on December 10, 1848, by an overwhelming and indubitable popular mandate. At the end of his term Louis-Napoléon Bonaparte, had his opponents—both republican and monarchist—arrested, and he took power by force on December 2, 1851. The Second Republic lived for another year but the next step was inevitable. On December 7, 1852, the dictator abolished the Republic, proclaimed the Second French Empire and took the title of Napoléon III. The new emperor of the French encouraged a great march toward material progress, which marked the triumph of the Industrial Revolution in France, but his adventurous international policy was a serious source of discontent for French public opinion.

Crimean War, 1854–1856

Historical background

The Crimean War, which lasted from 1854 to 1856, was a pointless war initiated by the ambitious Napoléon III. Toward the end of the 1840s war broke out between Russia and Turkey. The French had many interests in the Near East: they had often furnished money and advisers to the sultans, they claimed protection over the Turkish Christians and staffed and financed Christian missions and they carried on a huge volume of trade. On March, 28, 1854, France joined with the Turks, and so did anti–Russian Britain, whose settled policy was to uphold Turkey and the Near East against

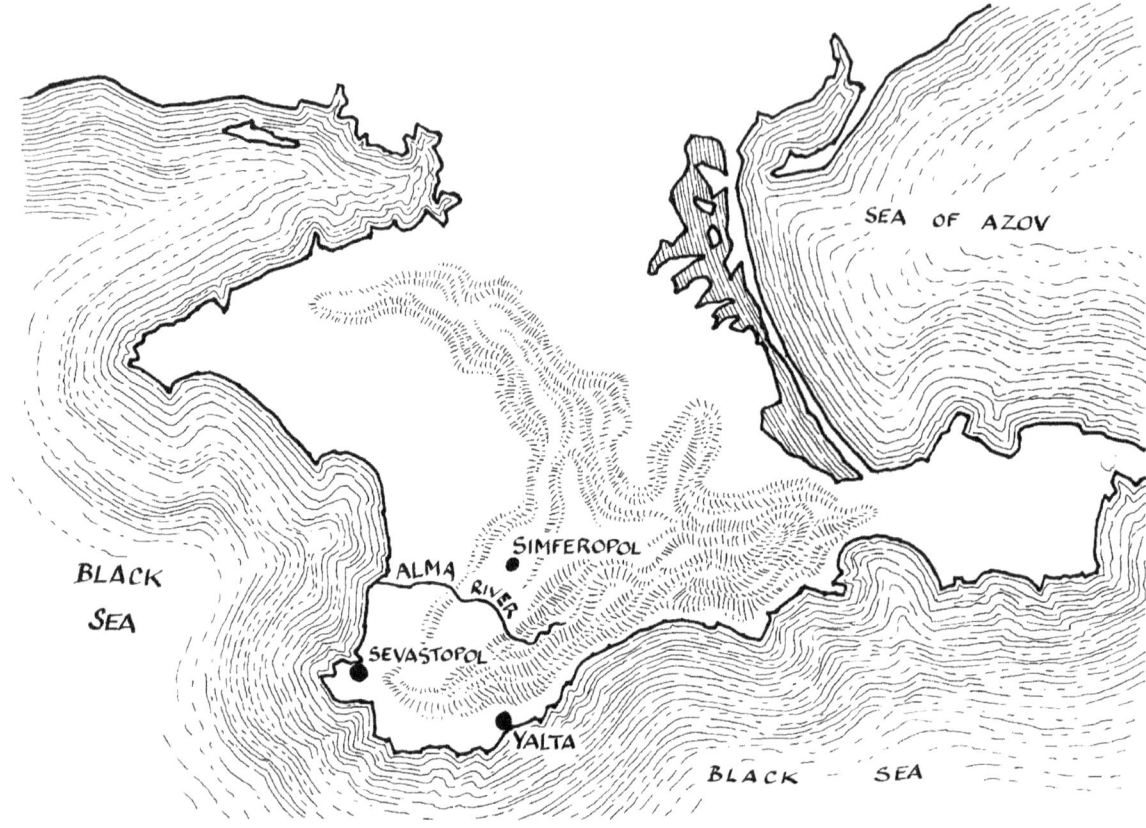

Sketch map of Crimea, 1854–1856

penetration by Russia. After having blockaded the Russian fleet in both Baltic and Black seas outlets, the Allies decided to strike in Russia itself. On September 14, 1854, the Allies landed in the Crimean Peninsula, where all the important fighting was confined. The landing was uncontested, and the Allies scored a victory at the first battle near the Alma River (September 20, 1854).

The siege of Sevastopol

After the victory of Alma, it was decided to concentrate on the capture of Sevastopol, the great Russian port-fortress with its arsenals, shipyards and naval installations. It was originally anticipated that the port would fall after a short cannonade. In fact the siege of Sevastopol proved to be a long and painful operation—it lasted 349 days from October 1854 to September 1855. Actually, more than a siege, Sevastopol was a dreadful war of attrition. It was conducted in terrible conditions, as French and British troops were totally unprepared and badly provided with stores and equipment needed to resist the winter rain, cold, wind and snow. The siege operations were not only thwarted by the tempests of the Crimean winter, soon cholera and frostbite took a heavy toll on all the armies. Helping to prolong the siege was the fact that Sevastopol was never fully isolated. The defenders had access to convenient lines of supply so that ammunition, food, weapons and fresh troops could be moved in as reinforcements, while the attackers had to rely upon long naval supply lines from their homelands. Another miscalculation was underestima-

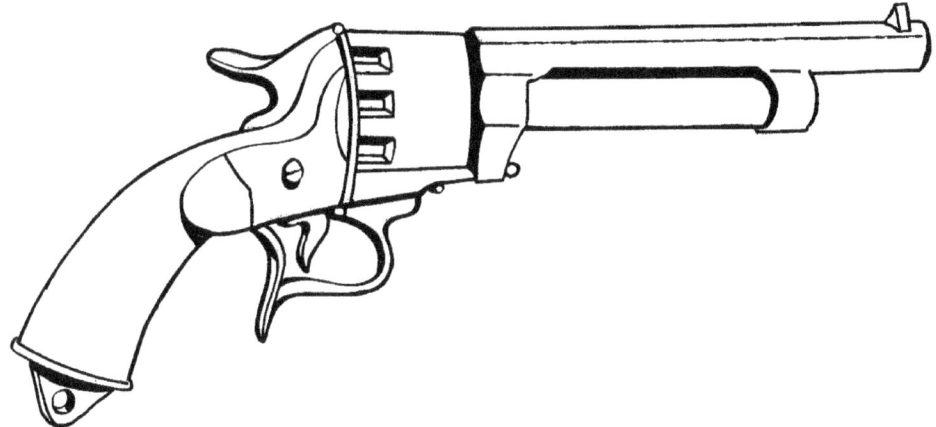

Le Mat revolver 1856. Invented by the American Samuel Colt in 1836, the revolver is a firearm in which a cylinder, with a series of chambers bored centrally through it, revolves about a central axis; each chamber contains a metallic cartridge which may be presented to the firing mechanism in turn.

The depicted revolver—designed in 1856 by the army doctor Jean Alexandre François Le Mat—had two barrels and could fire 9 rounds. It weighed 1,450 grams (51.1 oz), and was 340 mm (13.4") in length. Produced by the Girard & Fils Company of Paris, it was issued to army and Legion officers.

tion of the fortifications of Sevastopol. These were formidable, due to the genius of engineer and commanding officer Todleben. They included a series of forts, earthworks and batteries, all bristling with artillery, and defended with ditches and obstacles. After a long an appalling siege, the fortress was taken, the Russian army evacuated Sevastopol, and the tsar sued for peace. A congress of all the great powers made peace at Paris in March 1856.

The Legion in the Crimean War

For the Crimean War Napoléon III ordered the formation of two Foreign Legion regiments, the 1st from Sidi-Bel-Abbes commanded by Colonel Bazaine and the 2nd from Sétif under Colonel De Caprez. Each regiment included two battalions, and the four battalions constituted the Deuxième Brigade étrangère (2nd Foreign Brigade). The battalions were regrouped at Algiers and arrived at Gallipoli, Crimea, in July 1854. The men were kept in the rear for second-line duties, as the Legion's reputation among the top leadership of the French army was still very low. The first enemy the soldiers met was a cholera epidemic which ravaged the ranks of both the British and the French armies. Before any combat took place, some 200 legionnaires had died, and among the first victims was Marshal de Saint-Arnaud. He was immediately replaced by General Canrobert, who had briefly commanded the 2nd Legion Regiment in 1849.

The Legion unit was incorporated into General Canrobert's division while the remainder was used on ordinary line of communication duties. In September 1854, the battalion de marche moved southward and was engaged at the battle of the Alma, on a high and rugged ridge on the south side of the Alma River. The battle began on September 20 by a frontal attack against 40,000 entrenched Russians well supported by artillery. In their sector, the foreign legionaries fought with calm and efficiency, and with the support of North African Zouaves, they outflanked and successfully disorganized a part of the Russian formations. Having

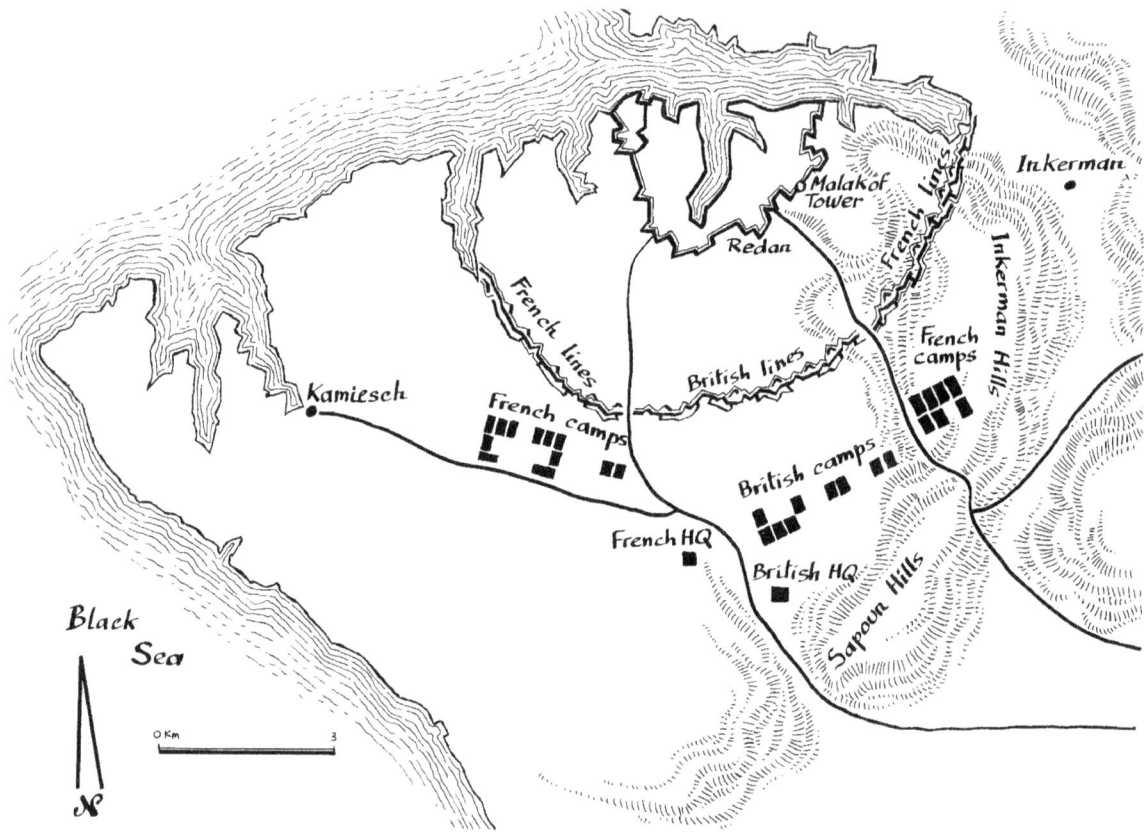

Sketch map siege of Sevastopol, 1854

opened a breach in the enemy lines, they were followed by Canrobert's main infantry force and artillery, therefore obliging the Russian general Menchikov to withdraw to Sevastopol. At the Alma the Foreign Legion's discipline under heavy enemy fire had impressed Canrobert, but casualties were high: 5 officers wounded and 55 men killed and wounded.

After the battle of Inkermann in late October 1854—mainly fought by the British with only a few French units engaged—the siege of Sevastopol began. Now General Canrobert engaged the whole of the Foreign Brigade and the two regiments, the one under Colonel Viénot, and the other under Colonel Caprez, were engaged at the grueling siege of Sevastopol. In the winter of 1854–1855, the Legion was deployed into positions to the southwest of the city. They established siege fortifications including gun batteries, trenches and communications saps in bad weather and often under enemy fire. On November 5, 1854, the 1st Regiment repulsed a strong Russian counterattack, saving a British unit from destruction, but at a cost of 12 officers and nearly 150 men.

During the long winter months there were numerous small raids and counterraids, either for reconnaissance purposes, to destroy works constructed or dug, or for retaliation. Between these actions there were lengthy weeks of inaction in muddy trenches. The legionaries suffered enormously from boredom, cold (there was a lack of fuel, winter clothing and blankets) and disease (cholera, dysentery and typhus). Their time was spent in digging and reinforcing their trenches and earthwork positions, in fitting into their shelters ovens, stoves and other heating devices, in robbing dead bodies in no-man's-land, and in complaining that there were not enough fighting. They attracted a good deal of attention, as much for their great fighting spirit and efforts to make their existence more bearable as for their bad manners, their excesses of all sorts, their enthusiastic foraging and pillaging, their exotic slang and their heavy drinking bouts. There is a famous anecdote that illustrated their inexhaustible thirst: It is reported that during an inspection, General Canrobert was shocked to discover a glassy-eyed legionary with a hangover parading in the snow with no boots and black-polished feet; the man had sold his footwear for drinks, and hoped nobody would notice.

In the night of January 19 to 20, 1855, the Legion repulsed another Russian sally. This was followed by a series of attacks against Russian trenches, but it was not before early May 1855 that a large-scale offensive was resumed. The Legion played a full part in the various assaults around the Schwartz Redoubt and Malakov Tower. Colonel Viénot, the chief commander of the 1st Foreign Regiment, died on May 2,

Legion officer in Crimea, 1854–1856

Mud in the trench (Sevastopol winter 1854–1855). The siege was a dreadful war of attrition, which foreshadowed the terrible deadlock of the trench warfare of World War I (1914–1918).

1855. His name was subsequently given to the home of the Legion ("Quartier Viénot") at Sidi-Bel-Abbes, and after 1962 at Aubagne near Marseilles.

The Legion distinguished itself on several occasions, notably by successful assaults on May 1 and June 7 against Russian entrenchments. On Saturday, September 8, 1855, at noon, after a heavy artillery bombardment, the final attack on the city was launched and the Malakov Tower was assaulted and conquered. In the meantime the Russians had burnt their fleet and evacuated Sevastopol, bringing the siege to an end. During the operation, the two Legion Regiments suffered the loss of 12 officers killed and 66 wounded, as well as 1,625 legionaries and NCOs killed or wounded, not included the casualties caused by exposure and sickness. The siege had been indeed an epic of human endurance and fortitude, and the legionaries had suffered, in common with all the other besiegers, from low temperatures, snow, ice, wind and exposure.

After the evacuation of Sevastopol by the Russians, the port was occupied by the Foreign Legion Brigade now commanded by General Bazaine, formerly a sergeant in the Old Legion. There was a grand review of French troops in which both Regiments of the Brigade took part. The town was partly destroyed, and totally empty—all inhabitants had fled—quite fortunately for them. Indeed the occupation was marked by large-scale looting and exactions. After a period of static trench warfare under cramped miserable conditions the spirit of the men rocketed skyward. The legionaries, who for several months had survived on poor food and in cold, filthy, muddy trenches, took up winter quarters in the empty city. For a while, they lived in cosy houses, slept in comfortable beds with clean white sheets, and gorged themselves on pillaged food and drinks. For no other reason than fun, they misbehaved, acting like Vandals and mercenaries in the Middle Ages in breaking, burning and destroying anything they could not loot, stupid excesses which did no good to their already stained reputation. This "princely" life did not last long, however, and, after two years' absence, the Legion was rapatriated to its home depot in Algeria.

New medals were awarded to veterans with the claps *Alma*, *Inkermann*, and *Sebastopol*. The victorious Second Empire was in a benevolent mood and, as a measure of reward, Napoléon III decreed that all foreigners who had fought for France would be allowed to become naturalized Frenchmen if they wished to do so. A number of legionaries, probably having little prospect of ever going back to their own country again, took advantage of this offer, but a larger number chose to stay in their own family: la Légion étrangère.

After the Crimean War the badge of the Legion, the "seven-flamed grenade," appeared. The grenade itself had always been the mark of elite units in the French army. It was officially adopted in 1882.

Kabylia, 1857

Reorganization of the Legion

In January 1855 Napoléon III undertook to reorganize the Legion, and announced the creation of a second Foreign Legion exclusively raised from Swiss volunteers for whom he had a high opinion; this new corps was to consist of two infantry regiments of two battalions, plus a battalion of *tirailleurs* (riflemen) uniformed in red and green. This new force, organized near Lyon in France, was to be placed under the leadership of his personal friend Colonel Oschenbein. However, recruiting was disappointing and the original scheme soon clearly appeared much too ambitious. In April 1856, a more realistic design was selected. The brigade returning from the Crimea was reshaped into a single regiment designated Deuxième Régiment étranger (2nd Foreign Regiment) with three battalions based at Sidi-Bel-

Abbes, while the Swiss were redesignated Premier Régiment étranger (1st Foreign Regiment) with two infantry battalions and two companies of *tirailleurs* based at Philippeville. Soon units of both regiments were engaged in a major campaign of "pacification" in Kabylia.

The battle of Ischeriden

A proud, courageous and independent people the Berbers (or Kabyles, the original inhabitants of North Africa) had always resisted foreign invaders both Arab and French. The French had attempted to control Kabylia on several occasions. Since 1838, 14 expeditions had been launched. The Foreign Legion had been engaged in May 1851 at Fedj-Menazel and at M'Harka, but none of these operations had ever succeeded in breaking all resistance and only the fringes of the Kabylian Mountains had been penetrated. On the outbreak of the Crimean War, the French garrison in Algeria was reduced, rebellious Berber tribes took advantage of this and there were

Swiss volunteer of the "Second Foreign Legion," 1855. The volunteers of the unsuccessful Swiss Legion wore a red and green cap, a green-grass skirted tunic with red shoulder straps and red trousers. The weapons included model 1840 rifle and model 1842/1853 carbines both with sword-bayonet. The colors adopted by the short-lived "Second Foreign Legion" were green and red. Interestingly they were taken over by the French Foreign Legion proper, and they are retained today, green symbolizing hope and red sacrifice.

several revolts and insurrections. In 1857 the French planned to put the finishing stroke to resistance in the Kabylia Mountains, before devoting their efforts to fully developing Algeria. It was decided to crush the rebellious Kabyles once and for all.

To subdue the Berbers, a large force was gathered, including the 54th Infantry Regiment, 2nd Zouave Regiment, and two battalions of the 1st and 2nd Foreign Regiment, placed under command of General MacMahon. This army—totaling some 35,000 men—was divided into four columns. After having fought their way through the barren and difficult Jurjura Mountains, the columns captured the villages of Tacherahir, Beklias, Afensou and Imaseren and obtained the submission of the Beni-Ratten tribe at the end of May 1857. In June 1857 the French army was stopped in front of a large ridge, on top of which was a fortified village called Ischeriden. This natural fortress was defended by about 4,000 Kabyle warriors. The French occupied the valley but an open stretch of land had to be crossed before the ridge, a sharp, craggy one, could be scaled. The battle took place on June 24, 1857, and the Legion performed extremely well. The first attack was launched by the regular *lignards* (54th French infantry Regiment) and the 2nd Zouave Regiment. Exposed to a sustained and terribly deadly fire they suffered heavy casualties; those who were not dead or wounded retreated or sought cover behind rocks, and the attack was a failure. Then MacMahon engaged the Legion Battalion. Using their expertise acquired in fighting in broken terrain, the legionaries ascended the rocky slope making use of any available cover, and finally they assaulted the top of the ridge with the bayonet; their impressive self-control and determination gave a new impulse to infantrymen and Zouaves, who rushed to the top. After a fierce close-range combat that lasted about half an hour, the encircled Kabyles were defeated. The operation cost the Legion one officer killed, three officers wounded, 8 men killed and 87 men wounded. This impressive feat-of-arms, performed under the very eyes of General MacMahon, added to the Legion's reputation of hard-fighting soldiers. The charge of Ischeriden, a splendid example of discipline under fire, made a deep impression on senior French officers. The place served as the key to that part of Kabylia and after it fell the hardcore of resistance crumbled. After a month of skirmishes and sporadic bouts of fighting the rebels were subdued, the fighting died down, the French troops occupied the main villages and Kabylia was pacified.

After the feat of Ischeriden, in July 1857, the Legion units marched back to their home depots at Sétif, Sidi-Bel-Abbes, and Philippeville. General MacMahon went on inspection at Sidi-Bel-Abbes, thanked the troops and the Legion received a new Color as a reward. On the flag the following battle honors were inscribed: Constantine 1837, Mostaganem 1839, Mouzaia 1840, Coleah 1841, Djidjelli 1842, Zaatcha 1849, Alma 1854 and Sevaspotol 1855.

The year 1858 was rather quiet in North Africa, and the Legion continued minor police and occupation duties and construction work, before being engaged in another of Napoléon III's ventures, this time in Italy.

Italy, 1859

Historical background

In the 1850s, Italy was still a deeply divided and weak country made up of several kingdoms, small duchies, principalities, free cities and the Papal States. Some rulers, however, wanted a *Resorgimento* (rebirth), leading to unification and establishment of a central government. Napoléon III, who had always supported the *Resorgimento*, signed an alliance with Victor Emmanuel II, the king of Piedmont-Sardinia. Tension mounted with Austria—the country that occupied much of northern Italy—in early 1859, and war broke out.

For the Italian campaign the Foreign Legion furnished the 2nd Regiment, composed of four battalions totaling 60 senior officers and 1,400 legionaries, most of them experienced veterans of the Algerian campaigns and the Crimean War. In early May 1859, the 2nd Regiment was reinforced with the undermanned First Swiss Foreign regiment and, together with the 2nd Zouave Regiment, they formed the 2nd Brigade under the command of General Castagny. This brigade was incorporated into General Espinasse's 2nd Division in MacMahon's 2nd Army Corps. The campaign was short and successful for the French. By the end of May, MacMahon's 2nd Army Corps was deployed in the valley of the Po River. On June 3, a detachment of the Legion made a reconnaissance at San Martino and captured a bridge over the Ticino River, which flows into the Po. At night the army camped at the village of Turbigo and the French army planned an attack on the small market town of Magenta.

Foreign Legion grenadier, Italy, 1859. In 1855 Napoléon III confirmed by decree that the French infantry would wear a double-breasted capote (greatcoat) regardless of the season or the theater of operation. By force of tradition, this cumbersome, warm and heavy, standard combat dress would be worn by the French infantryman until 1939.

Magenta

The battle of Magenta was fought on June 4, 1859, near the Ticino River, about 16 miles west of Milan. The Franco-Piedmontese forces—headed by Napoléon III—defeated the Austrian field marshal Gyulai's army.

Both Foreign Regiments played a leading part in the victory, marching on the left wing of the French army. Their advance was at first fairly rapid and unopposed but it slowed down near the town when the attackers bumped into numerous Austrian outposts, which had to be dealt with. The terrain was favorable to the defense as it was wooded and interspersed with numerous smallholdings, barns, farmhouses and vineyards. It was close country warfare in which cavalry and artillery were of little use. Magenta was an infantry battle with numerous skirmishes, attacks on improvised strongholds and bayonet charges. Colonel Chabrière was killed and Major Martinez came to the fore as the dominant leader of the 2nd Foreign Regiment. He rallied the legionnaires, and breathed fire into them. The result was a superb assault which forced the Austrians to withdraw. The Legion then attacked the firmly held city. The legionaries dashed over the railway station and entered the town proper; after fierce and confused house-to-house fighting the Austrians were forced to retreat in the evening.

The Legion had taken a vital and prominent part in the battle and, of course, losses were heavy. The 1st Regiment counted 5 officers and 44 legionaries killed and wounded. The 2nd Foreign Regiment suffered 9 officers killed (including Colonel Chabrière) and 250 NCOs and legionaries killed and wounded. The triumph of the Legion was total. The despised desperadoes and mercenaries had proved their worth in a major battle in Europe.

Once Magenta was captured, the road to Milan was open. On June 5, 1859, the French army and the Foreign Legion entered Milan to an enthusiastic reception. For years, the pillaging of Sevastopol and the women of Milan were to become cherished memories in the hearts of the Foreign Legion veterans. The undermanned Swiss 1st Regiment stayed in Milan in garrison, hoping to recruit, but this was a failure. No Milanese enlisted in the Legion; all they wanted was the rapid departure of those burdensome guests who were too popular among their wives and daughters. After Magenta the 2nd Regiment (placed under command of the meritful Martinez, now promoted to the rank of colonel) participated in the two-week pursuit of the Austrians.

Solferino

The French army continued to press the retreating Austrians in an easterly direction. For about two weeks no fighting of note took place between the opposing forces, during which time it rained almost incessantly. Both sides, acting on completely erroneous premises, were about to engage in an unpremeditated battle, each opponent, respectively, believing that he only faced the van or rearguard of the enemy. Suddenly both armies crashed headon in a chance meeting near a village called Solferino, near the town of Castiglione delle Stiviere south of Lake Garda. The major battle of the Italian campaign took place on June 24, 1859. The battle of Solferino amounted to a terrible frontal clash of two huge armies deployed on a broad front of 20 kilometers, both sides being equally surprised and therefore compelled to give battle on ground not of their own choosing. The Franco-Piedmontese army—officially commanded by Napoléon III himself—totaled 118, 000 men and 320 field guns; their opponents—commanded by Emperor Francis of Austria—counted 120,000 soldiers and 451 guns. Here again victory was achieved by the courage and endurance of soldiers and NCOs, not by the blundering emperor and

Drummer, Italy, 1859

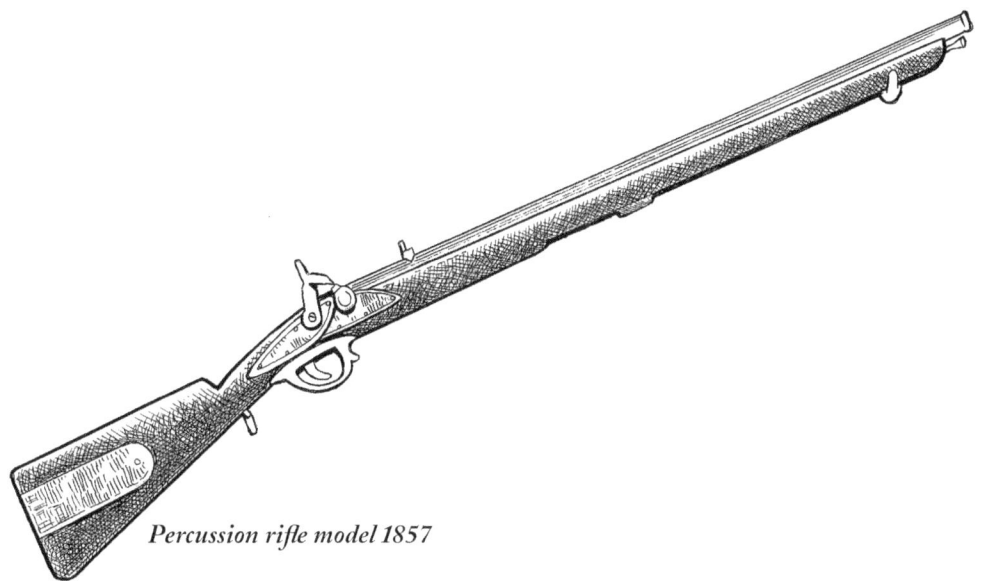
Percussion rifle model 1857

his generals. The 2nd Foreign Regiment—deployed in the center of the battlefield—fought on the hill of Cavriano, which was several times lost and retaken at high cost. By noon the fighting had reached something of a stalemate as the legionaries were halted by a strong enemy party entrenched behind the stone walls of a cemetery. Only when reinforcements were brought up did the battle turn in favor of the French. By the end of the day, the Franco-Piedmontese army won the day, but the victors were too exhausted to pursue their defeated adversaries.

Solferino was a terribly bloody and savage battle: wounded enemies were callously neglected and left to die, some were sought out and dispatched; some prisoners were also subjected to ill-treatment and a few were shot out of hand. The Legion lost 6 killed and 40 wounded, which was very light compared to the total French losses: 2,491 killed, 12,512 wounded, and 2,292 missing or prisoners. Austrian casualties amounted to 3,000 killed, 10,807 wounded and 8,638 missing or taken prisoner. The butchery at Solferino resulted in the creation of an international humanitarian organization and convention. The International Movement of the Red Cross, founded in 1864 at the Swiss civilian businessman Henri Dunant's instigation, remains today a neutral humanitarian organization devoted to the care of the sick and wounded. The Geneva Convention, signed by many nations in 1864, is still today intended to define and protect the right of civilians and prisoners of war.

Aftermath

In spite of his military success, Napoléon III was shaken by the heavy casualties of Solferino. Alarmed by the growing military power of Prussia, the emperor quickly concluded an armistice on July 7, 1859, bringing an end to this bloody war.

After the Italian campaign, for the first time, the glorious 2nd Foreign Regiment, no longer ignored and unwanted, was rewarded in being given permission to participate in the prestigious military parade on Quatorze Juillet (July 14, French national day) in Paris for a brief moment of glory. Medals for bravery were also granted. Ten legionaries were awarded the prestigious Legion d'honneur Knight Cross and 33 of them awarded the much coveted Médaille militaire (Military Medal). In August 1859 the 2nd Foreign Regiment, under Colonel Martinez, returned to Sidi-Bel-Abbes, while the Swiss 1st Regiment returned to Philippeville.

French field gun about 1859

At the end of 1861, Napoléon III's unsuccessful Swiss experiment was abandoned. The remnants of the 1st Regiment were incorporated into the ranks of the 2nd Regiment. This unit became the Légion étrangère proper. It came under the command of Colonel Butet, who replaced Martinez. The Legion's home was fixed at Sidi-Bel-Abbes.

Mexico, 1862–1867

Historical background

In the early 1860s Mexico was torn by a civil war between the clerical and conservative Miramon and the liberal Garcia Benito de Juárez. Both parties borrowed money from Europe, and the victorious Juárez, legally elected in 1861, repudiated the loans. European bondholders and speculators demanded satisfaction from their governments. Great Britain, France and Spain sent a combined military force to Veracruz to collect debts in 1862, but Napoléon III harbored a more ambitious design. The emperor was determined to embark on a "crusade," partly for religious, partly for financial, partly for political reasons, to create a Catholic pro–French Mexican empire (with Austrian archduke Maximilian as its figurehead emperor) to counterbalance the growing power of the United States, which at that time was torn and paralyzed by the Civil War.

In May 1863, a French expeditionary force put Maximilian in power. He reigned for four years, but from the start everything had been miscalculated: the proud temper and courage of the Mexican people, the determination of Juárez, the number of troops required to reduce the country, and the obstacles offered by the climate, the difficult terrain and the outcome of the American Civil War. The chief of the French army, General François Achille Bazaine (1811–1888), conducted an able campaign but he never succeeded in subduing the Juarist guerrillas, and the feeble emperor Maximilian failed to attract any serious popular support. By the autumn of 1865 the U.S. government began to adopt a threatening attitude and the failure of the French operation was an accomplished fact. Reluctantly, Napoléon III withdrew his force in February 1867. Shorn of French troops, Emperor Maximilian was defeated, captured and shot in June 1867. Napoléon III's Mexican venture proved pointless and ended in a great loss of prestige—another war fought for nothing.

The battle of Camerone, April 30, 1863

In 1862, the French expeditionary forces had secured a corridor between the port of Vera Cruz and the city of Puebla well inland. No further advance could be made on Mexico City until Puebla was captured, but the city resisted for many months. It was at that time that the French Foreign Legion came upon the Mexican scene.

In late 1862 the Régiment étranger was based at Sidi-Bel-Abbes where everything was quiet, and—thunderstruck to be left out of the French expedition—Legion officers petitioned Napoléon III. What the Legion did not know was that French military authorities had seriously considered handing over to Maximilian the whole Corps, in the same way that Louis-Philippe I had ceded the first "Old" Legion to Maria-Christina of Spain in 1835. However, because Napoléon III had not agreed to this plan, it had been dropped. Instead, in January 1863, a Régiment étranger de marche (task regiment) was raised; this was composed of two battalions divided into seven companies and a headquarters company (in all about 2,000 soldiers) placed under command of Colonel Jeanningros. Jeanningros was a highly regarded personality. He had entered the French army at the age of 14. He had fought at Moulay-Ismael (Algeria) in 1835, and a year later served in the Zouave Corps. Many times wounded—and owing to his courage, military skills and experience—he was promoted to the rank of colonel commanding the 43rd Infantry Line Regiment. In March 1862 he volunteered to serve in the Foreign Legion.

Officers and men were jubilant at the thought of loot, exotic women and glory. The Foreign Legion task force disembarked at Veracruz on March 26, 1863, where they quickly revised their opinions of exotic Mexico. Instead of taking part in the siege of Puebla, the Legion was charged with protecting convoys in eastern Mexico in the so-called *Tierras calidas* (Warm Lands), between Veracruz and Puebla, a region which was constantly attacked and threatened by Juarez's *guerrilleros*. Colonel Jeanningros's force was divided into several units stationed along the road at Veracruz, Tejeria, La Soledad, and Chiquihuite. This French-held "corridor" was vulnerable to guerrilla raids, and indeed the whole of Mexico, outside the few cities and towns garrisoned by French troops, was unsafe. The portion of road placed under the control of the Legion represented a stretch of about 85 kilometers in a sweltering area of stagnant marshes, unhealthy forest with occasional bleak and dry uplands covered with cactus scrub. Desolation was complete: there was no entertainment and no serious fighting. Only the blazing sun, diseases, irritating patrol actions, convoy escorts, and occasionally sudden and bloody skirmishes with an invisible enemy. Soon the legionaries dropped like flies from *vomito negro* (fever), pestilences and diseases as the siege of Puebla dragged on and on.

In late April 1863, in a small hamlet named Camerone, the Foreign Legion's

Legion fusilier Mexico 1863. The rifleman wears the square-peaked casquette with white cover, black chin-strap and white neck-cloth. Alternative headgear was a local Mexican sombrero. Around the neck he has a blue neck-stock. Behind the tunic he wears a white collarless shirt. The tunic—called a basquine—is fastened by a row of nine buttons. It is dark blue, short and could be worn open; it has a yellow collar with red piping, and the shoulder straps are green. A long wide blue or red body sash worn under the belt was introduced for the first time. The baggy trousers were red, often with leather reinforcement patches between the thighs, and tucked into fawn leggings above white, buttoned leather gaiters. Equipment includes a drinking bottle covered in dark grey cloth and a black leather waist-belt supporting a single black pouch for ammunition and a black scabbard for the socket bayonet. The weapon is a model 1860 percussion rifle.

greatest epic took place. At the end of April 1863, Colonel Jeanningros at his headquarters at Chiquihuite received word that a convoy of siege material, artillery munitions, and 3 million gold francs for the besieging army at Puebla would leave early on the next day from the village of Soledad marching in his direction by the route El Sordo, Palo Verde, Camerone, Paso Ancho and Paso del Macho. Jeanningros was ordered to send troops down the road to protect the convoy. This cumbersome column—commanded by Captain Cabossel—was composed of 60 mule-drawn carts stretching along 5 kilometers and proceeding very slowly on a bad and dusty track. What the French did not know was that Colonel Francesco de Paula Milan, the territorial commander of the Juarist forces in the region, had also been informed about the convoy by his network of spies. The secret apparently had leaked some time before the convoy was due to depart, certainly in sufficient time for the local leader to muster a force of about 800 horsemen and 1,000 infantrymen. An ambush near the Joya River, 5 kilometers north of Camerone hacienda, was laid to capture the convoy and seize the money.

Colonel Jeanningros ordered the 3rd Company of the 1st Battalion to clear the road and meet the convoy. This unit, composed of Poles, Germans, Belgians, Italians, Spaniards, and a few Frenchmen, had fallen to 62 legionaries due to disease. It was headed by Captain Jean Danjou. Two other officers from the HQ company, *sous-lieutenants* (Second Lieutenants) Maudet and Vilain, volunteered to accompany him. Captain Jean Danjou was born on April 15, 1828, at Chalabre (*département* of Aude). After graduation at the French military school of Saint-Cyr, he served in Algeria in the 51st Infantry Regiment and volunteered to serve in the Foreign Legion in 1852. An experienced officer, a veteran of Algeria, Crimea, Italy, and Morocco, a holder of the Honor Legion Cross, he had lost his left

Sombrero

hand at Sevastopol, and he wore an articulated wooden prosthesis fixed to his wrist.

Early on the morning of April 30, 1863, Danjou's small troop left Chiquihuite on a 24-hour patrol. The mission was to reach Palo Verde and to secure the path of the supply convoy. The men were lightly equipped, carrying their rations on mules, and were armed with their model 1857 percussion rifle-muskets and 60 rounds per soldier. After a few hours marching, the column reached the French-held post of Paso del Macho commanded by Captain Saussier who, seeing how small Danjou's company was, offered a grenadier platoon as reinforcement. Danjou—thinking it would only weaken his colleague and totally ignorant of the fact that Colonel Milan's had been spying on him since his departure—kindly refused the offer and the small troop set off again. At about 5 A.M., the 3rd Company marched right in front of the deserted hacienda (farmhouse) of Camerone. As a precaution, the company was split into two squads, which marched in extended order around the hamlet in search of elusive enemies. None appeared and the squads regrouped about one mile beyond Camerone. Then Danjou's company halted for breakfast. The water for coffee was almost boiling when the Legion sentry spotted Mexican cavalry approaching, and suddenly the

Legion officer in Mexico. By the time of the campaign in Mexico, officers often wore the popular tunic of zouave cut. This was dark blue with gold knots on the sleeves. The loose-cut trousers were red. The képi was red and blue with gold rank piping.

3rd Company was charged by a strong party of Milan's horsemen armed with lances and swords. Totally surprised, the legionaries repulsed the attack by firing volleys. Danjou then deployed his men on the southern side of the track behind a thick edge of cactus. A second cavalry charge was repulsed and, fearing to be encircled in open terrain, Captain Danjou ordered a hurried retreat through the thick cactus scrub back to the nearest cover: the deserted farmhouse of Camerone. In this first phase of the battle 16 legionaries were killed or captured, and—equally disastrous for the party—the two mules carrying food, water and spare ammunition had broken loose, became separated from the company, and galloped off. After moving painfully and slowly through the undergrowth with the Mexicans pressing close on them, the remaining 46 men—of whom several were already wounded—and their three officers took cover in Camerone. Danjou's decision to retreat to the hacienda was dictated by his sense of mission. He chose to block the road between Milan's force and Captain Cabossel's supply convoy and, by doing so, drew the Mexican forces to his small group. As he had no idea how strong the opposing

2. The French Foreign Legion at the Time of Napoléon III, 1852–1871

Legion sergeant, Camerone, 1863. The weapon is a carbine model 1853T with bayonet-sword model 1842.

force was, he probably wanted to gain time by holding back the enemy.

The hamlet of Camerone consisted of a partially derelict two-storey hacienda with partly ruined gates, breached walls made of adobe enclosing a square corral (about 50 m × 50 m) and several equally collapsed buildings, barns and sheds on the other side of the track. Unfortunately Mexican snipers had gotten there first. Deployed in the main building, they fired with U.S.–made repeating Sharp and Spencer carbines at the legionaries (armed with single-shots). The French had no other option than to seek cover in the northwestern corner of the hacienda within the ruins of lean-to outhouses. The position was hurriedly barricaded and openings were filled with planks, beams and available debris of all kinds. Already suffering casualties, Danjou's 3rd Company was rapidly and completely encircled by Milan's cavalry, who now had dismounted. By 9:00 A.M., Colonel Milan demanded the surrender of the 3rd Company, but this request was rejected. It is believed that Danjou—even though knowing his situation was hopeless—made each and every legionary swear to him that they would never accept capitulation.

The second phase of the battle began, this time in the farmhouse. The Mexican attacks were renewed and the rate of fire increased, causing casualties on both sides. Captain Danjou was killed at about 11:00 A.M. by a sniper firing from the upper

storey of the farmhouse. Second Lieutenant Vilain took over command and continued directing the defense with determination. The number of killed and wounded increased hour by hour. About noon the heat became unbearable, and suddenly trumpets and drums were heard. These sounds raised the besieged company's hopes. Was it Captain Saussier from Paso del Macho or Lieutenant-Colonel Giraud from La Soledad or Captain Cabossel's escort coming to their rescue? Unfortunately no relief approached, but rather Milan's three battalions, a reinforcement of about 1,000 infantrymen. Again the Juarists demanded the surrender of the 3rd Company, and again this was rejected. Colonel Milan became impatient. He ordered this small troop to be quickly wiped out and then to proceed to attack the supply column. At high cost, the French managed to repulse several

Mexican Juarist, c. 1863. The Juarists had only a few regular military formations, and most of the units were of a "territorial" nature in that they lived and operated in the same district. They simply mustered when called upon for a particular operation and then dispersed again to their homes when the raid was done. They were thus totally familiar with the sectors in which they operated and had the support of the local population. As civilian territorial guerrilleros they did not wear uniforms. Armament varied; it was mainly from the United States (Remington and Winchester carbines), or purchased in other foreign countries or captured from the French.

assaults. Fighting raged in the courtyard in the blazing noontime tropical sun. Survivors, including the wounded, all tortured by thirst, repulsed charge after charge, frequently at the point of the bayonet in the breaches and rubble of the battered barns. At about 2:00 P.M. Vilain was killed. Second Lieutenant Maudet took over, and, seizing a dead man's weapon, he fired like a common rifleman at the enemy. Another call to surrender was made, but was answered by a rude word. Then the Mexicans brought up straw and put it afire. Choked by thick and stifling smoke, tormented by sun and thirst, Maudet and his 12 surviving legionaries rejected another demand to surrender at 5:00 P.M. and, after a brief lull, continued to fight. In spite of steady firing by the legionaries, the Mexicans slowly closed in. One hour later, confined to one of the miserable sheds, exhausted, assaulted and under fire from all directions, Maudet had only seven, then four men alive. After 15 minutes of desperate combat, when they had shot their last round, Maudet gave the order to fix bayonets. In a display of defiant courage, knowing that all was hopeless against such odds, the last men of the 3rd Company charged with the bayonet into the ranks of hundreds of Mexicans massed in the corral. Swamped by sheer weight of number, Maudet and legionary Catteau were wounded at once, but an enemy officer named Combas (ironically a Frenchman serving in the Juarist army)—astonished by such gallantry—prevented his men from firing at Corporal Maine, Private Wenzel and Private Constantin. Maine, speaking in Spanish, said that the three survivors would accept surrender provided they could keep their weapons and that the injured Maudet and Catteau be taken care of. It is said that the chivalresque Combas replied in French: "To men like you, one cannot refuse anything." The exhausted Maine, Wenzel and Constantin were presented to Colonel Milan, who greeted them. They thought, however, they would face a firing squad for having inflicted so many casualties. To their great surprise, they were well treated and later released. Another man, Private Lai, lived to tell the story of the action: the badly wounded drummer escaped by feigning death under a pile of dead comrades. Twelve prisoners of the 3rd Company were later handed over to the French under an exchange agreement. During the battle 52 officers and men of the 3rd Company had died in action or later of their wounds. The price was extremely high but the mission was accomplished: Captain Cabossel's supply convoy was safe. Hearing gunfire in the distance, it had turned back to safety at La Soledad. Danjou's 62 men had held off about 1,800 Mexicans for 11 hours, inflicting between 300 and 500 dead and wounded—the exact number is still unknown. The following day, May 1, 1863, a relief column was sent to Camerone, and, among the smoking ruins, Colonel Jeanningros's men found only dead naked bodies as the Mexicans had stripped the legionaries of their weapons, uniforms and equipment.

The legacy of Camerone

The battle of Camerone was over and the Camerone legend started. Corporal Berg, one of the survivors, later declared to Colonel Jeanningros: "The 3rd company of the 1st battalion is no more, Colonel, but it has done enough so that one might henceforth say: it contained nothing but good soldiers!"

Of all the scores of battles of the Legion, the battle of Camerone—after all, only a minor incident in the Mexican campaign—is the most highly regarded. It is extremely important in the history of the Legion because it helped to create a reputation of loyalty, bravery, courage and self-sacrifice. One may ask: why has a defeat been singled out in this way instead of a victory? The answer is that in the Legion it is always the spirit that counts and is remembered, not so much the deed itself. The "Camerone spirit"—that is to refuse to surrender and

Mexican horseman, c. 1864

fight till the last round and till the last man—was to leave a profound mark on the Foreign Legion. Many Camerones were subsequently fought by the Corps and the *spirit* was still very much alive as late as 1954 during the ill-fated battle of Dien Bien Phu in Indochina. "*Faire Camerone*" (that is, fighting with the Camerone spirit) became one of the leading principles of the French Foreign Legion. Before Camerone the Corps was recognized as a tough fighting force but the legionaries had a (often deserved) bad reputation. The conventional army's commanders did not take the Legion seriously, and they often regarded it as a collection of unreliable thugs and dangerous looting mercenaries.

Camerone also contributed materially in establishing strongly rooted traditions and self-esteem. Danjou's wooden hand was found two years later at Tesuitlan in possession of a Frenchman curiously nicknamed l'Anglais (Englishman) who agreed to sell it for 50 piastres to a Legion officer. Another source says the artificial hand was found right after the battle of Camerone in the hacienda. Whatever, the wooden hand was brought back to Sidi-Bel-Abbes in 1867 at the end of the Mexican campaign. It became the most sacred relic of the French Foreign Legion, the very symbol of its esprit de corps, symbolizing loyalty, gallantry and final defiance in the face of hopeless odds. Danjou's wooden hand was displayed in the hall of the Legion's home at Sidi-Bel-Abbes until the Corps moved its depot to Aubagne (near Marseilles, southern France) in 1962.

At Colonel Jeanningros's request, Napoléon III approved inscription of *Camerone 1863* on all Foreign Legion flags and banners, a tradition still alive today. The emperor also ordered the placing of a commemorative plate in the Hôtel des Invalides in Paris bearing the names of Danjou, Vilain and Maudet in golden letters. For unknown reasons this order was executed only in August 1949 at the initiative of General Blanc, director of the Invalides, the French army museum. In 1938 a commemorative plate was placed on Danjou's house in his native village of Chalabre. April 30 became the revered and traditional *Camerone Day*, the most important ceremonial holiday of the Legion. Each year on April 30, Colonel Danjou's legendary hand is paraded and the heroic story of the Camerone battle is read aloud to every Legion unit, wherever they may be, as the climax of impressive military ceremonies, generally followed by a heavy drinking bout. Today the hacienda of Camerone has practically disappeared as a railway line now runs through the courtyard where the 3rd Company fought to the end, but each year on Camerone Day a ceremony takes place there attended by French residents in Mexico and Mexican officers. There is a commemorative marker, placed in 1892, bearing this inscription in Latin: "They were here less than sixty / Opposed to a whole army / Crushed by its mass / These French soldiers / Lost their lives but not their courage / On April 30, 1863."

The end of the war in Mexico

Camerone did not mean, of course, the end of the Mexican campaign, which lasted until 1867. The epic standoff at Camerone made a deep impression on the French army command in Mexico, but in spite of this the Legion remained engaged in unrewarding missions, including going on patrol, hunting guerrilleros, undertaking "pacification" and occupation duties, and convoying escorts in the most unhealthy part of the country. Diseases took a steady toll and by February 1864, the effective strength had sunk to 11 officers and 800 men out of the original strength of over 2,000. On Colonel Jeanningros's request the Legion was strengthened with fresh troops from Algeria and Mexican recruits. The corps was reorganized and composed of four infantry battalions, a company of Mexican volunteers, a mounted scouting company, and a mountain artillery battery of six small howitzers

Mexican campaign medal, 1862–1867

Santa Isabella hacienda near Parras, the Legion suffered another disastrous defeat, rather similar to Camerone. The 2nd Battalion (eight officers and 177 legionaries under command of Captain Brian) was ambushed by a party of 1,500 Juarists. The example of Camerone had apparently taken root and only one officer and 81 men survived. Of those taken prisoner, 40 died in captivity. Other engagements took place, notably Huichapam (October 1866) and Perral (November 1866) but the war was already lost.

By April 1865, the American Civil War was over, and the United States then took a deep interest in the Mexican affair, openly aiding Juárez. They gathered a force of 30,000 soldiers on the northern bank of the Rio Bravo River while the U.S. Navy entered the waters of the Gulf of Mexico. To avoid a clash with the Americans, Monterrey was evacuated, and French troops withdrew from northern Mexico. Of course Juarist troops flooded into the territories the French vacated. Soon Napoléon III ordered the retreat of all French troops from Mexico. In February 1867 the Foreign Legion embarked for home at Veracruz. The humiliating and pointless Mexican campaign had cost the Legion 31 officers and 1,917 NCOs and legionaries who perished either in combat or of disease.

carried by mules. With this new force Jeanningros at last obtained permission to take part in active operations in the field. The Legion was able to pacify the region of Puebla and repel Juarist forces led by General Porfirio Diaz. In the winter of 1864-1865, the Legion took part in operations launched in southern Mexico against the fortress of Oaxaca. Jeanningros's troops were successfully engaged at Matamoros, San Luis Potosi and Saltillo. Reinforced with the 4th Battalion from Algeria, the Legion participated in the siege of Monterrey in June 1865, almost on the frontier of the United States. In February 1866, at

The Legion, 1867–1870

On returning from Mexico the Foreign Legion took up its old duties in Algeria. The three battalions were based at Mascara, Sidi-Bel-Abbes and Saida. This period was not the best for the Legion. The quality of the leadership always declined somewhat in peacetime. The Corps did not get a fair chance to consolidate and progress; it tended to fade into the background. Of the several commanding officers who were appointed, of whom some stayed only for months, some were distinguished leaders,

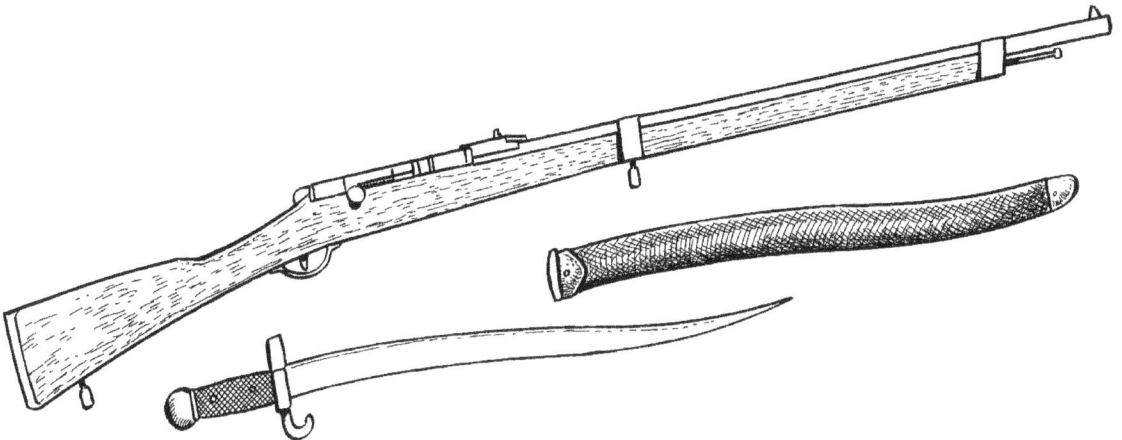

Chassepot 1866 needle-rifle with bayonet. By 1866 a new weapon was issued to the French army and to the Legion. This was the MAS Chassepot fusil d'infanterie M66 which had been designed about 1857 by Antoine-Alphonse Chassepot (1833–1905). The breech-loading rifle was built by the Manufacture d'Armes de Saint-Etienne (MAS, National Weapon Factory of Saint-Etienne, near Lyon). It was used by the French army from 1866 to 1874, when it was gradually replaced by the 1874 Gras rifle. It had a caliber of 11 mm (0.43"), single action, and a weight of 4.1 kg (9.13 lbs.), a range of almost 1,000 meters, and an average rate of fire of six rounds per minute.

but others were less than mediocre. Many were place-seekers, carreerists with political ambition only hungry for promotion and advancement, and thus they regarded the Legion only as a useful stepping-stone. In garrison, officers were remote figures, and the men were largely supervised by senior NCOs and the dreaded *adjudants* (warrant officers) who exercised an iron discipline, and sometimes abused their authorities, giving rise to the horror stories, all too often found in novels about the Legion. The legionaries' great vice was drunkenness, and they were often tempted to desert; desertion had always been a serious problem in the Legion, and this would remain so until late in the 20th century. Indeed many men joined without having the slightest idea of what they were doing. Disappointment, hardship, iron discipline and training were for many unbearable. After a few months service some got fed up or bored and deserted. By doing so they did not feel they were traitors—they saw themselves not as Frenchmen who betrayed their fatherland but merely professionals breaking a business contract. In wartime desertion was considered a serious crime, which could result in the death penalty; but in peacetime this could be punished more or less indulgently. Deserters were generally incorporated into the dreaded Bat'd'Af (short for Batallions d'Afrique), disciplinary units placed in remote parts of the north African desert, notably at Tataouine, where conditions were particularly harsh.

In 1868, a 4th Foreign Battalion was set up. There were some scattered skirmishes and raids against dissident Algerian tribes, notably in the region south of Oran in 1867, but, on the whole, the northern part of Algeria was pacified and the first stage of the French conquest was over. The legionaries were occupied in monotonous hard marching, boring patrols, dull occupation duties, and policing actions in little remote forts. Mostly they engaged in back-breaking construction work. In peacetime the legionaries exchanged rifle and bayonet for shovel and pick. Everywhere the Legion was garrisoned, the legionaries erected fortified positions, notably small forts for control duty, but they also constructed bridges, roads and tracks, railways, tunnels, military hospitals, administrative offices, and schools and civilian buildings.

In this period the "Boudin" became the official marching song of the French Foreign Legion. (See Appendix for the music and translated lyrics of the Legion's marching song.)

Although created for "duty outside France," the Legion took part in one of the most disastrous wars fought on French soil: the Franco-Prussian War of 1870.

The Franco-Prussian War, 1870

Historical background

In the 19th century, Germany was still a profoundly divided land comprising many duchies, kingdoms, principalities, bishoprics and free cities. It would become a powerful sovereign state in 1871 after a series of aggressive wars backed by brilliant diplomatic moves, largely due to the skills and efforts of the Prussian chancellor Otto von

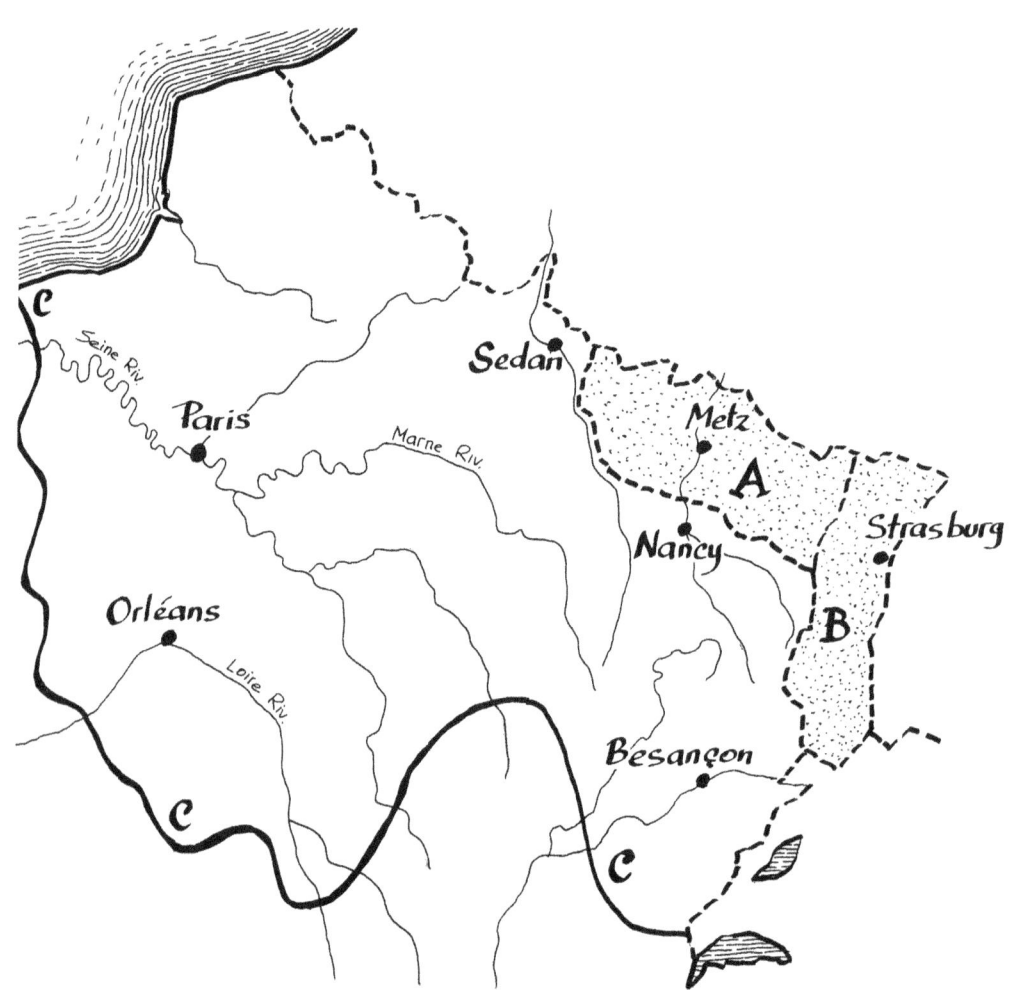

Sketch map of the 1870 war. The map displays the northeastern part of France. A (a large part of Lorraine) and B (Alsace) indicates the two provinces annexed by Germany. The line CCC indicates the zone occupied by the Germans from 1870 to 1873. This zone was recovered by France after the payment of a war indemnity.

Bismarck (1815–1898). Napoléon III—fearing Prussia as the leader of a united Germany and anxious to regain his waning prestige—made the foolish mistake of declaring war on Prussia on July 19, 1870. In a chaotic state of mobilization and logistical confusion, lacking a clear plan of attack and with little intelligence of the enemy, Napoléon III ordered an advance on Berlin, but the Prussians quickly seized the initiative in the field and invaded northeastern France. French defeats followed in quick succession at Wissembourg, Froeschwiller, Forbach, Metz and Sedan. Napoléon III himself fell prisoner and personally had to sign the act of capitulation. After a short custody in Germany, the defeated emperor, a bitter and sick man, ended his life in exile in England, where he died in 1873.

As soon as news of the capture of Napoléon III and the capitulation of Sedan reached Paris on September 4, 1870, confusion was total. The republican leader Léon Gambetta proclaimed the fall of the Second Empire and the creation of the Third Republic (1870–1940). The new French republican government decided to continue the war. Paris surrendered after an appalling siege that lasted from September 1870 to January 1871. Peace between the newly created French Third Republic and the newly created German Second Reich was reached on signing the Treaty of Frankfurt on May 10, 1871.

The Legion in the 1870 war

On August 22, 1870, it was decided to create a 5th Legion Battalion, to be engaged against the Prussians for the duration of the war. Composed of seven companies (about 1,600 men), it was raised from foreigners living in France and sympathetic to the French cause. Placed under the leadership of Commandant Victor-Joseph Arago, the battalion included Austrians, Swiss, Belgians, Italians, Spaniards, Poles, and Serbians but, obviously, no Germans. They included the Serbian prince Karageorgevitch, the future king of Serbia Peter I who served as second-lieutenant in the 1st Foreign Regiment under the pseudonym of Kara. About the same time, two others battalions (2,000 legionaries) were raised from the available troops in Sidi-Bel-Abbes in Algeria. As nothing was properly organized and coordinated, these ill-equipped units landed in Toulon (southern France) only in early October 1870.

The 5th Foreign Legion Battalion was incorporated in the 15th Army Corps, about 20,000 strong, commanded by General De La Mottery, and engaged in the region of Orléans. At first, in mid–October 1870, they were deployed to defend the village of Arthenay. Gradually, under enemy pressure, they were forced to retreat to Orléans where they defended the suburb of Bel-Air-les-Aides. When Commandant Arago was killed, the disorganized battalion withdrew to the suburb of Bannier. The situation was confused and soon desperate. Under heavy artillery fire and encircled by overwhelming infantry, the badly battered 5th Foreign Legion Battalion lost two-thirds of its complement. A breakout was planned, but this was only partially successful. Many were killed, wounded and taken prisoner. Others hid and escaped to the French lines. On October 19, remnants of the 5th Foreign Legion Battalion were merged into the other two "Algerian" Foreign Legion Battalions at Pierrefitte. These units were regrouped and redesignated Régiment de marche de la Légion étrangère (RMLE, Foreign Legion Task Regiment). They were incorporated into the Loire Army, 60,000 men strong under the command of General d'Aurelle de Paladines, and regrouped at the military camp of Salbris. On November 9, 1870, at a place named Coulmiers, about three miles from Orléans, they defeated the Prussians commanded by General von der Thann and reoccupied Orléans. The idea now was to march and relieve the besieged capital of France. Two new armies—hastily raised by General Chanzy (at the Loire River in the south) and General Faidherbes (in the North)—were to converge on Paris. Unfortunately, due to lack of coordination, poor leadership, unpreparedness, and bad weather (the winter of 1870-1871 was particularly cold), these rescue armies never reached Paris. On December 2, 1870, they were defeated by the Prussians at Loigny. The badly disorganized Loire Army withdrew to Orléans, and the RMLE was ordered to cover its retreat. At Cercottes-Chevilly, on December 4, the Legion launched a bayonet charge and repulsed a Bavarian regiment, allowing General d'Aurelle de Paladines's force to win precious time. This sharp action halted the enemy, but only temporarily.

On December 17, 1870, from a total of 3,600 legionaries engaged at the beginning of the campaign, only 1,000 survived. The rest were dead, wounded, sick, incapacitated, taken prisoner or missing. By that time the survivors were hastily reinforced with 2,000 Breton infantry volunteers. On January 7, 1871, the new "Foreign" Legion Regiment (which consisted of only one-third foreigners) was shipped by train from Vierzon to Montbéliard near Besançon in the Jura Mountains, not far from the Swiss border, to reinforce General Bourbaki's Eastern Army. The journey was long and appalling, undertaken with little

Legionary, France, 1870

food, spotty accommodation and in bitter cold against a background of civilian panic, military disorganization and total confusion.

The Foreign/Breton Regiment was incorporated into the 39th Régiment de ligne (French Infantry), a part of General Bourbaki's army (85,000 strong), and deployed at

Sainte-Suzanne Hill, west of Montbéliard. The frozen hill—swept by wind, snow storms and enemy bullets—was taken by the Legion in an action which gained the admiration of General Peytavin, who declared: "The Foreign Regiment on its own has done the job of a whole division!" The Legion's success marked, however, only a local and, in the end, a futile victory. The Prussian lines had not been broken and the enemy counterattacked. Boubaki's force, wretchedly equipped and ill-commanded, was defeated and pushed back over the frontier into neutral Switzerland and there ignominiously disarmed on February 1, 1871.

Sainte-Suzanne Hill was the Legion's last action in the war against the Germans. Short of food and ammunition the 39th Régiment de ligne and the Foreign Regiment, in the middle of total chaos, were forced to retreat back to the city of Besançon. On January 28, 1871, Paris surrendered and France capitulated.

The war with Prussia was over but fighting went on as a French civil war broke out in Paris. The so-called Commune was a spontaneous revolutionary insurrection caused by a variety of political and social factors. The fighting in Paris was atrocious, beyond anything known in any preceding

Legion headgear (France, winter, 1870-1871)

Legion corporal, 1870

French and Parisian revolutions, and, in the end, the Commune was crushed in a terrible bloodbath. It is estimated that between 20,000 to 30,000 of its members were shot without trial, while another 35,000 were arrested, hastily tried and condemned to imprisonment or deportation.

In order to suppress the Parisian rebels and bring a rapid end to the civil war, President Adolphe Thiers and the National Assembly—after bargaining with the occupying Germans—frantically called in troops from all over France. On March 27, 1871, the 39th Régiment de ligne, which still included the Foreign Legion units (by that time totaling 66 officers and 1,003 NCOs and legionaries), was shipped by train from Besançon to Paris. The troops were incorporated into the so-called Paris Army, and engaged in suppression of the rebels. Against a background of exacerbated political passion resulting in atrocities perpetrated by both sides, the Legion participated to several skirmishes on the outskirts of Paris at Courbevoie and Neuilly and then inside Paris. It is difficult to know precisely to what degree the Legion participated in the harsh repression of the 1871 Paris Commune as the Legion itself remains rather discreet about it. For several weeks the Corps was probably engaged in street fighting, urban skirmishes, and assaults on desperately defended barricades in the Gare du Nord, Villette and Buttes-Chaumont neighborhoods. Were there perhaps also foreign legionaries who, together with the soldiers of the government's army, slaughtered the last Communard rebels in the midst of the graves of the Père-Lachaise cemetery on May 27, 1871? Given the silence and the apparent embarrassment about this operation, it seems that crushing the Commune was one of the dirtiest missions of the countless dirty operations ordered by French governments to be carried out by the French Foreign Legion. There was no glory and nothing to be proud of about the actions, as civil wars are always savage and brutal. The bloodbath of the Commune remains something of a taboo subject, and, even today, the Legion authorities and Legion historians prefer to quickly and quietly turn this unglorious page of their glorious history.

In June 1871, the survivors of the Franco-Prussian War, decorated with medals, returned to their home depots in Algeria. The 5th Battalion, whose strength had considerably decreased and which in any case had been raised only for the duration of the war, was formally disbanded at Saida in December 1871.

3

Colonial Conquests, 1872–1914

French Expansion

In the 19th century, and particularly after 1870, the most industrially advanced European powers took part to a wide movement of aggressive imperialism and predatory colonialism. With the development of the Industrial Revolution the Europeans needed goods of a kind and in quantity that preindustrial handicraft methods simply could no longer supply. Under the principle of protected trade, it was thought necessary to exercise political influence in areas in which one did business.

The expansion of France overseas had begun in 1831 with the conquest of Algeria. Although the French public was little concerned or interested in distant conquest, the expansion continued during the Second Empire. After France's humiliating defeat in 1870, the government of the Third Republic worked to regain France's place as a leading power in Europe by providing it with a worldwide colonial empire. At the beginning of the 20th century, France possessed four major colonial blocks. Built by Jules Ferry and his successors, the French Empire was the second largest in the world. It included the following:

- Afrique du Nord française (ANF, French North Africa, or Maghreb) including Morroco, Algeria, and Tunisia.
- Afrique occidendale française (AOF, French West Africa) including Mauritania, French Sudan (today Mali), Senegal, Niger, Guinea, Upper Volta (Burkina Faso), Ivory Coast, Dahomey, Cameroon and Togo (after 1918).
- Afrique équatoriale française (AEF, French Equatorial Africa) including Chad, Ougangui-Chari (today a part of Central African Republic), Gabon and Congo-Brazzaville. In addition France possessed in Africa the French coast of Somalia (Djibouti), the Comores Islands, the Seychelles Islands, Madagascar and the island of Reunion.
- Indochine française (French Indochina) including Vietnam (Tonkin, Annam and Cochin China), Laos, and Cambodia.

In the 1880s and 1890s, the Foreign Legion (together with the Colonial army) played an important role in the conquests overseas. Wherever there was a particularly difficult, dirty, unrewarding or dangerous job to be done, the Legion was the first to advance and the last to retreat.

French canonière *(gun-boat), c. 1892. In the colonies, rivers often offered the most obvious routes for either exploration or military advance.*

The Legion in Algeria, 1872–1884

Uprising in Algeria

The French defeat of 1870 had, of course, encouraged North African tribesmen to revolt. During the absence of their comrades, who were engaged in the ill-fated battle of France, the 3rd and 4th Foreign Legion Battalions had to face local uprisings in Kabylia, on the Moroccan border in the southern part of Oran Province, and at the edge of the Sahara Desert. Faced with superior forces, the small number of French occupation troops and garrisons were on the defensive and only able to take measures to contain the general rebellion. As soon as the war with Germany was over, French troops were rushed to Algeria. Several punitive

Colonial medal. The Médaille coloniale was instituted in 1893 as a reward for soldiers and sailors who took part in colonial conquests.

Zouave, about 1900

expeditions were launched and the rebels were soon hunted down and dispersed after a series of limited actions and violent skirmishes. The Legion—whose units were stationed at Géryville, Saida, Mascara and Sidi-Bel-Abbes—was engaged in the southern part of Oran Province to subdue the Ouled Sidi Cheik tribe. By August 1871, although many rebels safely slipped over the mountainous Moroccan border into the traditional refuge of France's enemies, the revolt began to die down. By January 1872, things quietened down further, and the last of the rebel leaders came in to sue for peace. The situation was now under control.

In 1871 Colonel de Mallaret was appointed commander of the Légion étrangère and many of the abuses which had sprung up were curbed and a calmer atmosphere was achieved. There was no serious fighting in Algeria, a large part of the country was pacified, and colonization and economic development proceeded. The strength of the Legion was limited to four battalions of four companies each, and the legionaries—for lack of enemies—served as a labor corps for about 10 years. This inactivity led the men astray into dangerous idleness, drunkenness and alcoholism, and some attempted to desert. The legionaries were put to work to develop the Algerian colony. They erected bridges and roads and helped build railways and also military and civilian buildings. They also built fortified positions, control posts and checkpoints particularly in the plains, mountains and deserts. These strongholds served as bases for the military, administrative, commercial and cultural

A Legion fort in Algeria (end of 19th century)

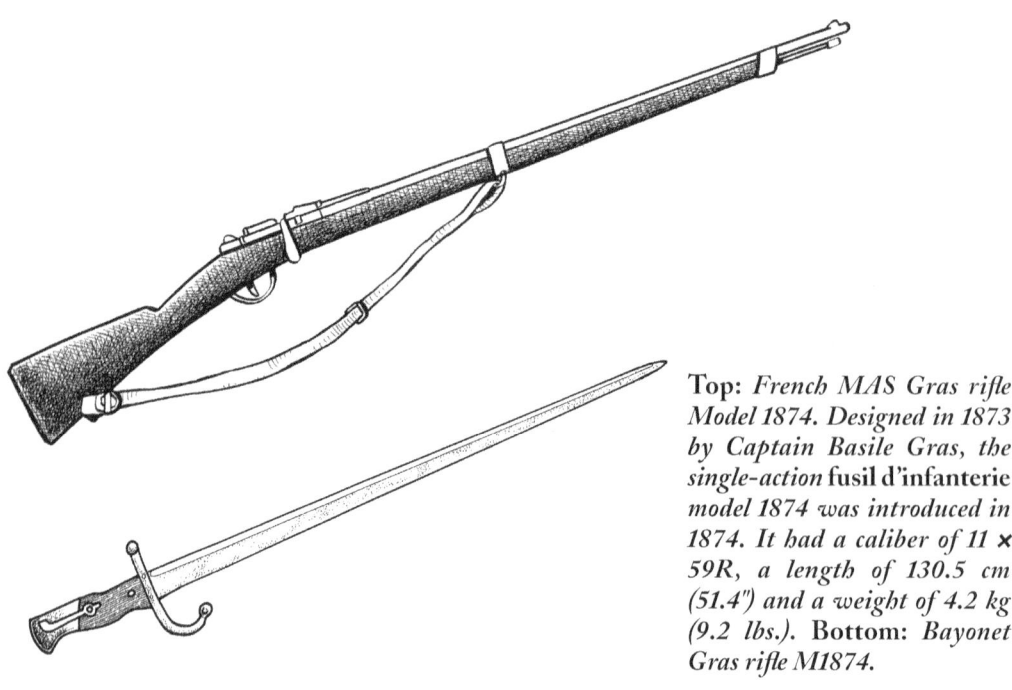

Top: *French MAS Gras rifle Model 1874. Designed in 1873 by Captain Basile Gras, the* single-action fusil d'infanterie *model 1874 was introduced in 1874. It had a caliber of 11 × 59R, a length of 130.5 cm (51.4″) and a weight of 4.2 kg (9.2 lbs.).* **Bottom:** *Bayonet Gras rifle M1874.*

exploitation of the surrounding area. They were intended to impress the local inhabitants and deter them from rebelling and they acted as refuges in time of troubles. A typical Foreign Legion fort at the end of the 19th century usually accommodated a garrison of 20 to 40 men with a varying number of native auxiliaries; it was located either in an oasis in the Sahara desert by a crossroad on the plains or on a pass in the mountains.

Mounted companies

The legionaries were rescued from their role as laborers in 1881, when Colonel François Négrier became chief of the Legion. Négrier—probably one of the Legion's greatest commanders—had served as senior colonial officer in the Chasseurs d'Afrique. He was an officer of energy and foresight, he took a deep interest in the Foreign Legion and—having influence in higher places—he was able to revitalize the Corps. Négrier wanted soldiers, not laborers, and he made changes and introduced innovations. He put a stop to a rather depressing period and raised the Legion to a new pitch of

Bourgeron. The so-called **bourgeron** *was a hard wearing, lightweight and readily washable fatigue suit including cap, white blouse and trousers. The man also wears the Legion dark blue* **ceinture** *(sash) around the waist. This piece of cloth (with a length of 4.20 m and a width of 40 cm) was originally worn in the 1830s by French troops in Africa supposedly to protect their stomach from infections. The blue belt made its appearance in the Legion in the early 1880s, and it has become ever since a distinctive piece of the legionary's uniform.*

efficiency. He formed a sincere attachment to it and a high regard for the fighting ability of the legionnaires. The Foreign Legion has Négrier to thank for revitalizing it more than any other French officer.

Négrier instituted the first *compagnie montée* (mounted company). This unit, a form of mounted infantry, was fitted with one mule for each of two men; the mule carried the *barda* (food, water, tent, equipment and ammunitions, and own barley), and one man rode while his mate walked at the stirrup or marched ahead of the column as a scout on vanguard and reconnaissance duty. The men changed places every few hours; the officers rode on horses. This successful experiment, simple and effective, helped put an end to the debilitating long marches, which wasted the soldiers' strength before battle. Négrier also reorganized the defense of convoys, and he introduced light field artillery. At night the column halted for bivouac on the top of a hill, tents were set up, and the temporary camp was protected by a *murette*, a small screening wall, about 1 meter high and 0.50 meter wide, erected by the men, who piled up rocks and stones. The first mounted company was so successful that others were created. The *compagnies montées* became formidable weapons against the rebellious tribes of North Africa.

In 1881 a law was passed permitting Frenchmen to join the Foreign Legion for the first time. Many had already enlisted as Swiss or Belgian, but now because entry could be made openly, the Legion could attract a larger spectrum, and the corps gained in cohesion.

By then the French were engaged in mapping the whole of Algeria, and the surveyors and cartographers working in dangerous areas had to be protected by armed escorts. In April 1882 a significant attack occurred at Haci-Bel-Salem near the dry salt lake of Chott Tigri, south of Oran. A geographic survey party headed by Captain de Castries escorted by two rifle companies and a Legion mounted company (totaling about 300 men) was ambushed by a large force of Arab rebels led by their leader Bou Amama, who sought to oust the French from Algeria. Several charges were repulsed by the French armed with Gras rifles, and fighting lasted for seven hours. In the end the Arabs plundered the convoy and withdrew, leaving many dead on the ground. On the French side casualties were high: two officers and 49 men dead and two officers and 26 men wounded. The survivors were saved by a rescue columns headed by Colonel Négrier. Two Legion battalions were then sent in search of the dissident Bou Amama and his tribesmen, but they had disappeared over the Moroccan border.

After this action North Africa entered a period of relative peace broken only by occasional local uprisings, which were easily quelled by the Legion mounted companies. In the ensuing years the legionaries had far more work to do than fighting, their activities, again, being mainly centered round the various road construction schemes. Only the mounted companies operated near the fringes of the Sahara. In the period September 1892 to June 1893, and again in February 1894 to January 1895 the Legion's *compagnies montées* were sent to the Sudan for pacification duty against dissident Arabs in the desert, through which the French authorities planned to construct a transcontinental railroad track. The mounted companies proved their worth again by covering the extraordinary total of 12,000 miles under hard conditions and in difficult terrain during an exploring mission through Guinea, Senegal, Upper Volta (today Burkina Faso) and Sudan.

Back in December 1883, the Legion was expanded and divided into two units, each with four battalions: the Premier Régiment étranger (1er RE, 1st Foreign Regiment) stationed at Sidi-Bel-Abbes; and the Deuxième Régiment étranger (2eme RE, 2nd Foreign Regiment) stationed at Saida, Gerryville and Tiaret. Apart from occasional incidents in the foothills on the edge of the desert where the tribes were not fully pacified, the legionnaires were employed either in training, garrison duty or roadmaking.

By the end of 1883, Colonel Négrier was instrumental in persuading the French military authorities to include the Legion in the expeditionary force to the Far East. As a result the two battalions were shipped, and became heavily committed to a new challenge in a remote Asian country.

Indochina, 1883–1918

Historical background

Indochina is a huge peninsula that stretches for 3,000 kilometers, from southern China to Indonesia. It includes Laos, Cambodia and Vietnam—itself divided into northern Tonkin, central Annam and southern Cochin China. One of the key motivating factors that encouraged the French to undermine the authority of the Vietnamese emperors was their treatment of Roman Catholic missionaries, but it was also spurred by the desire to control trade. The French seized the eastern part of Cochin China in 1862, Cambodia in 1863 and the western part of Cochin China in 1867. After the fall of Napoléon III in 1870, the colonization drive was continued by the Third Republic with the conquest of Annam and Tonkin in 1883–1884. This was achieved after a war with the Chinese. By 1887, China declared that she was prepared to accept the overlordship of France in Vietnam and the war came to an end. The conquest of Indochina by the French was completed by the establishment of the Union générale indochinoise (Indochinese General Union). These colonies were commonly referred to as Indochine française (French Indochina).

Fighting against the Pavillons noirs

The 1st Battalion of the French Foreign Legion (600 men strong) left North Africa in September 1883 and reached the port of Haiphong in Tonkin one month later. From there it was deployed at Hanoi before moving up in a northern direction to chase the Chinese, joining the forces that were being gathered under the command of Admiral Amédée Anatole Courbet (1827–1885).

Their opponents were Chinese irregulars known as the Pavillons noirs (Black Flags) as this was the predominant color of the banners which they carried. Originally the Black Flags were a religious sect named Tai-Ping, which had merged with other Chinese sects such as the *Long Knifes* and the *White Water-Lily*. They had become fearless mercenaries and irregular troops employed by the Chinese authorities. Generally their discipline was poor and loot was their chief motivation; the various gangs were independent of each other and only joined together temporarily for a specific campaign, raid or operation. When the French began their penetration of North Vietnam, the Black Flags—about 25,000 men headed by a warlord named Lun-Vinh-Phuoc—were hired by the emperor of Annam. They were loosely organized, being small units of unequal size, each under its own leader. They were professional mercenaries capable of putting up serious resistance at times in terrain of their own choosing. They had a tendency to be unstable and unreliable, and they fell in with a master plan—whenever there happened to be one—only when it suited them. Their allegiance to the Chinese authorities was somewhat of a fiction, but they eagerly took all the weapons and supplies sent to them from China. These included mainly old-fashioned arms, although a few of the more modern types of fire weapons and artillery did trickle through to them. Their anarchical organization handicapped them when it came to regular pitched battles, and of course, their favorite tactic was guerrilla warfare, using hit-and-run attacks, quick raids and ambushes. The Black Flags were, however, not a "paper" force. On the contrary, they proved a hard nut to crack for the French.

French marsouin *(marine), c. 1885*

In August 1883, Admiral Courbet had subdued the emperor of Annam by seizing his capital, Hue, and a French protectorate over Annam and Tonkin was established. But the northern province was still occupied by the Pavillons Noirs, who held several fortresses. Courbet, with about 5,000 soldiers, including *marsouins* (navy infantrymen) and the 1st Legion Battalion, launched a large operation to defeat them. Three particular attacks on fortified works remain historically attached to the conquest of Tonkin by the French Foreign Legion: Son Tay, Bac Ninh and Tuyen Quang.

Son Tay

Son Tay is situated on the Red River northwest of Hanoi. From Hanoi, Admiral Courbet divided his force into a naval convoy, including seven steam gunships and 30 supply junks and barges sailing the river, and an infantry column marching along the Mandarine Road with, of course, the Legion in advance guard. Son Tay was occupied by about 25,000 Black Flags and regular Chinese. The city was heavily fortified. The external defenses included a 5-meter-wide moat filled with water; a 4-meter-high fence made of sharpened bamboo and a 5-meter-high earth wall. The citadel (fort within the town) had another 5-meter-wide ditch full of water, and a 5-meter-high stone wall. In addition the fortress included several outposts consisting of rough earthworks-cum-barricades, screening the main positions.

Admiral Courbet decided to concentrate his attack on the weakest spot, the main gate, with the Legion at the front. The operation began in the early morning of December 15, 1883, by a heavy bombardment, which soon caused the gatehouse to collapse. The breach was assaulted at high cost, and, after two hours of fierce fighting, a group of legionnaires led by a Belgian sergeant named Minnaert charged with the bayonet and leapt through the line of defense. In spite of this breakthrough, the

Black Flags' garrison did not surrender. The defenders were many times the strength of the French troops and stiff fighting went on in the narrow streets for the whole day and a part of the night. Nonetheless, step by step the Chinese defense collapsed, resulting in the evacuation of the citadel late in the night, and the retreat of the Chinese into the surrounding jungle. The French troops mastered the last defenders and the tricolor was hoisted over the fort. The victory was achieved mainly by the Legion, which suffered 10 killed and 48 wounded. In clear medieval fashion, the fighting was followed by the pillaging of the well-supplied citadel by the *marsouins* and the legionnaires.

Bac Ninh

In February 1884, the 2nd Legion Battalion (headed by Major Hutin) arrived at Haiphong to reinforce its sister unit, the 1st Battalion. The French had now decided on an all-out policy of conquest. Both Legion units were engaged with the rest of the French expeditionary force in the seizure of the fortress of Bac Ninh, situated on the Song Cau River 30 kilometers northeast of Hanoi. The French force totaled some 5,500 men, including navy infantry and the 1st and 2nd Battalions of the Legion; there were also about 6,000 coolies (hired porters) who carried supplies and equipment. Local spies had informed the French about the defenses of the Chinese citadel, which included 24 detached small forts, fortified redoubts and barricaded villages defended by some 15,000 regular Chinese troops. The intelligence was cleverly exploited and the operation carefully planned. A part of the French force acted as a flanking pivot for the advance and the other led the main attack. On the march to Bac Ninh, the Legion formed the advanced guard dealing with the patrol and ambush activities of the enemy. The various positions and outposts defending Bac Ninh were captured one by one. After a short pause to form up, the attack on the fortress began on March 12, 1884. The gate of the citadel was smashed by artillery and legionaries of both Legion Battalions and naval *marsouins* immediately poured in. After short, sharp hand-to-hand fighting the Chinese regulars—apparently much less determined than the Black Flags of Son Tay—fled in disorder. Sergeant Minnaert, the hero of Son Tay, distinguished himself again by fighting at the head of his men and by planting the tricolor on top of the main building; he became one of the numerous legendary heroes of the Legion, and one of the most decorated legionaries for his bravery, rescue actions, and other feats of arms.

After the two defeats of Son Tay and Bac Ninh, in May 1884, the Chinese recognized the protectorate of France over Annam and Tonkin. The northern frontier cities of Cao Bang, Lang Son, and Khat Ke were evacuated by the Chinese and occupied by the French. The war would have ended but suddenly, in June 1884, the Chinese broke the agreement, a French column was massacred at Bac Le, and hostilities were resumed.

By that time, the 1st and 2nd Battalions of the French Foreign Legion embarked on an exhausting period marked by patrols, raids, skirmishes and ambushes, as gangs of elusive Black Flags ceaselessly roved about the interior of the country. The legionaries quickly adapted to the difficult demands of dense jungle warfare along twisting narrow paths, with visibility down to a few yards and evasive enemies lurking within. They often provided the spearhead of operations, which took a heavy toll from death, wounds and tropical diseases. During one of these operations, in November 1884, the Legion attacked fortified positions defended by 1,200 Chinese at Yuoc. The defenders fled and the nearby abandoned fort of Tuyen Quang was occupied.

Tuyen Quang

Tuyen Quang, situated in a small basin on the Claire River about 130 kilometers

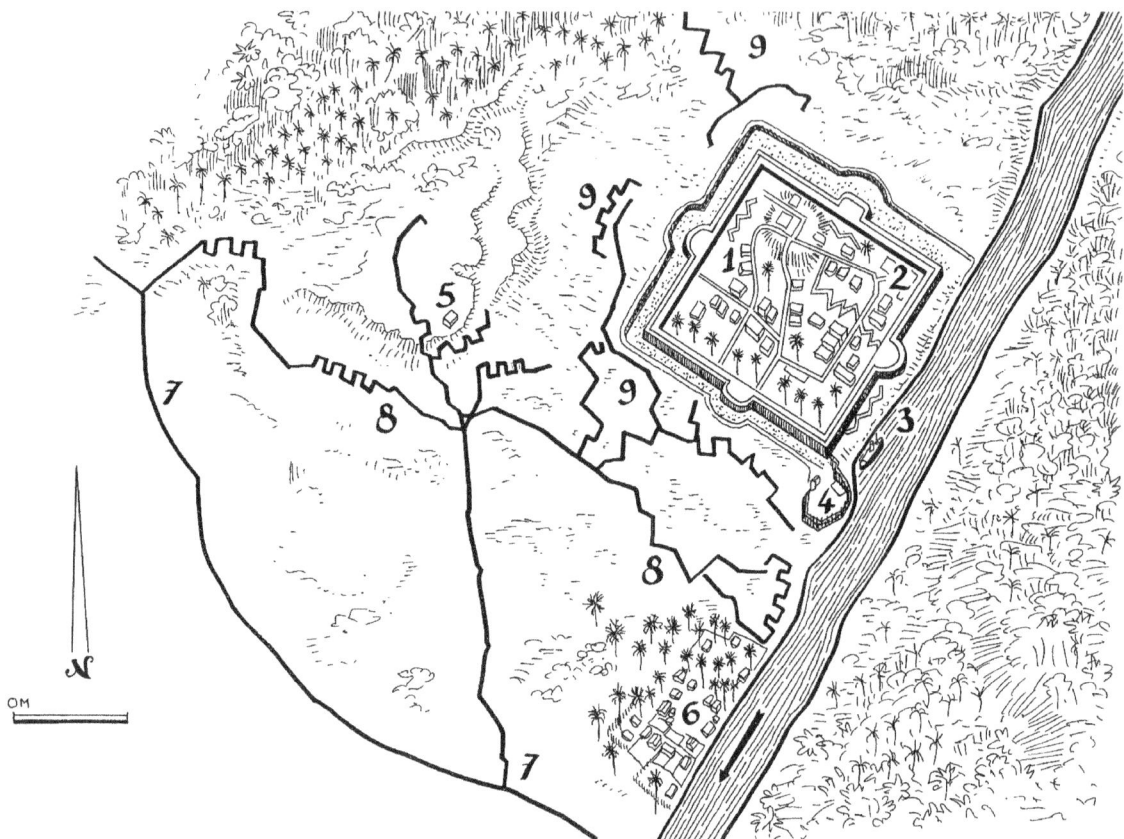

Ground plan, siege of Tuyen Quang. (1) Fort of Tuyen Quang consisting of a square perimeter (about 270 m × 270 m) composed of a 3-meter-high neglected stone and brick wall with small redans on each face; it was hemmed with a dry ditch, which was partially filled, and a fence of sharpened bamboo. Inside the fort there was a kind of village with various quarters, houses, pagodas (sacred religious towers), a hospital (2) and a small hill (called the Mamelon) serving as outlook. (3) Gunboat in Clear River. (4) Pagoda of the Tirailleurs; south of the fort, near the Claire River, a barricaded group of small buildings. (5) Advanced blockhouse (simple work made of earth and wooden beams) placed west of the fort on a small hill and serving as a forward defense post manned with 20 riflemen. This untenable position was rapidly evacuated. (6) Village. (7) Chinese first parallel. (8) Chinese second parallel. (9) Chinese approaching trenches.

northwest of Hanoi, represented a key position in the mountainous and forested hinterland of Tonkin. The ruined and neglected fort was soon repaired by the French, and a small garrison—totaling 624 men placed under the leadership of Commandant Dominé—was left behind to occupy it. This included two companies of the Legion headed by Captain de Borelli and Captain Mouliney, a total of eight subaltern officers and NCOs and 390 legionaries. These men would resist assaults from about 20,000 well-armed Chinese from January 20 to March 3, 1885.

They had a few artillery pieces, and all men were armed with 1874 type single-shot rifles and carbines with a total of 320,000 rounds. They had food and water for four months, and they awaited additional supplies, which would permit them to hold out for another six months. It was this small garrison which wrote another famous page in the epic history of the Foreign Legion.

Patrols were sent into the jungle around

the fort in search of the enemy, but the Chinese seemed to have disappeared. But while the French were fortifying Tuyen Quang, the enemy was not idle. Lun-Vinh-Phuoc, the chief of the Black Flags, had become Chinese general and commander of a large force of Black Flag mercenaries and regulars from the Yunnan Army. As they were not united this movement took some time to form, but it did progress. For months the Chinese silently filtered through the jungle, building up their strength around the isolated fort. By the end of December 1884 the position was totally encircled and even the Claire River had been blockaded by sampans, which formed an effective boom, denying the use of the river to the French. On January 20, 1885, with 20,000 men and numerous artillery in position, the attack began. Hordes of Chinese launched themselves against the French defenses, but the attackers were held at the outer walls with heavy casualties. When they realized that the fort was a far harder nut to crack than they had anticipated, the Chinese changed their tactics and resorted to 17th-century Western classical siege technique, in the purest traditional of Vauban. South of the fort, they established two small forts and a long parallel trench where they positioned artillery pieces. Until the end of January 1885 they fired at the fort and dug other zigzagging trenches in the direction of the forward blockhouse. The blockhouse stood increasingly isolated from the fort, and it had to be evacuated. Of course the position was immediately occupied by the Chinese, who placed artillery there. They continued to dig trenches in the direction of the fort and fired with their guns. Under constant bombardment, the garrison began to suffer casualties. The Chinese also dug a tunnel leading under the wall of the citadel and, in the early morning of February 13, 1885, exploded a mine making a wide breach in the French defense. The breach was then assaulted, and after fierce hand-to-hand fighting, the French managed to repulse the attackers. The breach was promptly consolidated with rubble, rocks and wooden beams. In the meantime Commandant Dominé had sent a call for help carried by a volunteer messenger who succeeded in passing through the enemy lines.

A few days later, another mine exploded under the western wall, and when the French rushed to take their fighting position a second mine exploded, and then a third one, destroying another part of the defensive wall and causing great carnage: Captain Mouliney and 12 legionaries were killed, and 30 were severely injured. This action was immediately followed by a large wave of Chinese infantry attacking the smoking ruins. Momentarily thrown into confusion, the legionaries and the *tirailleurs* were speedily rallied by their officers and were ready in time to meet the assaulting party. In confused and deadly fighting, the garrison launched a bayonet charge and repelled the assault. The following day, after a heavy artillery preparation, the Chinese launched another attack and succeeded in penetrating inside the fort. Again there were individual struggles and hand-to-hand fighting, and a Legion charge with the bayonet eventually contained, ejected and threw them back. The following days were quieter, marked by sporadic cannon and musketry fire. While the French were licking their wounds, the Chinese concentrated on pushing their trenches forward. In spite of pressure, stress, and casualties, the morale of the besieged was quite high as Dominé was informed by a messenger that a relief column was on its way. This was also known by the Chinese who intensified the pressure on the fort, which by now was seriously weakened with large breaches in the walls. On February 21, mines were exploded, breaches made or widened and assaults furiously launched again. The main attack was now launched, and disaster was avoided only by equally furious hand-to-hand counterattacks and fighting in the breaches, which succeeded in ejecting the attackers. Seeing that the

Chinese hesitated, the garrison launched a sharp and audacious sortie on the night of February 23-24. The besiegers were thrown into confusion, some trenches were swiftly cleared, and two of their black silk banners were seized and brought in triumph back to the fort. Stung by this impudent sally, the Chinese recovered themselves and prepared a final attack. From February 25 to 28 there were three major assaults accompanied by mines and thundering artillery. They were all repulsed, but, by now, the garrison of Tuyen Quang was exhausted and it is doubtful whether they would have been able to hold out much longer. However, they would not have to face the fate of Danjou's men at Camerone as help was on the way. The rescue brigade, about 3,000 Algerian and Tonkinese *tirailleurs*, navy *marsouins*, and legionaries, commanded by Colonel Giovanninelli, had left Lang Son on February 16. In bad weather the column had to march a long way in difficult mountainous and jungle terrain. Their advance, which lasted for two weeks, was unopposed, rendered arduous only by the difficult geography. But, 15 kilometers before Tuyen Quang, the column approached two barricaded villages called Hoa Moc and Phu Doan defended by a strong party of Black Flags, who put up a stubborn resistance. The fortified positions were attacked and taken at the high cost of 27 officers and 600 men killed and wounded. In the valley, the besieged garrison in Tuyen Quang and the Chinese besiegers heard the distant gunfire; the former had new heart, the latter had had enough. During the night of March 2, they silently withdrew and disappeared into the mountains. In the afternoon of the next day, March 3, 1885, the rescue brigade relieved the fort. The memorable siege battle of Tuyen Quang was over. The garrison had held out for 36 days. A total of 48 men were killed, including two officers, 28 were severely wounded, including 8 who later died, and 118 were lightly wounded.

The end of the conquest

After the siege of Tuyen Quang, the Legion in Southeast Asia was reinforced by two additional battalions, the 3rd and the 4th. These units of the Foreign Legion remained in Tonkin for another 10 years. The 1st battalion occupied the region of Cao Bang; the 2nd the region of That Khe; the 3rd the sector between Tuyen Quang and Ha Giang; and the 4th the region between Lao Key and Yen Bay. During this period there were no major battles, only sporadic actions, ambushes, raids, and local expeditions against irregular Chinese gangs, Annamite pirates and opium smugglers who pursued their own sort of uncoordinated guerrilla warfare against the French. The Treaty of Tien-Tsing in 1886 marked the end of the war between France and China. The Chinese reluctantly recognized a French protectorate over both Annam and Tonkin. As gangs of Black Flags refused to lay down their arms and continued to be a nuisance, and a threat which impeded the pacification and colonization of Tonkin, the 2nd and 3rd Battalions were formed into a *Régiment de marche* commanded by Colonel Négrier. This force was engaged with mitigated success at Bang Bo and Lang Son. Ambushed, the column had to withdraw, and thanks to the legionaries the fighting retreat was raised above the level of a rout. The French did not succeed in completely pacifying the jungle mountained at the border of northern Tonkin and China. For years, the battalions of the Legion, now regrouped and designated Régiment de marche d'Afrique au Tonkin (RMAT, African Task Regiment in Tonkin), were busy patrolling the length and breadth of the province searching unorganized and elusive gangs of irregulars and bandits that roamed the land. There were countless patrols and long exhausting marches in the jungle and few skirmishes and ambushes, as the guerrilla bands invariably melted away before the French forces only to reassemble

once they had passed on. By 1895, although outbursts of local resistance in one form or another still occurred, the French regarded the conquest of Indochina as complete. By 1897, the colonization and development of the land commenced in earnest, and most Foreign Legion units were repatriated to Algeria. In recognition of its work in the conquest of Indochina, the Régiment de marche d'Afrique au Tonkin was decorated with the prestigious Légion d'Honneur.

The French occupation forces in Indochina, mostly colonial and navy infantry and a few Legion units, were then dispersed to man a chain of small forts and posts for control and maintenance of order duty. By the end of 1907, the province of Tonkin was pacified, only disturbed by minor operations in 1909 against local pirates headed by a certain chief De-Tham. The most serious outbreak during this period was the attack on the city of Lang Son by about 1,000 Chinese bandits and pirates. In response the French government reinforced the Indochina occupation army by sending three Legion battalions, which greatly helped the local colonial French troops to restore order. This Legion force was maintained in Indochina and designated Cinquième Régiment de la Légion étrangère (5th Regiment of the Foreign Legion) in 1930. Between the world wars, the legionaries settled in to a relatively quiet life made up of construction projects, patrols, and minor police duties. The 5th Regiment settled into garrison

Legion infantryman, Tonkin, 1885. When the Foreign Legion was engaged in Indochina in 1883, legionaries wore the same uniforms as in Algeria. The Legion stocks ran out rapidly in Tonkin, and replacement uniforms came from the **Infanterie de marine** *(marines). The depicted legionary wears a white pith colonial helmet; a dark blue naval jacket; a white shirt with a low-standing collar; light linen trousers for summer wear; the Legion's blue sash worn around the service belt; and white canvas gaiters. The black chest-pouch (called* **cartouchière de poitrine Négrier***) contained 12 or 14 packs of cartridges for the Gras rifle; it was made by the men themselves from various materials, oilcloth, canvas or leather when available. The weapon is a Gras bolt-action single-shot rifle introduced in 1875 as a replacement of the older Chassepot rifle.*

Left: *Tonkinese tirailleur, Indochina, 1885. During the operations in Indochina, the French recruited units of natives* **tirailleurs** *(riflemen) serving as auxiliary troops. Headgear, dress and footwear were largely local civilian with only the addition of a dark blue military naval tunic, black leather service belt with ammunition pouch, and a rifle with bayonet.* **Right:** *Chinese "Black Flags," Indochina, 1885.*

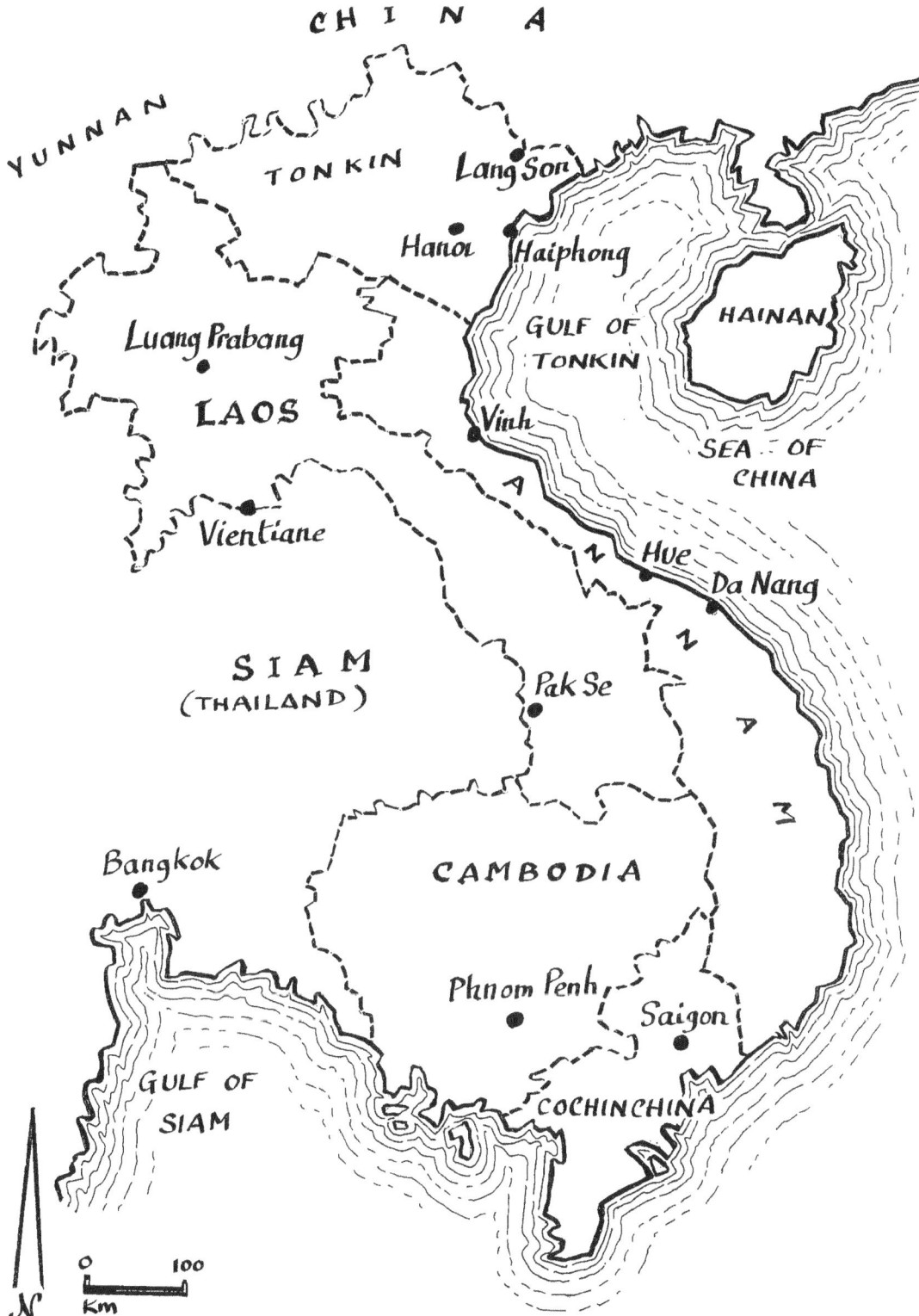

Sketch map of Indochina

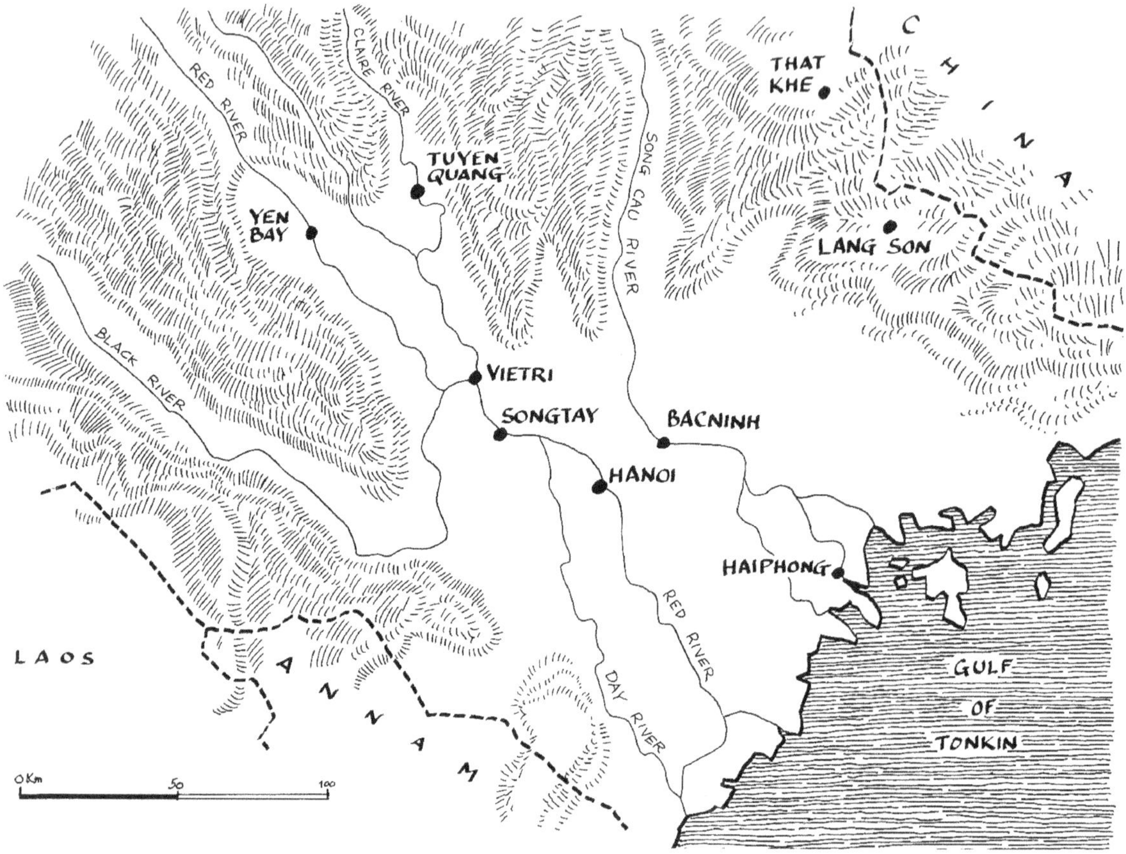

Sketch map of Tonkin

Officer with colonial helmet, Tonkin, 1883

duty in far more congenial circumstances than were enjoyed by their colleagues in Algeria. This "easy" life in the tropical sun came abruptly to an end in 1940 when French Indochina was invaded by Japan, as we shall see in Parts 6 and 7.

Dahomey and Sudan, 1892–1894

Historical background

As early as the 17th century, several French trading posts had been established along the southern coast of the kingdom of Dahomey. Until the 18th century, the principal activity involved trade with local kings of black slaves who were shipped to America, giving this region its other name of Slave Coast.

Since the second half of the 19th century there were German and French trading companies established on the Dahomian coast at Ouidah and Porto-Novo. The European commercial rivalry was exacerbated by the Franco-Prussian War of 1870. Under cover of civilian commercial trade, the Germans furnished King Behanzin of Dahomey with modern rifles, artillery, ammunition and experts to train his army. With a comparatively well-armed force of about 15,000, the determined and hostile Behanzin soon began to pose a threat to French commercial interests in the region. Treaties and agreements had been made, but not completely adhered to. In the early 1890s, tension between France and King Behanzin had reached an alarming level. When Dahomian troops raided the French posts, disturbing trading activities, France decided to send troops to protect its nationals and defend its commercial settlements.

To this must be added that King Behanzin continued an ancient tradition that involved sacrificing human beings ostensibly for religious purposes but in fact mainly for public amusement. Ghastly ceremonies were held in which large numbers of victims were annually slaughtered by beheading, mainly those unfortunates who had been captured but were not fit to be sold as slaves. All the neighboring tribes for many miles around lived in fear of this ruthless and blood-thirsty tyrant. Reports of these human sacrifices had filtered through to European countries, and of course had caused great outrage. The French believed that it was their duty to eradicate such primitive, barbarian and cruel practices. Therefore the French had a convenient and strong moral excuse—as well as economic grounds—for their brutal military intervention.

The operation

The expeditionary corps to Dahomey was organized by the French navy. It was composed of 4,000 "colonial" soldiers, under the command of General Dodds, detached from the Ministry of Navy and Colonies. This force also included a Foreign Legion battalion of 800 legionaries headed by Commandant (Major) Faurax. The mission was to subdue and dethrone Behanzin (nicknamed by the troops *Bec en Zinc*, that is, Zinc-Mouth), by capturing the capital of his kingdom, Abomey, and then to establish a pro–French government.

The task force arrived at Cotonou on August 26, 1892. From Cotonou the legionaries, the colonial *tirailleurs*, and their light field artillery were shipped by inland steamboats to Porto Novo, the capital of the territory of King Tofa, who was pro–French. Tofa provided a detachment of native scouts who led the way. From there, on September 1, they proceeded on foot across pestilential

Legionary in Dahomey, 1892

marshes and tropical bush, their western flank covered by the *canonnière* (steam gunboat) *Topaz*, sailing over the Oueme River, which shadowed their advance. The march was unopposed but slow and exhausting. The swamp and bush gave way to thick jungle with only narrow paths. The French had little intelligence about the intentions, moves and strength of the Dahomians. By day the column wound its way slowly forward like a long snake. At night when the expeditionary force halted, trenches were dug and sentries posted in anticipation of an ambush. On September 19, the French force was attacked for the first time by a large party (about 4,000) of Behanzin's force near a small place named Dogba. The assault was pressed home with determination and nearly overwhelmed the French. The defender's line shuddered, but discipline and cohesion were maintained and steady firing was kept up. After two hours of fierce combat, and a Legion charge with fixed bayonets, the defenders beat back their attackers. The Dahomians broke off the action and retreated northward, leaving behind them about 800 killed. On the French side, the engagement had cost 45 killed (5 legionaries) and 60 wounded (10 legionaries including the Legion commandant Faurax who died a few days later from his wounds). After the battle, to their great surprise, the French had taken two female prisoners and found 20 dead women among the bodies of the attackers. These were fighting females of Behanzin's personal guard. Every three years it was the custom that all young unmarried women of the kingdom would gather at Abomey; the prettiest of them were selected for Behanzin's harem, some were given as wives and mistresses to his officers, and the rest formed into a special combat guard.

Behanzin's Amazon, Dahomey, 1892. The uniform of the Amazons consisted of a full skirt and blouse, with a cartridge belt slung either over one shoulder or at the waist. A haversack and a water bottle hung by their sides. Apart from miscellaneous firearms, an Amazon's arms consisted of short swords, machetes, knifes, spears, and bows and arrows. Souvenirs of active service frequently dangled from their belts in the form of human skulls or bones.

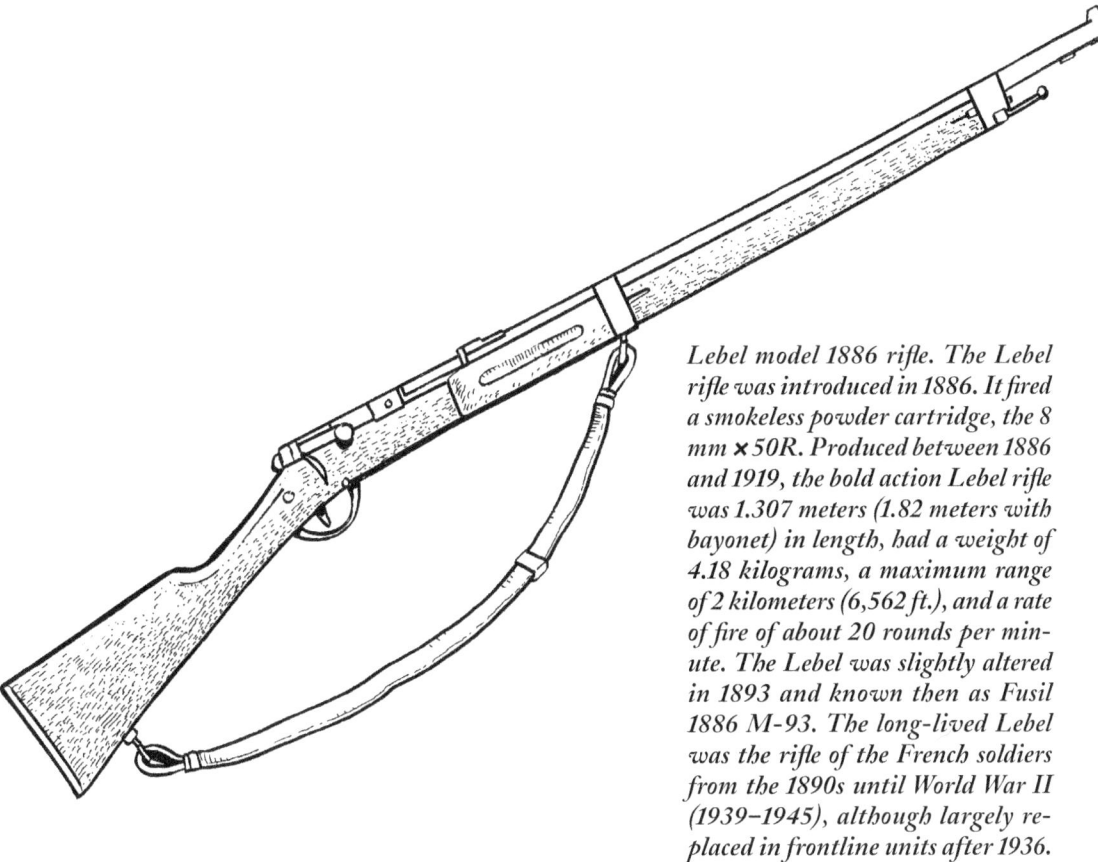

Lebel model 1886 rifle. The Lebel rifle was introduced in 1886. It fired a smokeless powder cartridge, the 8 mm × 50R. Produced between 1886 and 1919, the bold action Lebel rifle was 1.307 meters (1.82 meters with bayonet) in length, had a weight of 4.18 kilograms, a maximum range of 2 kilometers (6,562 ft.), and a rate of fire of about 20 rounds per minute. The Lebel was slightly altered in 1893 and known then as Fusil 1886 M-93. The long-lived Lebel was the rifle of the French soldiers from the 1890s until World War II (1939–1945), although largely replaced in frontline units after 1936.

Selected primarily for their physical ability, toughness, and ability to bear adverse conditions, the women warriors were divided into small units, each about 300 or 400 strong. Generally armed with modern weapons, e.g., U.S.-made Winchester repeating carbines, each unit had its own flag, and some had a detachment of drums for parades. Female officers were properly appointed and wore a white headdress to indicate their rank. The female guards (probably totaling some 2,000 in 1892) formed an elite unit, equal to and sometimes demonstrating even more courage than their male counterparts. Behanzin's female guards were promptly nicknamed *Amazons* by the French, after the ancient Greek legendary female warriors.

After the indecisive battle of Dogba, the French reorganized and the column resumed its advance northward at the same slow rate along the forest paths. The next serious action occurred on October 4 at the village of Porguessa where the column was ambushed. After a moment of confusion, the French wavered and gave ground but quickly recovered. The village was assaulted and cleared by the Legion. Until October 6, there sporadic fighting, assaults and attacks occurred, which were repulsed, costing Behanzin 250 soldiers and 30 fearless Amazons. After the clearing of Porguessa, the column moved on, but from then on there were skirmishes with the enemy almost everyday. Before reaching Abomey the French force progressed very slowly as they had to cross a thick forest, which proved very difficult for the passage of supply convoys and artillery and extremely favorable to enemy snipers, skirmishers and Amazon ambushers. The French also began to run short of water, and they had to fight for each source of water in the forest. They sent a messenger forward to demand Behanzin's surrender; this was refused, and General Dodds resumed his advance. Another clash occurred at a place called Koto, costing the French 20 killed. On November 6, the exhausted column reached the city of Kana where it rested and waited for reinforcements and additional supplies. After a final short march through the tropical forest and several ambushes, the path to the capital, Abomey, lay open. Again Behanzin was urged to surrender but no reply was given. The town was taken without a fight on November 16. For unknown reasons, King Behanzin had chosen to leave after setting his palace and several buildings afire. Two days later General Dodds proclaimed the overthrow of Behanzin (who ultimately was captured in 1894) and invited the inhabitants of the kingdom of Dahomey to accept the protectorate of France. As they reasoned that French domination could be no worse than Behanzin's tyranny, the Dahomians rather readily accepted French rule. King Behanzin was held prisoner at Fort Tartenson (Martinique island) from 1894 to 1889.

A few years later, when commanding in Indochina, General Dodds recognized the role played by the Foreign Legion: "The Legion is an élite troop upon which one can always rely in any circumstances. Without it I could never have achieved victory in Dahomey." The campaign had indeed been very costly for the Legion battalion. Counting about 800 men at the start of the campaign, the battalion had suffered some 450 casualties, including 410 wounded or incapacitated by disease and 40 combat deaths. This task completed, the Legion marched southward to the coast to reembark for Algeria.

Dahomey became a part of Afrique occidentale française (AOF, French West Africa).

As for the Germans, they did not intervene, probably because they reasoned that Dahomey was not worth an open conflict with France. They held the neighboring territory of Togo, and this colony was placed under French control after the German defeat of 1918. Dahomey and Togo remained French protectorates until 1960.

Madagascar, 1895

Historical background

Madagascar is a large island located in the Indian Ocean, separated from Africa by the Mozambique Channel. The French had established the trading post of Port-Dauphin in the 17th century, and King Louis XIII by a royal edict of 1642 had declared Madagascar a possession of the French crown. When the queen of the Hovas, Ranavalona I, violently chased out the Europeans, the French responded by sending in a task force. After an operation that lasted for one year, the French succeeded in imposing a fragile protectorate over the island in 1885. The conquest was followed by a period of pacification, which had only limited results. The French only controlled the Bay of Diego-Suarez in the north and the islands of Nossi-Be and Sainte-Marie. Over Madagascar itself they enjoyed only a vague and contested protectorate which proved difficult to enforce. French authorities alleged that the terms of the treaty had not been carried out, and when troubles and turmoil continued, the French decided to intervene again in 1895.

The operation

The expeditionary force which operated in Madagascar in 1895 was organized by the French Armée de terre (ground army). This force was composed of the 200th Infantry Regiment, which was a special formation including units drawn from 12 different French home regiments joined together for the occasion. As a gesture, the navy was allowed to be represented by two battalions of Algerian *tirailleurs*. In addition there was one Foreign Legion *bataillon de marche* (task

Legionary in Madagascar, 1895

battalion) attached to General Metzinger's brigade. This included 22 officers and 818 legionaries placed under the leadership of Commandant Barre—and thus known as Bataillon de marche Barre. The expeditionary force totaled 21,600 soldiers under command of Army general Duchesne whose mission was to submit the queen of the Hovas and to install the protectorate of 1885 by marching on Tananarive. The capital of Madagascar is situated in the middle of the island in the central mountains, and the best approach to the town lay on the east side of the island at the port of Tamatave (today Taomasina), but the best defenses were located here—or so the ill-informed organizers of the expedition believed. The French thought that the Hova army was large (about 40,000), well armed and well trained. Actually the Malagash army was more impressive on paper than in reality. Although the route between Tamatave and Tananarive was both shorter and better, the totally misinformed French felt it was wiser to go in through the "back door" and so chose to land at Majunga, a primitive port on the northwestern coast in the Sakalavas territory. As this tribe had always been the enemy of the Hovas, it was anticipated that they would assist the French, or at least remain neutral and provide scouts, guides, a labor force and porters. From Majunga, it was then planned to proceed on foot in a southernly direction to Tananarive following the valleys of the Ikopa and Betsiboka rivers. This "wise" plan was not only based on wrong intelligence but also prepared based on a total ignorance of local conditions. The terrain was extremely difficult, there were no roads nor even tracks, only occasional narrow paths, making the expedition's heavy field artillery pieces (90 mm Bange and 120 mm Baquet) completely useless. Moreover, the climate was hideous.

80 mm mountain gun, c. 1895. Colonial warfare required special guns for mobility in difficult terrain. A common feature of colonial mountain guns was that they had a rugged and straightforward design, were rather light, and could be quickly broken down in several loads for animal draft.

After its arrival at Majunga, the expeditionary corps had to cross the marshy region of Boueni, infested with mosquitoes, flies and other pests. The French force quickly suffered very heavy casualties from tropical disease, which they were not equipped to deal with. The operation in Madagascar was one of the oddest and most ill-prepared of the expeditions during the period of French colonization and in the history of the Foreign Legion. It was a battle waged more against nature and epidemics than against an organized and determined enemy, as illustrated by the astonishing number of casualties. Twenty soldiers were killed in combat, and no fewer than 5,736 died of tropical diseases and heatstroke. It is, however, noticeable that the Legion's casualties from disease were much fewer than those of the line troops. The legionaries were, on the whole, tougher, hardened and accustomed as they were to extreme climates and bad water; their sanitary discipline was therefore better, and they did not mingle with other units in camps. Even so they suffered 266 men dead of disease and only five killed in combat.

The Legion's Battallon de marche Barre was regrouped at Oran in early April 1895, embarked aboard SS *Liban*, and arrived at Majunga, Madagascar, on April 23, 1895. The unit, attached to the brigade commanded by General Metzinger, bore more than its fair share of combat and track building during the advance.

The distance between Majunga and Tananative is about 350 miles, and the progression through the jungle proved extremely slow owing to the tropical heat, humidity and difficult terrain. There was no opposition as the Hovas melted before the French expeditionary force. After having secured the small town of Morovoay, the French force moved in a southeastern direction, the Legion leading the way. On June 1, 1895, a bare ridge named Hauteurs Dénudées (Naked Heights) was reached. On June 6, there was a light skirmish at a ford over the Betsiboka River. A few rounds were shot and the Hovas broke and fled; the ford was crossed with difficulty because of the strong current and the width (450 m) of the river. On June 9, there was a first engagement with the Hovas army at Mevatanana, a village placed on top of an almost perpendicular cliff. The Hovas army controlled the narrow valley along which the French force had to pass and the position seemed impregnable. After a short cannonade and an outflanking move by the Legion, the Mahs ran and the village was taken. A few days later the small town of Suberbieville was reached. The countryside had been depleted on purpose to delay the French. Villages were abandoned by their inhabitants so that neither information nor material help could be given to the invaders, supplies having been removed and all crops destroyed. All food and equipment had thus to be brought forward carried by local porters. The enemy tactics, based on *hazou* (forest), *tazou* (disease) and *fazou* (fire) proved extremely efficient. The intense strain of tramping in full marching order through hilly jungle on rationed food, the crossing of rivers and streams infested with crocodiles and the plague of mosquitoes and flies were telling. Fever began to take a fatal toll. By June 1895 the expeditionary corps had already suffered 10 percent in casualties due to tropical disease, and the soldiers who were not infected were exhausted by marching through the difficult jungle. At this stage it was obvious that the soldiers needed a respite. It was decided to take a break, and, in order to improve communications, to build a track fit to take two-wheeled mule carts between the port of Majunga and Suberbieville in order to bring up supplies and evacuate the sick. All troops had to lend a hand and, needless to say, the legionaries played a major role. Issued with shovels and other tools they were ordered to build the stretch of track between Beratsanana and the Mandroya River, appalling work under the tropical sun and work disturbed now and then

by snipers. On July 16—the roadway now fit for small carts to use it—the difficult advance through the forest was resumed while the Legion remained engaged in road work. On August 20, the expeditionary corps reached the small fortified city of Andriba, which was taken after a few artillery rounds were shot. On August 23 the exhausted French took Mangasoavina where they halted for rest. By then the number of sick soldiers reached alarming proportions, (two-thirds of the army) and it became clear that if things went on like this no French soldiers would ever reach Tananarive. It was decided to create a *colonne légère* (light column or task force) which would only carry food, water and ammunitions for a quick raid on the capital. The legionaries resumed their place in the front force, and, not surprisingly, made up the spearhead of the column. Although suffering less from fever than other units, the Legion's *bataillon de marche* was reduced to 19 officers and 330 legionaries. The light column was ironically baptized *Marche ou Crève* ("march or die") as it had henceforth to be totally self-supporting; this title became a popular catchword, and was applied later on many occasions to Legion marches in difficult conditions through hostile countries. The task column departed on September 14, 1895. Taking over the lead, the Legion moved eagerly forward, probing scouting paths suitable for the *colonne légère*. Two days later they reached the Ambohiminas mountain (height 1,500 m) and a place named Tsinaindry, a fortified village on a slope dominating a defile, constituting the last serious obstacle before Tananarive. The "march or die" column was divided into several units, which outflanked the entrenched Hovas. Several actions were launched, but these were more skirmishes

Hova warrior, 1895. The Madagascar natives usually wore the lamba, a dress which consisted of a large sheet of cloth, usually white, folded around the body somewhat in the style of the ancient Roman toga. Over this some of them occasionally wore a jacket or a dress, frequently of European pattern, which produced a curious effect. The most frequently worn headgear was a large straw hat. Equipment varied and armament ranged from modern rifles to old-fashioned muskets.

than large battles. As ever, since the start of the campaign, the Hovas tended to run at first contact. News that the French had forced the Tsinaindry defile caused panic in the Hova capital and the aged prime minister and the queen ordered all subjects to fight in a final battle. Tananarive—at last—was reached on September 28, 1895. The town was attacked from the south and the east and after a short cannonade and a few skirmishes, a white flag was hoisted. The Hova army disintegrated, the soldiers disappeared into the jungle or merged into the civilian population. After negotiating the town was taken and occupied by the French. The day after the Malagash capitulation was official. The mission was accomplished.

The Legion had formed the advanced guard of the expeditionary force along almost the entire route. General Duchesne thanked the Legion officers by declaring: "It is owing to your men and to you, gentlemen, that we are here. And if I ever have the honor of commanding another expedition, I surely shall take with me at least one battalion of the Foreign Legion." In October 1895, the Legion's task was over and the men marched back along the route they had helped to construct to Majunga. By December 1895 all Foreign legionaries—except those in hospitals—were rapatriated to their home depot in Algeria. Madagascar remained a French colony until 1960.

The Legion at the Turn of the 20th Century

By the end of the 19th century, the Foreign Legion had achieved a good reputation and gained a solid cohesion. A common bond was certainly engendered by marching, hard fighting and suffering in trying and remote environments. The endless desert and barren mountains of North Africa, the lush forests of Equatorial Africa, the exotic marshes, paddyfields and jungles of Indochina had a special mystique but they were markedly inhospitable battlefields. Mountains, jungles, deserts and tropical marshes created extreme conditions for warfare, making logistics and endurance more difficult than in any other kind of terrain. This breathtaking environment often made ideal hideouts for native guerrillas, who waged hit-and-run warfare which prolonged campaigns and disrupted communications.

The North African desert was a scorching, arid ground by day which became an equally unwelcoming, freezing world at night. In daytime the desert was like a furnace with temperatures often up to 40 degrees Celsius, at night sometimes down to 5 degrees below zero Celsius. Thirst was hellish and the other name of the Sahara in Arabian language was and still is *Tanezrouft* (Land of Thirst); many legionaries died of thirst. Compared to the well-fed British Tommy and the vitamin-supplied American GI of World War II, the legionary of 1900 was provisioned extremely poorly. In noncombat conditions, army regulations stipulated three warm meals served daily. In combat conditions, however, large groups of men campaigning for long periods in difficult terrain made feeding difficult. Many a unit suffered from starvation and lack of vitamins resulting not only in death (from, for example, scurvy, beriberi) but also declines in health and, possibly, morale. Depending on conditions, it was more or less difficult to provide regular hot meals and fresh vegetables. Eating out of cans was not always appetizing and the variety of canned food was extremely limited, monotonous and not always of good quality. Captured food, plundered supplies and hunted game could improve regular military food but they also increased the hazard of dangerous diseases.

Legionaries and colonial troops, in a way, were similar to naval personnel in that they were fighting three enemies at the same time, the first being the natural surroundings, the second monotony and boredom, and the third the occasional enemy. Scorpions, snakes and sand flies (small creatures sucking blood) as well as jaundice, malaria, dysentery, and open sores often made life a complete misery. A wound or a fever—not necessarily serious—might often result in death as evacuation to a first-aid post could take days, in some cases even weeks. To say nothing of totally unsuited uniforms, which were much too thick and too hot, and bulky equipment, which was too heavy and too cumbersome. Until the 1930s, uniforms, footwear, weapons and equipment used by the French Foreign Legion were, on the whole, the same as those designed and used by the regular French infantry operating in Europe. Until the 1930s, either very few or no special items (like shorts, cotton shirts, and light tunics) were issued to meet the extreme conditions in which the legionaries operated.

Because of the difficult terrain in which the Legion was often engaged, units had to be self-supporting. Legionaries were—and had to be—supremely fit individuals. The Mounted Companies had mules, it is true, but many other units did not. Not only did they carry a considerable amount of personal kit and supply with them in their rucksacks (supply which the baggage train would usually carry for the traditional infantrymen), but they were also expected to scale snowy mountains, march through hot deserts or cross humid jungles and damp marshes while doing so. Many thought that in such conditions the white man could not work, let alone wage war, but the men of the Foreign Legion did both. Only the best of the best could endure such stress and hardship, and fight with spirit and determination. Not without reason, legionaries came to feel part of an élite, and they developed a sense of esprit de corps second to none, born of their fighting ability and their experience in mastering an inhospitable environment that few European armies could cope with. These extraordinary and amazing performances could be achieved only by extremely demanding physical training and harsh discipline. The Foreign Legion was—and still is—a military corps in which the letter of military regulations to the most minute and particular degree is strictly observed. It has always been the officers—and more particularly the NCOs'—task to see that training was practiced, traditions respected and exact regulations accepted—willingly or not. Officers and NCOs, in becoming military leaders, were considered tamers of wild beasts. First they had to totally break men who were far from being angels. A great emphasis was placed on endless drill and exhausting marches, which could last for days. Field punishment of various kinds was harsh, salutary and speedy; commanding officers and NCOs had wide powers for physically punishing soldiers on the spot for all minor derelictions; only more serious crimes were remanded for a formal court-martial with the possibility of heavy sentence. Owing to this, and to the lack of army supervision, abuses crept in from time to time, the incidents giving rise to lurid rumors of sadistic practices. The number of Legion discipline units in existence at any one time varied, depending upon the state of the Corps and its strength, but they indicated that the foreign legionnaires possessed a surplus of devilment and energy that they did not use up, particularly in peacetime and garrison duty. The discipline was (and still is today) harsh and strict, but a broken man, a dehumanized and brainwashed robot is nothing without a *spirit*. That is what the Legion has often achieved: to completely subdue the individual will but at the same time to provide a reconstruction of the personality by instilling—through harsh methods—a spirit which may be variously termed esprit de corps, or professional self-respect, or elitist pride or a certain idea of honor to the legionaries. Demanding training and discipline gave the legionaries an exceptional mental caliber, with a high degree of stamina to cope with the hardships that they encountered and the abnormal circumstances in which they lived and fought. This required exceptional men already having or rapidly acquiring a high sense of comradeship and a strong team spirit.

In the 1880s the famous maxim *Legio Patria Nostra* ("the Legion is our fatherland") was adopted. The Legion made no great effort to persuade its members to be loyal to France, as France was a country few of them knew and some of them disliked; instead, it was insisted that the first duty of a legionary was to be faithful to the Legion itself. Constant indoctrination assisted in keeping morale high, and stories of past victories won by the Legion, as well as individual legionnaires' feats of bravery and endurance, were drummed into the men. Until today the legionnaire's greatest degradation is to let the Legion down. And so paradoxically not all legionaries like France as a country and the French as a people, but most of them are intensely loyal to the Legion, extremely jealous of its reputation and would not allow it to be slandered in any way. The Legion, not France, is a family, a refuge, and a shelter for the homeless, the stateless and the runaways. The Legion takes them under its wing and gives them protection, security and often a meaning to their lives. However, the suicide rate has always been a problem in the Foreign Legion, particularly in remote garrisons where there is little to occupy the mind with when off duty. Drink, coupled with long and monotonous duty, often led to *le cafard* (melancholia or "blues") which could sometimes end in suicide.

No information about serving men—either a notorious criminal, a petty thief or a political personality—has ever been given in answer to any queries. A rigid barrier of silence, the cloak and protection of anonymity, became complete. This did not improve the Legion's reputation and standing, but at the same time it created an image of glamour and mystery.

By the end of the 19th century, without ever seeking it, the Légion étrangère, began to acquire a worldwide reputation. Memoirs and novels written by retired ex-legionnaires were published in their own countries, and information about the Legion's feats, battles, tough conditions and endurance appeared in all European countries. The Corps began to catch the imagination of the world, but rumors were distorted and fables magnified. Facts were strangely twisted and many authors and readers sometimes confused the French Foreign Legion with the dreaded Bataillons d'Afrique (African Battalions, in short Bat'd'Af). These were disciplinary units organized in light infantry battalions, in which French criminals, both civil and military (including Legion deserters) served as forced labor chain gangs in North Africa, the most notorious and dreaded place being Tatahouine. The conditions in the Bat'd'Af were extremely harsh and severe. Bad treatments, abuses, brutalities and inhumane discipline were often practiced, and these, when appearing in highly romanticized fictional accounts, were attributed to the Legion. In Victorian England, for example, the Foreign Legion became widely known when a novel titled *Under Two Flags* was published. This book was a best-seller and the forerunner of other similar romances about the Légion étrangère. Soon there could hardly have been anyone in the world who had not heard of both the illustrious and the "mysterious" Foreign Legion. This publicity was certainly not sought by the French military and civilian authorities whose policy was to operate the Corps as discreetly as possible.

The capacity of the Legion to survive and fight in a hostile environment was clearly demonstrated in April 1900 when the 2nd and 3rd Companies of the 2nd Foreign Regiment led by Colonel Ménestrel and Colonel Letulle, totaling 9 officers and 400 legionaries, undertook an audacious expedition in the Great Western Erg in the Sahara from El Goleah to Timimun, marching some 1,825 kilometers in the desert in 72 days. In July 1900 the Legion was attacked by Doui Menia tribesmen (about 300 horsemen and 600 warriors on foot); the Mounted Company of the 2nd Foreign Regiment, led by Legion chief Pauly, repulsed them. In September 1903, a supply convoy escorted by a few spahis and the same mounted company of the 2nd Foreign Regiment led by Lieutenant Selchauhansen, was ambushed by Bou Amana tribesmen between the oasis of Moungar and Zafrani. In extreme difficulties they fought for eight hours and succeeded in forcing the enemy to withdraw. By 1905, the situation along the border between Algeria and Morocco became increasingly dangerous and tense. The French were obliged to construct forts—notably Bechar, Forthassa and Berguent—to secure the region south of Oran from Moroccan raiders. Multiplication of the raids in 1907 led to the invasion and occupation of Morocco, as will be related in Part 5.

4

The Foreign Legion in World War I, 1914–1918

Historical Background

The situation in Europe in the late 19th century appeared relatively calm. Europeans experienced an unprecedented growth in material living standards. There had been no major conflict since the Franco-Prussian war of 1870, and statesmen prided themselves on having entered the age of diplomacy. But behind diplomatic compromises there lurked systems of attack and defense that had been erected in case arbitration should fail, and modern industry produced powerful weapons in massive numbers.

The pretext for World War I was the assassination of Archduke Franz Ferdinand, heir to the throne of Austria-Hungary on June 28, 1914, at Sarajevo in Bosnia. The fateful interplay of rigid alliances brought all the leading European powers into war. Military "experts" prophesied that it would last only a few months, but they proved to be wrong: this war would not end until four ghastly years later.

In December 1914, without any decisive victories, it was obvious that the war of movement was no longer possible. The western front stabilized along an enormous arc from southwestern Belgium near the North Sea to the Vosges Mountains near the Swiss border.

In order to maintain their position in the face of the enemy, the armies dug themselves in for the longest and bloodiest war of attrition in history. On the western front, 1915 was the first year of grueling trench warfare. The Germans went on the defensive while the primary concern of France was to expel the invaders from the national soil. The French thus planned to disrupt German fortified positions by taking the initiative with attacks in Artois and Champagne. The advances in military technology made these frontal offensives only suicide missions, which cost huge casualties for meager territorial gains. The entire concept of trench warfare in 1915–1918 evolved in reaction to the terrible efficiency of the machine gun. The combination of entrenched machine-gun fire, quick-firing artillery firing shrapnel projectiles and barbed wire inflicted prohibitive losses that stopped even the best-trained, best-disciplined and most enthusiastic attacking troops. Some 350,000 French soldiers were killed in 1915 alone. It was decided, at the instigation of General

Mangin, to engage the Foreign Legion, and large numbers of natives from France's colonies were also drafted. Between 1915 and 1918 some 500,000 men recruited in the oversea colonies fought in France: 250,000 came from North Africa, 150,000 from black Africa, and the rest from Madagascar, Indochina and other colonies.

The year 1916 saw events evolve further: the war of attrition became a war of exhaustion. Two gigantic bat-

French infantryman, 1914. The French army which went to war in 1914 retained the colorful uniform typical of the 19th century. The army had tried to adopt a more modern uniform, but French politicians demanded the retention of traditional kit. It still included a képi, a dark blue capote (overcoat) buttoned back to facilitate movement, red trousers, and brown gaiters. The weapon was a Lebel or a Berthier rifle with bayonet. Equipment included two leather ammunition pouches at the front, a bayonet scabbard, water bottle, a haversack—and later a gas mask. The leather backpack with a rigid frame contained a spare pair of boots, a blanket, a rolled ground sheet, a mess tin, food, entrenching tool, and various items, including, towel, extra socks, soap and a canvas hold-all containing comb and shaving kit. Each soldier—equipped with such "fighting order"—carried about 66 lbs. of equipment, making it difficult to get out of a trench, impossible to move faster than a slow walk and hard to rise and lie down quickly.

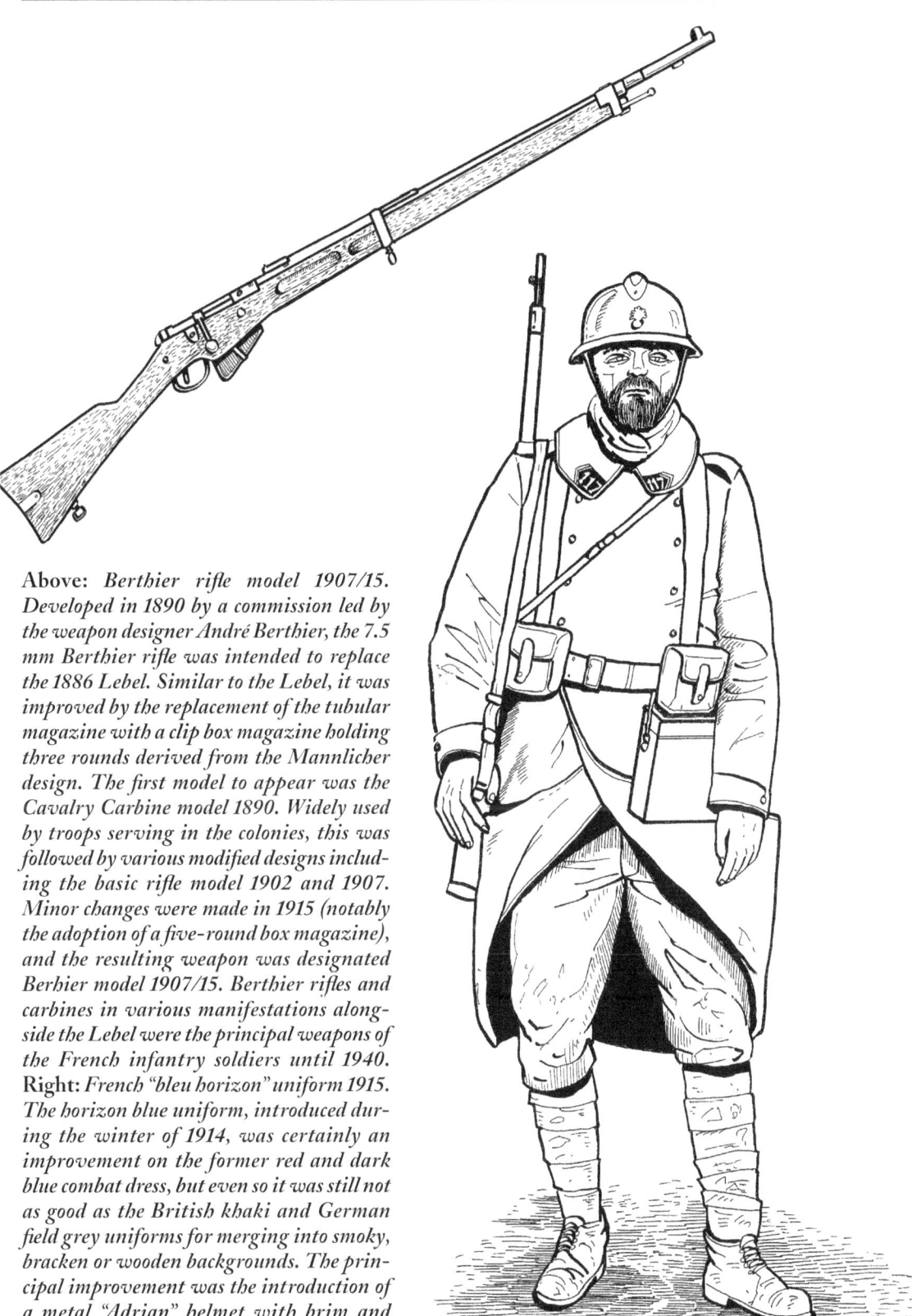

Above: *Berthier rifle model 1907/15. Developed in 1890 by a commission led by the weapon designer André Berthier, the 7.5 mm Berthier rifle was intended to replace the 1886 Lebel. Similar to the Lebel, it was improved by the replacement of the tubular magazine with a clip box magazine holding three rounds derived from the Mannlicher design. The first model to appear was the Cavalry Carbine model 1890. Widely used by troops serving in the colonies, this was followed by various modified designs including the basic rifle model 1902 and 1907. Minor changes were made in 1915 (notably the adoption of a five-round box magazine), and the resulting weapon was designated Berhier model 1907/15. Berthier rifles and carbines in various manifestations alongside the Lebel were the principal weapons of the French infantry soldiers until 1940.*
Right: *French "bleu horizon" uniform 1915. The horizon blue uniform, introduced during the winter of 1914, was certainly an improvement on the former red and dark blue combat dress, but even so it was still not as good as the British khaki and German field grey uniforms for merging into smoky, bracken or wooden backgrounds. The principal improvement was the introduction of a metal "Adrian" helmet with brim and crest.*

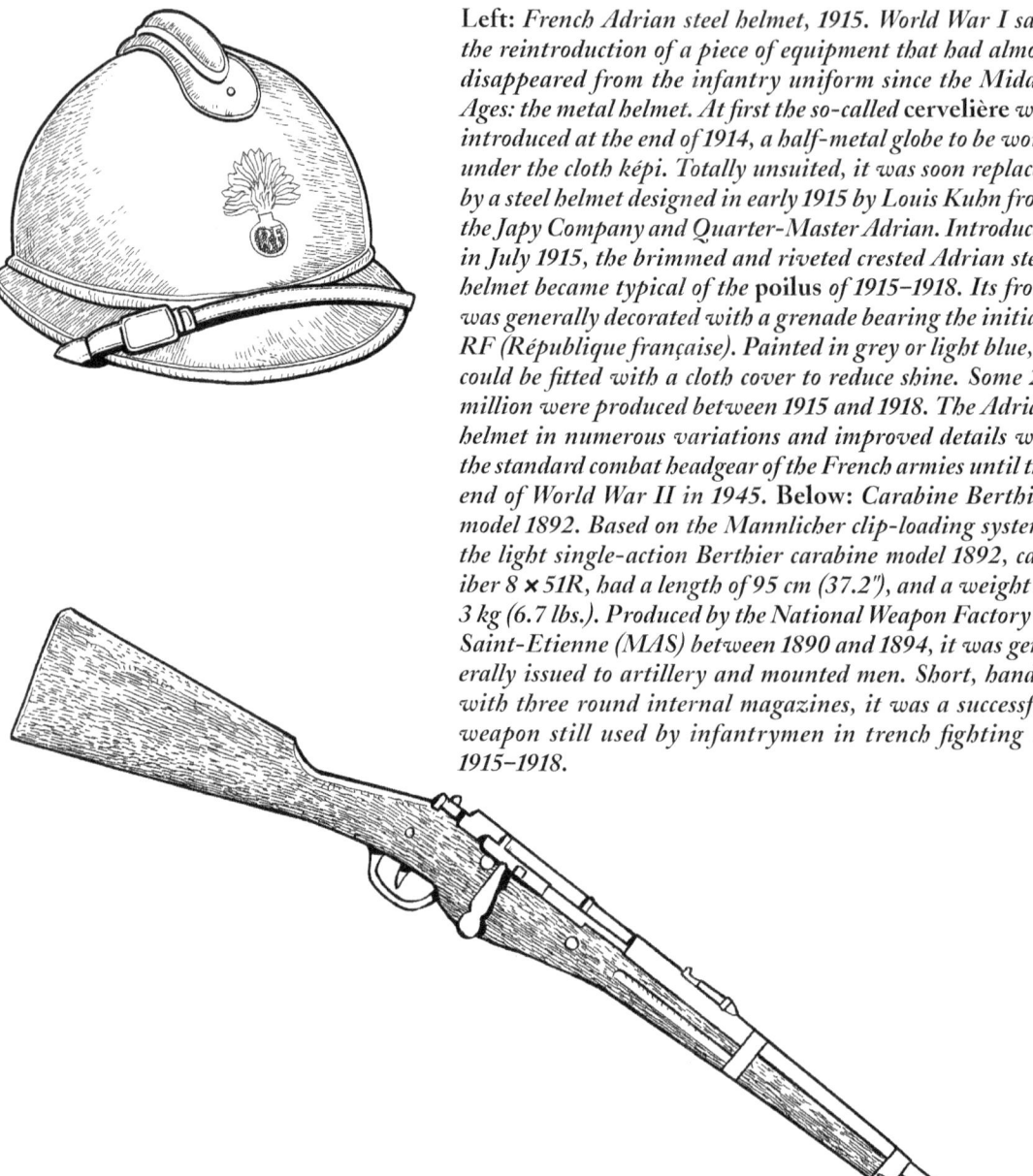

Left: *French Adrian steel helmet, 1915. World War I saw the reintroduction of a piece of equipment that had almost disappeared from the infantry uniform since the Middle Ages: the metal helmet. At first the so-called* **cervelière** *was introduced at the end of 1914, a half-metal globe to be worn under the cloth képi. Totally unsuited, it was soon replaced by a steel helmet designed in early 1915 by Louis Kuhn from the Japy Company and Quarter-Master Adrian. Introduced in July 1915, the brimmed and riveted crested Adrian steel helmet became typical of the* **poilus** *of 1915–1918. Its front was generally decorated with a grenade bearing the initials RF (République française). Painted in grey or light blue, it could be fitted with a cloth cover to reduce shine. Some 20 million were produced between 1915 and 1918. The Adrian helmet in numerous variations and improved details was the standard combat headgear of the French armies until the end of World War II in 1945.* **Below:** *Carabine Berthier model 1892. Based on the Mannlicher clip-loading system, the light single-action Berthier carabine model 1892, caliber 8 × 51R, had a length of 95 cm (37.2"), and a weight of 3 kg (6.7 lbs.). Produced by the National Weapon Factory of Saint-Etienne (MAS) between 1890 and 1894, it was generally issued to artillery and mounted men. Short, handy, with three round internal magazines, it was a successful weapon still used by infantrymen in trench fighting in 1915–1918.*

tles were fought at Verdun and on the Somme. The year 1917 was marked by two major events destined to exercise a far-reaching influence on the history of World War I and the fate of the world: the entry of the United States into the war and the Russian Revolution. At the end of September 1918, the German armies were at the point of defeat. The country found itself under threat of invasion, a revolution broke out, the German commander-in-chief Ludendorf resigned and Kaiser Wilhelm II was forced to abdicate and flee to the neutral Netherlands. A hastily formed transitory government sought an armistice, which was signed in a railway carriage at Rethondes near Compiègne on November 11, 1918. World War I was over at last. It had been a

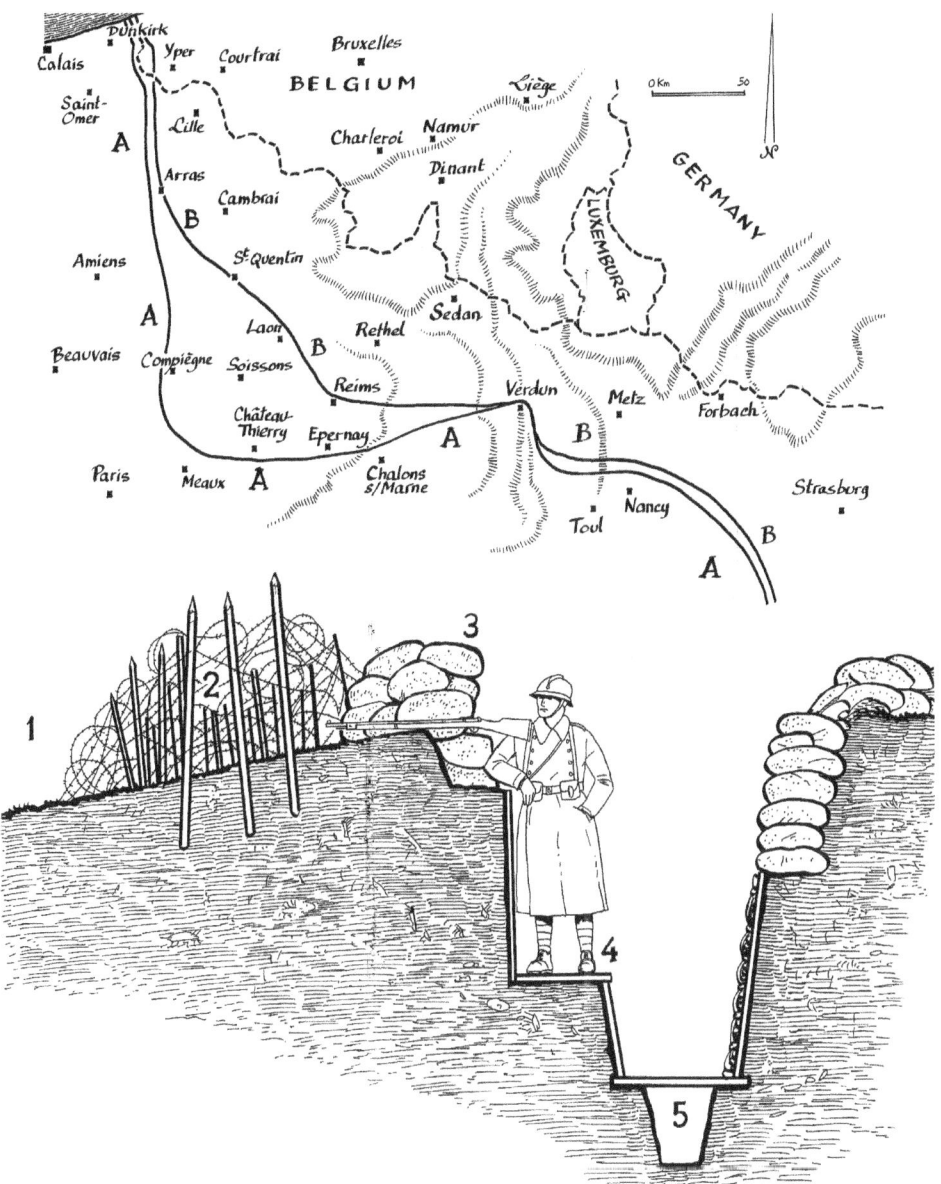

Top: *Sketch map of the western front, 1914–1918. The map displays the northeastern part of France. The line AA indicates the German advance of September 1914 and May–June 1918. The line BB indicates the approximate front line from 1914 to 1918.* Bottom: *Cross-section of a World War I trench. 1: No-man's-land; 2: Barbed wire entanglement; 3: Parapet made of sandbags; 4: Fire-step; 5: Drainage. The walls of the trench were supported by various revetments such as sandbags, XPM or wicker panels, planks, etc. Life at the front was not always hectic with constant shelling, offensive and counterattacks. Going over the top as part of a raiding party, or participating in a major offensive did not happen every day fortunately. The amount of military activity greatly varied, and there were places and times when combatants went for weeks or even months without seeing any action at all. The soldiers' time was divided into watches, stand-by, rest and duties (e.g., weapons inspections, bringing up supplies, digging latrines, laying barbed wire). Life in the trench was a constant struggle to dry out, drain and dig what the weather continually damaged and what enemy bombardments occasionally destroyed.*

Look-out men in trench. Daily life—or better said survival—in the trenches was both dangerous and boring, often grim, and always miserable, uncomfortable and precarious, with moments of humor, comradeship, tragedy, weariness, courage and despair. Even at rest, soldiers always had to be alert as one never knew what the enemy was up to.

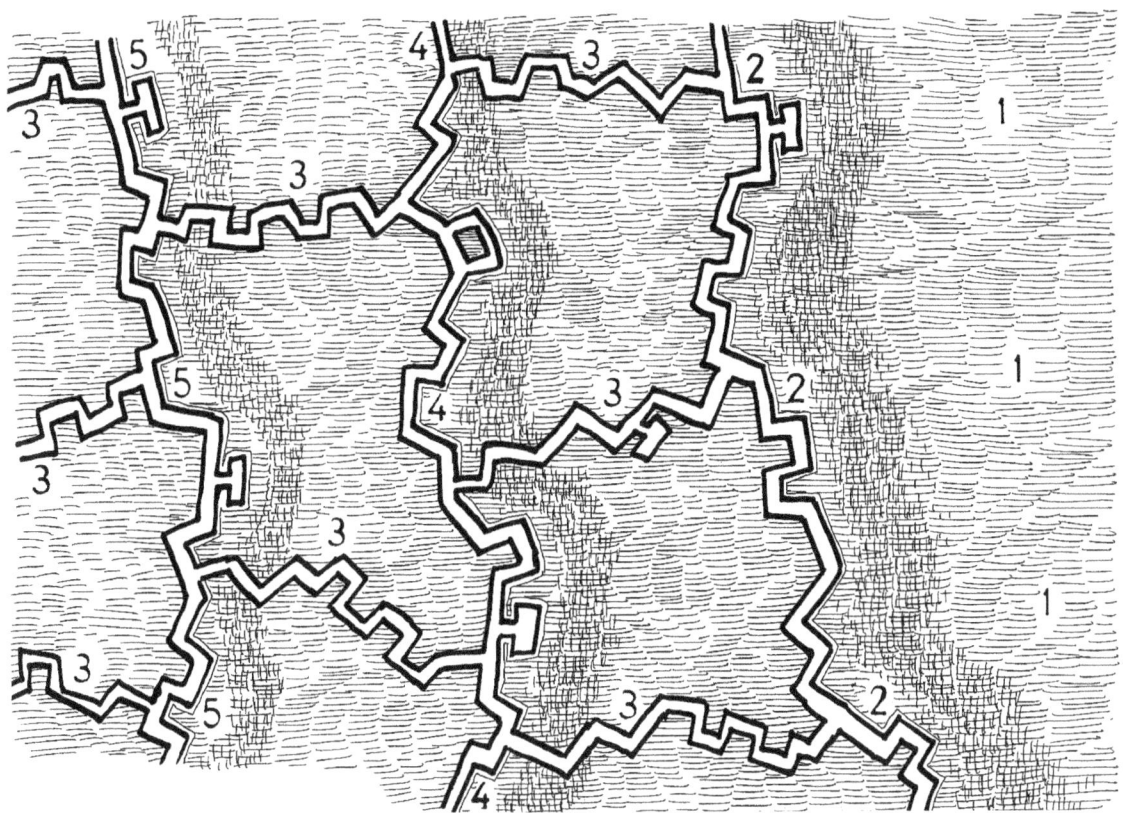

Trench network, World War I. 1: No-man's-land; 2: First line of trench; 3: Communication saps; 4: Second line of trench; 5: Third line of trench. The trench systems proliferated into labyrinths of incredible complexity, making sound and solid front lines on both sides. Behind the first delaying trench and outposts, some hundred or so yards, came a support trench, often so sited that the occupants could bring fire to bear over the heads of the soldiers of the fore trench and thus add firepower to break up any assault. Soon a third line was dug, about 20 yards behind the support line, called a bombing trench. Should the first trenches be conquered, counterattack parties deployed in the third trench could throw grenades at the intruders and retake the lost positions. All these combat trenches were, of course, linked together by zig-zagging saps or sinuous communication trenches provided with recesses, first-aid stations, dugouts and underground chambers for troops, who remained on instant call as reinforcements. Interval defenses included small forts in the form of T-head or D-head branches armed with machine guns with calculated and mutually supporting angles of fire to give all round defense should enemy troops break through the front line. This labyrinthine pattern could be repeated if needed to create an extremely complex system covering a large area that allowed for defense in depth. In some areas the defensive zone stretched up to 6.5 km (4 miles) back from the first sentry. At the rear of the complex there were local and fortified command posts or regional headquarters with observatories and telephones, ammunition and supply dumps, field kitchens, field hospitals, and other facilities, most of them buried underground. Farther back were quarters for reinforcement troops, and heavy support artillery batteries with their command posts and firing control centers.

terrible and enormous war, one of the bloodiest conflicts in history, and the only impressive results were the casualties. The total number of deaths attributable to the war has been estimated at 25 million. The Allies won, Germany was defeated but the war neither solved European problems nor achieved a lasting peace. World War I was not the "war to end all wars," as many politicians proclaimed it to be.

Raincoat 1916. Various items were issued to troops having to cope with the wet and muddy conditions of trench warfare. Always in short supply, these included wooden clogs, sheepskins, thick cloaks, heavy rubberized greatcoats, and raincoats.

4. *The Foreign Legion in World War I, 1914–1918* 97

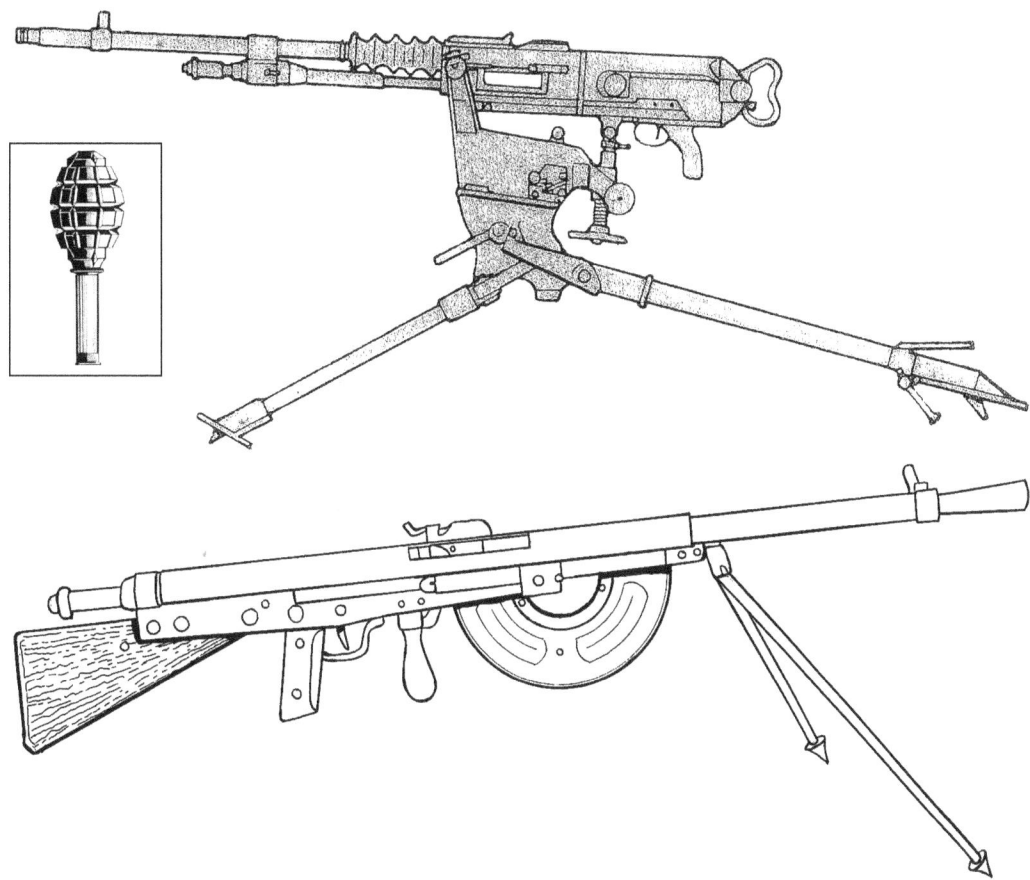

Top: *French Hotchkiss machine gun model, 1914. The heavy machine gun was developed in various versions, and widely used during World War I. The large casualties that machine guns could inflict did more than anything else to bring about the static position trench warfare that so characterized that war. The gas-operated Hotchkiss machine gun was big and heavy, weight was 23.58 kg (52 lbs.). It had a cyclic rate of fire of 600 rounds per minute. It used some of the propellant gases, diverted via a barrel port to operate a piston connected to an extractor and ejector, which disposed of the empty cartridge cases. At the same time a spring was compressed which, on reasserting itself, allowed a new round to be fed into the chamber on the breech mechanism's forward stroke. The Hotchkiss's main deficiency was the feed by flat strip clips holding 30 rounds of 8 mm Lebel cartridge model 1886. Being air-cooled it had a very heavy finned barrel to dissipate the heat generated by firing and so it did not require the encumbrance of water cans and condensers tubes needed by German and British designs.* **Inset:** *Hand grenade. Hand-to-hand combat in trench warfare saw the revival of the use of the hand grenade. Troops on the front, in early 1915, designed improvised devices such the French "racket" grenade, the British "jam tin" blast grenade or the German "nail bomb." Soon proper grenades were produced and issued to troops. Several types were used for various effects: smoke (filled with a mixture of hexachlorethane and powder) or tear gas, offensive (giving a strong blast) or defensive (exploding in a hail of lethal fragments within a range of maximum 20 meters from the burst). The hand grenade was—and still is—an efficient close-range weapon in confined spaces and trenches.* **Bottom:** *French Chauchat fusil-mitrailleur. The light machine gun 8 mm Chauchat was introduced in 1916. Fed by a half-circular magazine, air-cooled, and light enough (9.07 kg = 20 lbs.) to be carried by one soldier, it was intended to provide infantry squads with "walking fire," rate of fire was 250 rounds per minute. Although prone to jam, quick to overheat when delivering sustained fire, unreliable and inaccurate, the weapon, however, helped transform infantry assault tactics.*

Respirator TNH. The introduction of a new atrocious weapon, poison gas, brought a new element into warfare and became one of the horrors of World War I. Effects of combat poison gases varied with the substances used: they could be asphyxiating, lachrymal or blistering, causing violent nausea and faintness or slow-healing burns on the skin and in the respiratory tract, or they could attack the central nervous system. These symptoms were usually followed by utter collapse and incapacity and, in many cases, a more or less lingering death. Issued in February 1916, the French Respirator type TNH was designed by pharmacist Major Rodier, and manufactured by the Hutchinson Company. Some 510,000 were produced and issued to frontline troops until January 1917 when it proved no longer effective. It was then replaced by the gasmask type M2.

Nettoyeur de tranchée. *The so-called* **nettoyeurs de tranchée** *were special squads of "trench cleaners" whose task was to clear combat emplacements of the remaining enemy after a position had been conquered. Fighting dangerous hand-to-hand battles they were equipped with various close-range weapons including carbines, grenades, knives, bayonets, entrenching tools and improvised clubs whose heads were fitted with nails and spikes.*

Faby mortar 150 T model 1917. Trench warfare saw the revival and improvement of the infantry mortar. With its parabolical trajectory, a mortar could be placed behind a hill, in an entrenchment, or in a small steep-sided pit. It facilitated engagement of troops behind cover, in a ditch or concealed in a trench. A cheap substitute for the field gun, a mortar was composed of a barrel, a bipod and a baseplate, but many forms of mortars were used, notably the French lance-grenades and **Crapouillot** *(grenade-launchers), and the German* **Minenwerfer** *(mine-throwers). The French Faby mortar weighed 600 kg. It had a recoil system, and could rotate off its platform. A bomb of 17 kg was shot to a maximum range of 2 km with a rate of fire of four rounds per minute. Hundreds of these heavy mortars were issued to frontline troops in the trenches of France.* **Right:** *Renault FT17. The instrument that finally helped break barbed wire and machine-gun fire was the tank. Developed in Britain and France more or less concurrently and with little official support, the tank was a mobile fortress, an armored tracked combat vehicle designed to forge a path by force for infantry frontal attacks against entrenched positions. The Renault FT17, introduced in 1917, was a small light tank with a length of 4.1 m and a height of 2.14 m. It weighed only 6.5 tons, was capable of a maximum speed of 6 mph, and a range of 35 km. Armor was 6 mm to 22 mm. The vehicle had a crew of two (driver and commander/gunner). It was armed either with a Hotchkiss machine gun or a short 37-mm gun. It initiated the use of a revolving turret, universally adopted later by tank designers. Over 2,500 were produced, some of them still in service in the French army in 1940.*

Composition of the Foreign Legion in 1914

Recruitment

At the outbreak of World War I the French Foreign Legion was composed of the following formations:

- Two battalions posted in Indochina.
- The First Foreign Regiment (1st RE) based at Sidi-Bel-Abbès, and the Second Foreign Regiment (2nd RE) stationed at Saïda, both in Algeria.
- A *régiment de marche* deployed in Morocco recruited and trained by the two Algerian regiments; as Germany and France were now at war, all German citizens wishing to stay in the Legion were regrouped in this task regiment.
- Several mule-borne *compagnies montées* (administratively affiliated to the Algerian 1st and 2nd Regiments) operating as detached units in North Africa.

With the wildly patriotic climate that reigned in August and September 1914, Legion recruiting stations all over France were flooded with many idealistic volunteers of about 50 various nationalities (the most numerous being the Swiss, Spaniards, Luxembourgers and Belgians) who enlisted for the duration of the war with the goal of defending their fatherland of adoption. At the Palais Royal in Paris, Czechs organized a recruiting office. A young American named Georges Casmene published a declaration in the *New York Herald Tribune* on August 2 that led to the enthusiastic enlistment of 50 Americans. But the patriotic exaltation was accompanied by an exacerbated feeling of collective hysterical xenophobia. Many foreigners living in France—not only Germans, Austrians and Turks but also Hungarians, Serbs, Slovakians and Czechs and anyone speaking with a central European accent or having a non–French name—would be regarded *a priori* as a saboteur, a spy, and a potential enemy who would stab the French in the back. Fear of little known foreigners and both ridicule of and hatred for outsiders has long been evident everywhere, but, in wartime, it carries extra significance and seems to well up spontaneously in an outburst of xenophobia. When the official propaganda exacerbates this hatred of foreigners and demonizes them the result often produces an atmosphere of nationalistic hysteria. In such an atmosphere many foreigners were arrested (some molested) and interned in detention camps for the duration of the war. So the Legion was *also* a refuge for some foreigners who had reason to fear hysterical popular anger.

New Legion units

The more or less enthusiastic "duration only" volunteers were numerous enough to form two further *régiments de marche* trained and commanded by NCOs and officers drawn from the "Algerian" 1st RE and 2nd RE. These two new units were designated Deuxième Régiment de marche du Premier Régiment étranger (2nd RM/1st RE, Second Task Regiment of the First Foreign Regiment) based at Avignon, and Deuxième Régiment de marche du Deuxième Régiment étranger (2nd RM/2nd RE, Second Task Regiment of the Second Foreign Regiment) based at Toulouse. Each new regiment was composed of three battalions of freshly recruited and inexperienced volunteers bolstered by one battalion of "genuine" veteran legionaries who would provide a backbone. The two types of Legion soldiers mixed with difficulty. The "real" legionaries were for the most part hardened veterans of Indochina and North Africa. They were marksmen accustomed to march in full pack under the worst conditions, to advance without hesitation facing enemy fire and who, in defense, would hold out to the last man. They regarded with mockery and contempt the newcomers raised in France who had neither seen Africa nor passed through the barrack's gate at Sidi-Bel-Abbes. Many of them felt that the professional character of the élite Foreign Legion was being diluted by allowing amateurs and "soft civilians" to enter the ranks. Due to confusion during mobilization of the French army in 1914, large groups of single nationalities were formed, which encouraged particularism, rivalry and nationalism within the units—an error which the Legion had always avoided since the 1860s. Both volatile multinational regiments were trained at the military camp of Mailly in September–October 1914 by old-fashioned Legion reservists and *adjudants* (warrant officers) of rigid outlook who used harsh methods. Iron discipline, hard training, special demands for special treatment, general absence of military background, unrealistic expectations countered by brutal realities created tensions. Problems of language added to the confusion and caused many misunderstandings and a few laughable situations. For example, a group of 12 Cossacks—unable to speak French or even Russian—enlisted in September 1914 at the Legion depot at Toulouse; of course, they wanted to serve in the cavalry, but to their horror they found themselves in the infantry; when an interpreter who spoke their dialect was finally found, it was sadly explained to them that there was no Legion cavalry and the disappointed Cossacks were released. Resentment emerged between the battle-hardened professional cadres and the enthusiastic volunteers, many of whom were educated or politically liberal-minded men. Among these "idealist-amateurs" we may list a few celebrities. The American song and musical composer Cole Porter (1893–1964)—the man who composed the evergreen jazz song "Night and Day"—served in the Legion in 1917–1918, although other source says he never did but only pretended to so as to impress the ladies of the Parisian jet set. The American poet Alan Seeger (1888–1916), the father of the folk singer Pete Seeger, lived in France since 1912. He wrote his famous poem "I have a rendez-vous with death" and was killed in action in July 1916. The later statesman and politician Edouard Daladier (1884–1970) served in the Legion in 1914. The Luxembourgian cyclist champion, François Faber (winner of the Tour de France in 1909) enlisted in 1914 and was killed in action in 1915. The Swiss writer Frédéric Sausser (1887–1961), better known as Blaise Cendrars, author of *La Prose du Transibérien* (published in 1913), *L'Or* (1925), and *Moravagine* (1926) enlisted in 1914, was badly wounded and lost an arm in battle in 1916. The German writer Ernst Junger (1895–1998) served in the Legion in 1912–1913 under the pseudonym of legionary Berger; he later wrote *Jeux Africains* in which he described his experience in the Corps. The Polish artist Moses Kisling enlisted in 1914. Louis II Grimaldi, prince of Monaco (1870–1949), joined the Legion in 1914 for the duration of the war, and survived. He became the ruler of the small principality in southern France in 1922. William A. Wellman (1896–1975), later to become a movie director, served in the Legion in World War I.

The Foreign Legion thus entered World War I badly disorganized, as the confusion, bustle, enthusiasm and well-meaning, but sometimes misguided efforts of those early days at the Legion depots in France can be imagined. Soon enough, the hardship and suffering and the fighting and dying in grueling battles at the front welded all the illustrious personalities, unknown nobodies, experienced veterans and new legionaries together.

The number of volunteers available also enabled the raising of two other regiments. The Troisième Régiment de marche du Premier Régiment étranger (3rd RM/1st RE, Third Task Regiment of the First Foreign Regiment), based at Reuilly Barracks in Paris, with a strength of three battalions, was composed mainly of Belgians, Italians, Greeks and Russians; as the Legion could not provide cadres for this unit, officers were drawn from the Parisian *Gendarmerie* (uniformed police) and *Sapeurs-Pompiers* (Fire Brigade). As for NCOs, few regulars were available, and any volunteer who had previous military service in other armies or other wars—or claimed he had—was promoted. Needless to say, the inexperienced staff and officers made this unit one of poor military value.

At the same time the Quatrième Régiment de marche du Premier Régiment étranger (4th RM/1st RE, Fourth Task Regiment of the First Foreign Regiment) was formed in November 1914 at Nîmes and Montélimar, mainly made up of Italians, as Italy had not yet entered the war. One particularity of the 4th RM/1st RE was its command leadership, given to a grandson of the famous revolutionary Giuseppe Garibaldi (1807–1882), one of the leaders of Italian unification; five members of his family also enlisted, and the 4th RM/1st RE was popularly known as the Garibaldi Brigade and bore the star of Savoy on its regimental flag. In fact both 3rd RM/1st RE and Garibaldi 4th RM/1st RE had little to do with the Foreign Legion proper.

Given the scale of World War I involving millions of men, the contribution of the Legion was minimal, but wherever the Corps was engaged it performed rather well. All Legion units were sent to the front, which had stabilized to some extent by late 1914. All of them settled down to routine muddy, cold and wet trench warfare, with occasional patrol clashes, sniping and minor raids.

First Battles, 1914–1915

Garibaldi Brigade

The Garibaldi Brigade (4th RM/1st RE) was attached to the 10th Colonial Division, and deployed in the Argonne sector in December 1914. During the winter the unit took part to several battles. On December 14, at Maison-Forestière, and in the wood of Bois-Boland in the Argonne region, their attack was repulsed by German machine-gun fire causing high casualties. At Courtes-Chausses, a few days later, they broke through German trenches with the bayonet, but the Italians were only partially successful in this assault. In January 1915, the Germans began to press forward in the sector of Four-de-Paris. Some French positions gave way, so the Garibaldi was rushed there to fill the gap. They held the German advance but, after unsuccessful and costly counterattacks repulsed by machine-gun fire, they were unable to recover the ground lost. After two months of fighting the Garibaldi Brigade had suffered about 430 casualties—two Garibaldis, Bruno and Costante, being among those killed in action.

On March 5, 1915, Italy entered the war on the side of France and Britain. The Fourth Task Regiment of the 1st Foreign Regiment was disbanded at Italy's request, and the volunteers transferred to the Italian national forces.

3rd RM/1st RE

The undermanned and poorly commanded Third Task Regiment of the First Foreign Legion Regiment was deployed to the front along the Somme River in December 1914 and posted in the sector of Frise where they experienced a cold winter of muddy trench warfare. In March 1915, the 3rd RM/1st RE was posted in the plateau of Santerre. By that time many volunteers were transferred to their own national armies (mainly Russia, Belgium and Italy), and the regiment was reduced to only two battalions. In July 1915 it was decided to disband it, and active remaining personnel were transferred to the Second Task Regiment of the First Foreign Regiment. The 3rd RM/1st RE had thus only a short life, and had been allowed to wither away without being given the opportunity to prove itself in battle.

2nd RM/2nd RE

The four battalions of the Second Task Regiment of the Second Foreign Regiment were attached to the 36th French Infantry Division and deployed in the sector of Craonne in December 1914, where they, too, experienced a cold winter in trenches. In May 1915, the 2nd RM/2nd RE was moved to Reims and posted in trenches in the sector of Paissy. In July 1915, the regiment was withdrawn from the front and retired to rest quarters in Burgundy. By that time one battalion was disbanded as Russian, Belgian and Italian volunteers were transferred to their own national armies. The undermanned regiment joined the 2nd RM/1st RE and the Moroccan Division in early September on the Champagne front. On September 25 the regiment—temporary attached to the 10th Colonial Division—was ordered to attack the Wagram and Presbourg positions north of Navarin Farm and Souin Hill. See further below.

2nd RM/1st RE

After training at the camp of Mailly in September 1914, the four battalions of the 2nd Régiment de marche of the 1st Régiment étranger were deployed in November 1914 around the sectors of Prunay and La Pompelle in Champagne. There was no significant fighting but all the men suffered their first appalling winter of static warfare in rudimentary trenches. In May 1915 they were attached to the Moroccan Division and engaged in the Artois-Champagne offensives in the sector of Neuville-Saint-Vaast. Their objectives were Ouvrages Blancs and Hill 140 on Vimy Ridge. The attack started in the early morning of May 9 with an artillery barrage fired by 400 guns. The bombardment shattered the ground turning it into a hellish upheaval of muddy wasteland, torn fields, ruined paths and swampy shell craters. Then the legionaries "went over the top" with special squads equipped with wire-cutters to cut through with barbed wire, and grenade teams to silent German machine-gun posts. The regiment advanced slowly across the open and broken no-man's-land, and then suddenly the enemy opened fire with machine guns. The first and second battalions were battered to a halt and pinned down while the third battalion was successful in seizing an enemy post enabling the 1st and 2nd to move forward to Hill 140. The objectives were finally captured, but at very high cost; out of 4,000 men, about 1,900 were killed and wounded. As no French reinforcements came, the positions had to be evacuated, with heavy casualties again, after a German artillery bombardment and a powerful German

Lieutenant Colonel, 4th RM/1st RE, 1914. The képi was black and red with lace rank stripes gold and silver. The jacket was blue-grey with gold-embroidered grenades on the collar, and sleeves with full-sized rank stripes. The trousers, bright red with black seam stripes, were tucked into leather laced gaiters. Mounted officers wore spurs. Weapon was the M 1882 revolver in leather holster.

counteroffensive. On June 16, reduced to two battalions, the 2nd RM/1st RE was committed to attack in the sector of Givenchy, with hard fighting at Souchez, Carency and Cabaret Rouge. Here again the objective was taken—at the cost of 650 casualties—and again, lacking support, reinforcement and artillery backing, the legionaries were driven back by a German counterstroke. By June 18 the offensive was stopped and the French High Command considered a victory to have been won; in certain parts of the front the French army had achieved an advance of 2 kilometers. The casualties were 100,000, which meant 50 dead men per meter of ground.

In July 1915, the Moroccan Division and the 2nd RM/1st RE were withdrawn from the Artois front. They went into rest quarters in the comparatively calm sector of the Vosges Mountains and were reinforced by men of the disbanded 3rd RM/1st RE.

In September 1915, the 2nd RM/1st RE—now wearing a khaki uniform to replace the conspicuous blue coat and red trousers—was posted on the Champagne front, and there engaged in another major and costly engagement. On September 25, both Legion Regiments 2nd RM/1st RE and 2nd RM/2nd RE were ordered to assault the sector of the heavily fortified Navarin farm. Due to rainfall that transformed the area into swamps, and insufficiently supported by artillery preparation, they were not able to penetrate into the enemy wire network. As they rose up out of their trenches the legionaries ran headon into machine-gun fire, which withered their ranks and made the crossing of the open no-man's-land impossible. As ever, the Legion distinguished itself by extraordinary feats of courage and extravagant acts of bravado; it is recorded that the trumpeters (notably a certain legionary named Bouilloux) marched at the front of the attacking regiments through no-man's-land swept by heavy rainfall and German machine-gun fire, playing the Legion's song, the "Boudin." These efforts to encourage the legionaries forward were all of no avail because of persistent fire from machine guns. For two days the men were rooted where they were, unable to advance. When they were relieved their casualties totaled over 800, out of an original 1,600 going into battle. By September 29, 1915, the failed offensive was stopped. The remnant of the Foreign Legion was withdrawn and took its winter quarters away from the front. The color of the 2nd RM/1st RE was decorated with the Croix de Guerre with three palms, which amounted to the fourth such decoration that the regiment had been awarded.

Battles of the RMLE, 1916–1918

Creation of the RMLE

In October 1915 both 2nd RM/2nd RE and 2nd RM/1st RE were withdrawn from the front and, with other troops, took part in a review before the French president and King George V of Great Britain. By that time, in view of heavy losses and dwindling numbers (as more countries joined the war), it was decided to merge all Foreign Legion units in France into a single three-battalion formation. This new unit was designated Régiment de marche de la Légion étrangère (RMLE for short, Task Regiment of the Foreign Legion) and remained in this form and under this title until the end of the war.

The RMLE was officially on November 11, 1915, and adopted the flag of the 2nd RM/1st RE. It counted 3,115 legionaries placed under the leadership of Lieutenant-Colonel Cot. From December 1915 to June 1916, the RMLE, still attached to the Moroccan Division, was reshaped, trained and sent to occupy trenches in the sector of Roye-Lassigny. Now the Legion was fully recognized as an élite force to be employed as a spearhead in the fiercest fighting.

Belloy-en-Santerre, July 1916

The RMLE was engaged in an attack as part of General Joffre's offensive on the Somme front to relieve pressure on Verdun.

The unit was moved up to the edge of the battle and ordered to advance and take the heavily fortified village of Belloy-en-Santerre. On July 4, 1916, after a heavy preparatory artillery barrage, the leading battalion of the RMLE leapt out of its trenches and the legionaries "went over the top." In the pouring rain, and under sustained German machine-gun fire, the men crossed the 800-meter-wide broken no-man's-land full of muddy shell craters. The first wave was beaten to a halt, and the Second Battalion moved out into the attack and reached the outskirts of the village. The ruins of Belloy were taken after furious hand-to-hand fighting with bayonets and grenades in the streets, lanes, gardens and destroyed houses. The Legion took 750 prisoners, including 15 officers, but the cost was high, nearly one-third of the establishment—25 officers and 844 legionaries, among them the American poet Alan Seeger. After the war Seeger's father came to France in search of his son's remains, but the poet's body had disappeared, and Seeger senior bought a bell for the rebuilt church of Belloy-en-Santerre.

The Germans launched several serious infantry counterattacks supported by artillery fire but the ruins of Belloy-en-Santerre were held until July 6 when the Legion was relieved. Another attack took place in the sector of Chancellier on July 8 and 9, where the RMLE was engaged. Twice the

Corporal, RMLE, 1916. This corporal of the Régiment de marche de la Légion étrangère in combat order wears the model 1915 Adrian steel helmet (usually painted in light blue, later khaki), and a gas-respirator, which, when not in use, was stored in a rectangular metal box hanging from the waist-belt. The capote (greatcoat) was khaki, double-breasted, pocketless with a deep fall collar bearing a green collar badge with the cypher "1," as the RMLE had taken the regimental color of the Second Task Regiment of the First Foreign Regiment. The rank insignia (two stripes for corporal) was worn on the sleeve. Equipment included a brown leather belt with two ammunition pouches, braces, and knapsack. The weapon could be either a Lebel rifle or an 8 mm Berthier M1907/15 both fitted with a bayonet.

legionnaires leapt out of their trenches, and twice they were forced back again. These futile actions cost another 400 casualties. After these engagements the rump of the RMLE was sent for reorganization and a short rest to Maignelay (Oise). In autumn and winter 1916, the Task Regiment—rebuilt with new volunteers—went back to cold and muddy trenches in the sector of Plessier-de-Roye on the Somme front. Command passed to Lieutenant-Colonel Duriez.

Auberive, April 1917

When the French effort concentrated upon trying to crack the hard German lines between Soissons and Reims, the RMLE moved into position to the east of Reims. The next major engagement fought by the Task Regiment of the Foreign Legion was in April 1917, during the battle of Moronvilliers on the right flank of General Nivelle's Chemin des Dames offensive. The terrible lessons of previous frontal attacks had apparently been learned, and more sophisticated infantry assault tactics were used, with the emphasis on increasing firepower and better coordination between movement and fire support. Battalions included a company of machine gun, and each platoon had Chauchat portable light machine guns. On April 17, the Legion was ordered to take the fortified village of Auberive in the valley of the Suippe River, again under terrible weather conditions with wind and rain transforming the battlefield into a swamp of mud. After a thorough artillery preparation, the RMLE advanced, not in a single wave but in a small group of infiltrating skirmishers supported by machine-gun teams, riflemen and hand-grenade squads. Jumping from craters to collapsed trenches, the struggle bogged down and developed into a heaving mass of mud and men trying desperately to force their way forward, trench by trench. The fighting moved from one dugout to another, and frequently swayed backward and forward as the Legion's opponent, the German Infantry Regiment No.107, proved a hard nut to crack. It amounted to a grenade battle in which junior leaders and individual initiative played a large part. In spite of thirst, fatigue, lack of food and ammunition, and heavy casualties, the RMLE fought hand-to-hand in deep mud using 50,000 hand grenades. They succeeded in capturing 2 square kilometers of enemy-held ground, a total of 7 kilometers of trenches and saps, the ruins of the village of Auberive and a very strong position known as Bethmann-Hollweg, or Grand Boyau. A group of legionaries of the 6th Company led by the "Swiss" Adjudant-Chef Mader captured a German battery of seven heavy guns in an audacious raid using surprise and bluff.

Actually Mader was a German born in 1886 at Stuttgart. A mason drafted into the army of Würtemberg, the hot-tempered Mader had murdered a ruthless NCO who persecuted him, deserted and fled to Switzerland where he met an ex-legionary who advised him to enlist. Hunted by the police, Mader joined the Foreign Legion under a false Swiss name at Montbéliard. He was soon in Marseille and served in Algeria, in the 2nd Foreign Regiment at Saida and in garrisons in several small forts in the southern part of Oran Province. In 1914 the hunted criminal had become a sergeant owing to his good behavior. Officially a Swiss citizen, he was allowed to volunteer to serve on the western front in France against the Germans. After the feat of Auberive he was wounded in 1918 at Villers-Cotteret. After the war the discharged, amputed and married ex-legionary Mader worked as a warden in the Palace of Versailles. All his life, he spoke French with a very strong German accent and, during the occupation of France (1940–1944), pretended to be deaf and dumb to avoid problems with the Nazi police. He died a peaceful death in the early 1950s.

After three days and two nights of terrible hand-to-hand fighting in appalling conditions, the battle of Auberive came to a standstill through sheer exhaustion. Unfortunately for all their efforts, suffering and casualties, the legionaries were unable to hold the ground they had conquered. They were forced to withdraw on April 22, after German artillery and infantry counterattacks. In other sectors, offensives also failed to achieve significant gains or breakthroughs. The Nivelles offensives of spring 1917 ended in other pointless and costly disasters, which were followed by mutinies. The newly appointed general Philippe Pétain dealt with the revolt by court-martial and by stopping useless and costly offensives. Composed of volunteers and professionals who had chosen military life, the Legion was not shaken during the mid–1917 mutinies. Legionaries deserted individually when they were fed up, it is true, but the Legion, with its high morale, traditions and esprit de corps, did not experience wholesale mutiny. Legionaries had little care for what the average French draftees felt, thought, said and did. It seems that, on the whole, legionaries viewed the war with its endless carnage, hardship and suffering as an honorable duty and as yet another chapter in the Legion's history.

In May 1917 the exhausted Legion Task Regiment was relieved and sent to rest and reorganization at Pocancy (Marne). Command of the RMLE passed to Lieutenant-Colonel Paul Rollet, who replaced Lieutenant-Colonel Duriez who had been seriously wounded during the battle of Auberive. Rollet led a detachment of the RMLE (seven officers and 125 legionaries) with music and color-party to participate to the *Quatorze Juillet* (July 14th, Bastille Day), the illustrious annual national parade held on the Champs-Elysées in Paris. The Legion Task Regiment was awarded the Médaille militaire during a ceremony in the presence of President Poincaré.

Rollet, the Father of the Legion

The newly appointed chief of the RMLE was born on December 20, 1875, at Auxerre into a family with a strong military background. Paul Frédéric Rollet naturally chose to become a soldier. After two years at the Military Academy of Saint Cyr, Lieutenant Rollet served between 1899 and 1901 in the 91st Infantry Regiment in the Ardennes, after which he volunteered to serve in the Legion. Rollet remained in the Legion for most of his career with a short break between 1914 and 1917 when he served in the French infantry. He was a small and skinny man, with blue eyes, a *barbiche* (short beard), and a peppery character. A veteran of Madagascar (1902), and the Moroccan mounted companies (1905–1914), a very popular, brave and hot-tempered officer known for his *baraka* (good luck in Arab language), energy and enthusiasm, he was also famous for his eccentricities and unorthodox habits, which added to his personal fame and to the Legion's glamour. About him a host of anecdotes abound. It is told that he once helped a drunken legionnaire back to the barracks and smuggled him past the guards. He once sentenced an ill-disciplined man to detention (during which time he would receive no pay), and gave him money to send home to his family. On the French western front, even in the thick of combat, Rollet wore no helmet and carried no weapon; and even in wind, rain, snow or frost, he always wore merely his thin, pale khaki African uniform, reputedly with no shirt under his tunic; his "cuffs" being supported by threading a piece of string through the armholes of the jacket; these occasionally broke loose at unexpected, embarrassing moments. But Rollet was not only an exotic eccentric, he was also a brave soldier and a skilled organizer. He had distinguished himself in 1911 in Morocco and in the period before World War I in North Africa where he had built tracks in deserts and mountains, dug wells and—under Lyautey's influence—galvanized his

Legion captain, c. 1917. The captain wears the model 1915 Adrian steel helmet and the 1915 single-breasted greatcoat. He is armed with a sword and a pistol type 1892.

men. He also made fruitful connections and friendships with local Arab rulers. He instituted a (very popular) system allowing any legionary of the rank who considered himself to have been unfairly punished to complain directly to him without passing through the normal hierarchical procedure. When France was invaded in 1914, Colonel Rollet thought that his duty was to defend his fatherland. He left the Legion and served in the 331st Infantry Regiment, which he led in several major engagements in the Argonne in 1915, on the Somme front in 1916 and the Aisne River in 1917. After Colonel Duriez's death, he took command of the RMLE.

After World War I, Rollet commanded the 3rd Legion Infantry Regiment until 1926, and the 1st Legion Infantry Regiment until 1931, when he was promoted to brigadier-general, and then to the position of the Legion's first general-inspector, a title especially created for him. In his own words, Rollet divided humanity into three parts: the Legion; those who admired the Legion and could be useful to it; and the rest of the world, which was nothing in his eyes. Like Négrier before him, he devoted his enormous skills and energy to the Legion, and made tireless efforts on behalf of his legionaries. His motto was: "I give myself entirely to the Legion, the Legion gives itself completely to me," he put his words into action. Rollet organized unforgettable festivities for the Legion's hundred-year anniversary in 1931, and he created the Service du Moral et des Oeuvres de la Légion

(SMOL), a social service agency that provided homes and subsidies for veterans and that served as an influential network offering civilian jobs to ex-servicemen. He was a live wire, constantly dashing here and there in becoming a monument, a living legend, which earned for him the undisputed title *Père de la Légion* (Father of the Legion). Under his guidance, the Legion's morale soared, its traditions were further developed, and its fame and reputation grew tremendously. He served in the position of Legion inspector until his retirement in December 1935, after which he continued his work on behalf of his men, using his wide influence and reputation. In 1938 he became chairman of the World War I veterans association Gueules cassées (literally, "Ugly Mugs," disfigured ex-servicemen with horrible face wounds). Rollet died in Paris on April 16, 1941, and General von Stülpnagel, commanding officer of the German occupation troops in France, requested the honor of being present at his burial. After 34 years of service in the Legion, five times wounded in combat, 10 times mentioned in dispatches, the popular and legendary Father of the Legion was greatly mourned by all his men. Rollet—together with Conrad, Danjou, Viénot, Négrier, Amilakvari, Segretain, Jeanpierre and many others—belongs to the Legion's legendary personalities.

Cumière and Forges, August 1917

After a short moment of glory at Paris, the RMLE, led by its colorful new commander, took part in another battle in August 1917. Still a part of the Moroccan Division headed by General Degoutte, its mission was to retake positions lost in the spring of 1916 on the left bank of the Meuse River in the sector of Verdun. The attack, launched early on the morning of August 20, 1917, was supported by a creeping artillery barrage. The Legion took a German fortified position known as Ouvrages Blancs. Next they attacked the village of Cumière, which, without pausing in their stride, they cleared with bayonets and grenades. The legionnaires of the RMLE then forced their way forward to a brook near a destroyed village named Forges. This successful advance into enemy-held territory was far ahead of schedule. To a messenger sent by headquarters asking him where he was and what he was doing, Rollet replied that "the Legion had been given too closed objectives, and that he therefore had assigned a new task to his men." Without waiting for orders, Rollet immediately decided to exploit his success, and advanced his determined troops forward to capture Hill 264. The next day, August 21, the villages of Régneville and Forges were successfully assaulted, amounting to an advance of two miles, and taking 680 prisoners (including 20 officers), 10 77 mm guns, four 105 mm guns, and quantities of other materials. Casualties suffered by the RMLE were 52 legionaries killed, one officer killed and 271 wounded (including 20 officers)—light, by contemporary standards. And this points up even further the senseless waste that seems so much to characterize World War I. Rollet himself was lightly wounded in the arm by shrapnel, but as nobody dared to ask him to resign even temporarily, he remained in command. The Legion Regiment resisted counterattacks and airplane strafing, and it held its positions until September 4, 1917. After this successful engagement, the Foreign Regiment went into rest quarters at Vaucouleurs in Lorraine. On September 17, 1917, General Pétain reviewed the Moroccan Division and expressed his satisfaction about the RMLE legionaries' exploits. The red lanyard of the Légion d'honneur was added to the Foreign Legion Regiment's flag, a new decoration especially instituted for them.

Hangard-en-Santerre, March–April 1918

In winter 1917–1918, the Legion Regiment was placed in the entrenched sector of

Filey in Lorraine. They made a successful assault (January 8), resisted a gas attack (January 12) and went into rest quarters in March. After the peace of Brest-Litovsk with Russia, General Erich Ludendorf's forces launched powerful offensives on the western front in late March 1918. The Allied lines were breached in Flanders and on the Somme, and both French and British troops retreated in disorder and confusion.

The Moroccan Division (now commanded by General Daugan) and Rollet's RMLE were hastily rushed to the menaced Amiens sector. On April 25 the Foreign Legion Regiment was ordered to retake the wood of Hangard-en-Santerre, which had just been occupied by the advancing German 19th Infantry Division. The counterattack was launched jointly by the Moroccan Division, the RMLE and a few British tanks. Although primitive and small these tanks provided screens behind which the infantry could progress. The attack was a success but it was a tragic echo of previous battles, notably that of Auberive. The Germans had had enough time to get machine guns into action and inflict heavy loss to the RMLE. On the shell-churned no-man's-land, the three battalions were engaged one after another, each advancing as its predecessor was decimated by German machine-gun fire. Desperate hand-to-hand fighting in the forest went on for hours. In the end the Legion won the day, the Germans withdrew and the road to Amiens was securely blocked. When the engagement ended on April 28, casualties were appalling: 18 officers and 833 legionaries were killed or wounded.

The RMLE remained fighting in the sector of Hangard for a few days resisting several attacks. In early May 1918 the Task Regiment went for a short rest and reorganization to the region of Versigny and Ermenonville, north of Paris.

Soissons, May–June 1918

On May 27, another German large-scale offensive was launched, using artillery, poison gas and *Stoßtruppen* (special elite assault troops), which overran the Chemin des Dames and menaced Soissons. When the enemy reached the Marne River at Château-Thierry, the RMLE was quickly transported by truck on May 29 to plug the gap of Saconin-Breuil near Soissons. For four days and nights, a series of confused battles, assaults, counterattacks and skirmishes broke out on an ill-defined front between Montagne de Paris and Villers-Cotterets with positions changing hands several times. Plagued by bad weather with constant rain the Legion, however, successfully resisted the German attack, thereby stopping a threatening movement in the direction of Paris.

In early June, other sporadic defensive engagements were fought at Vivières, Saint-Etienne-Chelles, La Raperie, Coeuvres, Saint-Baudry and Ambleny. Contrary to their usual tactics, the French advanced without a preliminary artillery barrage, and therefore managed to take the Germans by surprise. The battle, which lasted until June 12, 1918, saw the German thrust contained and repulsed. A total of 17,000 men were taken prisoners and more than 300 guns captured, but it had cost the RMLE no less than 1,250 casualties.

Last battles, July–November 1918

Ambleny marked the last defensive battle. The German armies were now stopped, exhausted and retreating. The German high command based their immediate defensive hopes on the so-called Hindenburg Line, which was a series of well-defended positions stretching from the Schelde River to the Oise River. After the victories of July 1918, it was now Marshal Foch's turn to attack on all fronts. After a short break for reorganization, the RMLE, attached to

General Mangin's 10th Army, played an important part in a successful series of counterattacks between July 17 and 20 at the Plateau de Dommiers, Chazelles-Lechelles, La Foulerie, and Aconin. With no artillery preparation to alert the Germans, the attackers relied upon surprise. Legion infantry infused with the spirit of, *élan* supported by small Renault tanks and by strafing attacks of the 104th French Fighter squadron, went on the offensive. Steady fighting occurred, which went on day and night without respite, as German trenches, concrete casemates, machine-gun nests and artillery positions had to be assaulted one by one. Some 450 Germans were taken prisoners, 20 guns, and numerous other light weapons such as mortars and machine guns were captured by the RMLE. But the strength of the Task Regiment had sunk alarmingly owing to casualties—about 780 officers and men killed. The Task Regiment was reduced to about 700 men, and most companies were down to about 50 men, often without a survivor above the rank of sergeant. The men were almost out on their feet from fatigue and could hardly keep awake. On July 21, the RMLE was relieved, and it was reorganized in August. Fresh volunteers flooded in and by that time Lieutenant-Colonel Rollet commanded 48 officers and 2,515 legionaries, who were committed in the Task Regiment's last operation on the western front. From September 2 to 14, 1918, the RMLE took part in a major offensive against the heavily fortified Hindenburg Line. This last of the Legion's battles of World War I proved to be a splendid finish. In the sector of Laffaux, the legionaries gained all their objectives: capturing the fortified positions of Terny, Sorny, Neuville-sur-Margival and Vauxaillon. After a final, costly effort toward the Castle de la Motte and the village of Allemont, the Hindenburg Line was ultimately breached and the German forces retreated; they had come to the end of their spirit and resources. After 13 days and nights of combat, casualties, as may be expected, were high: 275 killed and over 1,500 wounded. There were rumors of a German surrender, and the decimated Task Regiment was withdrawn from front-line operations.

The armistice of November 11, 1918, which coincided with the Task Regiment's third anniversary, found the legionaries at rest in the quiet sector of Champenoux, near Nancy. On November 17, 1918, the survivors of Rollet's Foreign Task Regiment and Daugan's Moroccan Division held a triumphant parade in the village of Château-Salins in the reconquered province of Lorraine. On December 1, 1918, a detachment of the Legion entered Germany, at Hornbach, for a short and symbolic occupation duty.

The war—at least on the western front—was over. Too many facts and figures become dull and tend to bore, but one or two may be of interest to show the extent of the legionaries' efforts in World War I. Of 42,883 volunteers who had fought in the Legion, 6,239 were Frenchmen—as far as can be ascertained—and 36,644 were foreigners from over 50 countries. The total number of Legion casualties in World War I amounted to 157 officers and 5,172 legionaries killed. About 500 officers and more than 25,000 legionaries were wounded. Casualties thus equalled about 70 percent of the total who served.

At the end of the war the color of the RMLE was one of the most decorated in the French army. It bore new official battle honors: Artois 1915, Champagne 1915, Les Monts-Verdun 1917, Picardie-Soissonais 1918 and Vauxaillon 1918. On July 14, 1919, on the Champs-Elysées in Paris a detachment of the Legion participated in a large *défilé de la victoire* (military victory parade).

The Foreign Legion on Other World War I Fronts

The story of the French Foreign Legion during World War I would not be complete without mentioning three other theaters of operation: Gallipoli, Serbia and Russia.

Balkan campaign, 1915

The entry of Turkey into the war in 1915 meant that the Franco-British allies were cut off from their customary communication route with their remote Russian ally. A combined attack was prepared on the Dardanelles Narrows to reopen it. The naval attack proved a failure and the Allies decided on a landing on the Gallipoli Peninsula. The landing was only lightly opposed and the Allied forces were able to press ahead inland until strong Turkish resistance (organized by the skilled tactician and inspiring leader Mustapha Kemal) forced them back. From the start the operation met with grave problems, notably a lack of adequate artillery support and medical supplies. In spite of considerable efforts, suffering and losses, the Allies made only limited gains. Unable to break out, a stalemate ensued, resulting in static warfare in trenches where flies and other vermin caused more casualties than enemy bullets. The Gallipoli campaign, marked by high casualties, failed to achieve its aims. In London and Paris increasing concern led to a final evacuation. The ill-fated campaign was a disastrous "side show" that ruined political careers and military reputations, and wasted thousands of lives, French and British but also many ANZAC (Australian and New Zealand) troops.

In February 1915, the Premier Régiment de marche d'Afrique (1st RMA, 1st African Task Regiment) was organized for the Dardanelles operation, including two battalions of Zouaves and one battalion of the Legion (formed from two companies each drawn from the Algerian 1st and 2nd Foreign Regiments) placed under the leadership of Lieutenant-Colonel Nieger. The 1st RMA was attached to the French 156th Division which landed on the Gallipoli Peninsula in late April 1915. For nine months the Legion suffered high casualties, both from enemy fire (notably in the ravine of Kereves Dere) and from diseases (malaria, dysentery, diarrhea and stomach disorders) caused by appalling conditions in trenches in the summer heat. An offensive was launched in an attempt to break through the Turkish line, but the attack failed badly and the legionaries were savagely mauled. By June 1915, the Foreign Legion 3rd battalion of the 1st RMA were reduced to about 100 legionaries commanded by a staff-sergeant, Adjudant-Chef Léon, as all officers were incapacitated. By August 1915, the unit had practically ceased to exist when reinforcements came from Indochina in the form of a 700-strong Legion detachment.

Serbia, 1915

In October 1915, the 156th Division (including the RMA and the new Legion detachment) was withdrawn from Gallipoli and transferred to Serbia to fight the Bulgarians. The RMA and the Legion battalion endured an appallingly cold winter. By then, the Balkan operation was a total failure, and the legionaries fought in the rearguard all the way back during the retreat. A number of skirmishes and delaying actions took place in autumn 1915 at Monastir, Dent de Scie and Trana Stena. By the end of the year, only about 200 legionaries survived; the 3rd Battalion of the RMA was withdrawn to Greece and disbanded. Most survivors eventually joined the Régiment de marche de la Légion étrangère (RMLE) to continue waging war on the western front in France.

Russia, 1918–1919

After the revolution of October 1917, the enthusiasm of the Communist Bolsheviks was boundless. A new government, a new state and a new society were proclaimed, and the Red revolutionaries intended to conquer and change the world. Against a

Legionary, Gallipoli, 1915. The depicted legionary of the 3rd/ RMA engaged in the Dardanelles expedition wears a model M1886 colonial helmet with a khaki cover, the model M1877 dark blue capote, and light khaki drill trousers.

background of turbulence, discontent, futility and suffering, a movement of resistance ("White Russians" supported by the Western democracies) to the Bolsheviks sprang up in the wake of the revolution. A civil war raged for several years with much bloodshed and many atrocities committed by both sides. But the superior capabilities of the Red Army, newly organized and commanded by Leon Trotsky, settled the issue decisively in favor of the Communists. By 1920 the Bolsheviks controlled Russia from Murmansk in the north to Odessa and Baku in the south.

A battalion of the Legion—as part of the Allied intervention force—was engaged to fight the Communist Red Russians. Officially affiliated with the 1st Foreign Regiment, this Legion unit was created in autumn 1918 and composed of three rifle companies, whose men were local volunteers recruited for the duration of hostilities in the region of Archangel. Commanded by Major Vitrey (soon replaced by Major Monod) and a small cadre of NCOs from France, the units saw action between October 1918 and July 1919 when they successfully repulsed several Red Army attacks around the city of Archangel. When the Allies decided to withdraw their forces in October 1919, the small Foreign Legion unit was disbanded and most of its personnel passed into the White Russian army, actually into a formation commanded by General Boudenitch. They took part in fighting in the region of Petrograd (called Leningrad from 1924 to 1991, today Saint Petersburg). As a matter of interest it is reported that they fought with their French uniforms, badges, weapons and equipment.

5

The Foreign Legion Between World War I and World War II, 1918–1939

France in the Interwar Period

France in 1918 was among the victorious nations and it recovered the provinces of Alsace and Lorraine that it had lost in 1870, but the victory could not conceal the traumatism left by the war on its population. Losses were enormous in terms of human lives (1,322,000), and reconstruction took 10 years.

The period 1919–1939 saw the world make a dizzy passage from confidence to disillusionment and from hope to fear. It experienced a few years of superficial prosperity, abruptly followed by unparalleled economic disaster. For a time, in the 1920s, democracy seemed to be almost everywhere advancing. Then in the 1930s the new phenomenon of fascist totalitarianism began to spread.

The Bolshevik revolution of 1917 had destroyed the tsarist empire and resulted in the establishment of a Communist regime in Russia. This economic model—embodied in a planned economy and an egalitarian dream—soon became a dreadful, bloody and criminal dictatorship led by Lenin and later by Stalin. Communist Russia became the Union of Soviet Socialist Republics in 1922. It was proclaimed to be a "Paradise for Workers" and exercised a strong fascination on many people in Europe. Highly centralized Communist parties emerged everywhere (in France the Parti communiste français PCF) closely linked to the Russian Soviet regime. Another totalitarian temptation was running through Europe: ultranationalist fascism, founded in Italy by the dictator Benito Mussolini who seized power in 1922. His example was imitated in Germany where a racial-nationalist dictatorship was imposed after the seizure of power by Adolf Hitler's Nazi Party in January 1933. In France the period was principally an era of ministerial uncertainty marked by several serious crises, notably the world economic crisis of 1929 which aggravated social tensions, increased despair, strengthened nationalist discontent, and encouraged extremism, both Communist and Fascist.

Political changes in Germany were a

cause of increasing concern and mounting international tension. Hitler, by ignoring the conditions laid down in the Treaty of Versailles, swept away the dream of long-term peace. By the mid–1930s the French decided to defend their country at all cost and the fortified Maginot Line was built. By 1935, German rearmament was well underway, and the Rhineland was remilitarized. In 1938 Hitler annexed Austria and large parts of Czechoslovakia. On September 1, 1939, when Hitler's forces entered Polish territory, World War II broke out. However, before international affairs reached that date, France, confronting major uprisings in the mid–1920s, employed the Foreign Legion in operations in Morocco and Syria.

Morocco

The protectorate of Morocco

Since the French established themselves in Algeria in 1831, and through the 19th century, Morocco—with its slave traders, pirates, bandits and raiders who supported the Algerian rebels—had always existed as a thorn in the side of France. Between 1901 and 1906, after bargaining with Great Britain and Italy, France was given a free hand to pursue expansion in Morocco.

On August 7, 1907, a punitive French force landed in Casablanca, where Europeans had been massacred. This was evident to all as only an excuse as it was firmly believed that subduing Morocco would help to pacify Algeria, particularly the oasis and mountain regions south of the region of Oran where unruly Moroccan tribesmen disturbed French colonization by frequent raids, *razzias* and ambushes. That became perfectly clear when the intervention troops not only remained but attempted to penetrate the interior of the country. The 6th Battalion of the 1st Foreign Regiment took part to the conquest of Morocco in the summer of 1907 and its chief, Major Provost, was killed at the battle of Messiki in September. This first Legion unit was reinforced with two other battalions and the year 1908 saw several engagements. On April 16, a mobile column commanded by Colonel Pierron, including the 24th mounted company of the 1st Foreign Regiment, was ambushed at Menabha and 120 officers and legionaries were killed, including Lieutenant Coste. In May 1908 a punitive raid brought the Legion to the oasis of Beni-Ouzien where Lieutenant Jaegle was killed. Other engagements followed at Bou-Denib, Moulaya, Alouana, Sidi-Bel-Kacem and Khenifra.

In 1911 Fez was taken, but a serious crisis broke out with the Germans who held a claim to Morocco and who wanted to keep France out as part of a strategy to break up the understanding, reached in 1904, between France and Britain. A war was avoided when Germany conceded France the protectorate of Morocco in exchange for trifling territorial compensations in Congo and Cameroon. This settlement was supplemented by a Franco-Spanish agreement in 1912 which saw the creation of Spanish Morocco in the northern Rif region, stretching from Tangier to Melilla. The French protectorate of Morocco was established and the traditional native ruler, the Bey of Tunis, placed under close administrative and military guardianship. Together with the associated *départements* of Algeria and the protectorate of Tunisia, Morocco formed Afrique du Nord française (ANF, French North Africa) until the country was given independence in 1956. In April 1913, General Lyautey was appointed resident-general.

Lyautey

Louis Hubert Gonzalve Lyautey (1854–1934) had previously been staff officer under General Gallieni in Tonkin (north Vietnam) in 1884, and in Madagascar in 1897. He had commanded the French troops in the southern part of the province of Oran

French North Africa (from a 1938 atlas)

(Algeria), which he had more or less pacified in 1903. A brave soldier and a remarkable organizer who had written several books including *Le Rôle social de l'Officier* in 1891 and *Du Rôle colonial de l'Armée* in 1900, Lyautey was resident-general in Morocco from 1913 to 1925 with a short break in 1916 when he was appointed minister of war. Opposed to General Robert Nivelles's cult of costly *offensives à outrance* (offensives at any cost), which he thought insane, Lyautey was forced to resign. Through his celebrated

5. The Foreign Legion Between World War I and World War II, 1918–1939

Moroccan **goumier.** *The* **goums** *were created in 1908 by General Amade. They were originally recruited from Moroccan ex-rebels who had submitted to French rule. A* **goum** *(roughly equivalent to a large company) was generally composed of two French commanding officers, 16 NCOs (both French and Moroccan) and 160* **goumiers** *(riflemen). Three goums formed a* **tabor** *(a battalion). Three* **tabors** *formed a regiment. The most distinctive pieces of uniform were a light brown* **chèche** *(turban), the grey* **djellaba** *(cloak) with white, black and brown stripes, the* **gandoura** *(sleeveless overcoat),* **sarouel** *(large baggy trousers) and* **naala** *(sandals).*

and influential publications, Lyautey, who had a reputation as a challenging and troublesome military thinker, believed that a republican army needed a republican officers' corps and that the training methods of the French army were outdated. Soldiers were not brutes but Frenchmen and their training should strive for individual instruction. He persuasively set out the case for a broad perspective to be taken with regard not only to colonial conquest, occupation and pacification but also to political, social and economic development of colonial territories. He was thus not only concerned with colonial warfare but also with the establishment of a stable and secure colonial regime, and repeatedly put the emphasis on the role of the colonial soldier who had to be not only a conqueror but also an administrator, an overseer and an educator. First as commanding officer in Algeria and later as resident-general in Morocco, the influential theorist was given the opportunity to put his ideas into practice. Following the principle of *respecter les consciences et flatter les intérêts* (respect the consciences and stroke the interests—of the natives), Lyautey characterized his strategy as a "patch of oil spread," a step-by-step progression with attacks in spring and summer, and consolidation of conquest in autumn and winter by playing alternately on all the local elements, utilizing the divisions and rivalries between tribes and between their chiefs.

In 1908 local auxiliary units had been raised known as *Goums*. The men—called *Goumiers*—were recruited with ex-rebels and the local Moroccan population that was subjected to French rule, and officers and NCOs were drawn from the French army. Moroccan *Goums* (light cavalry and infantry) were raised and served in the French colonial army until 1956 when the country became independent.

After the conquest, Lyautey's soldiers were employed as key instruments in establishing an efficient, productive and contented colony. Lyautey, undoubtedly a thoughtful and humane officer, created a myth concerning colonial warfare that was too simple, benign and romantic to accord with reality. As a matter of fact he was to secure France's imperial interests as unequivocally as possible, and ultimately his strategy and method depended on the use of brutal force, *razzias*, reprisal raids, punitive military actions and oppression, apparently the only effective ways to bring recalcitrant tribesmen to submission.

The Legion at the Time of Lyautey

Morocco, 1914–1918

When World War I broke out, we have seen how Foreign Legion units, officers and NCOs were drafted to form combat regiments for the western front. All energies were directed toward training legionaries to fight in France. The Legion in Morocco was reduced to five battalions and three mounted companies of which a good three-quarters were either German or Austrian, personnel who were, of course, unsuited for the western front in France. French policy in Morocco was to maintain the status quo and to concentrate upon holding what had been conquered, which included a broad, wedge-shaped strip from Fez to Rabat and Casablanca and the narrow Taza Corridor from Fez to Oudja. The remainder of the country, particularly the mountainous areas, remained largely free of French control and virtually independent. Lyautey was ordered to retire his depleted garrisons into the coastal enclave. The resident-general refused to do so and managed during the war to maintain control over French-held parts of the country while still training and sending off to France all the troops the government demanded. This, however, did not happen without unpleasant incidents as some tribesmen, taking advantage of the French weakness, provoked local rebellions. The Legion's recruitment

Legionary with mule, c. 1911. The mule carried the **barda** *including various bags containing men's reserve clothes, a 20 kg "boudin" of barley, a tent with camping gear and greatcoats rolled together, cooking gear, a reserve of fuel (wood) for fire, and two cans of water.*

was at a very low tide as all European countries were committed fully to waging an all-out struggle in World War I, to which all fighting men available were drafted. Moroccan raiders, secretly armed by German agents, were free to come and go from safe refuges in the Atlas Mountains over the porous border with Spanish Morocco. Dissidents increased pressure and, as no recruits came through, a number of posts and forts had become extremely weak and vulnerable and so threatened that they had to be abandoned. While the world's attention focused on the war in Europe, the German and Austrian legionaries (together with criminals of the disciplinary Bat'd'Af, Senegalese *tirailleurs* and Moroccan *goumiers*) fought a forgotten war in the Moroccan highlands. The fort of Khenifra, for example, was continuously attacked practically throughout the whole of World War I, but it held on successfully until the end. The valuable mobility afforded the mounted companies compelled them to undertake exhausting patrols, escort duty, operations and forced marches to the rescue of besieged garrisons in the southern desert, in the Atlas Mountains and in the Taza Corridor. In August 1918 at a place called Gaouz, a withdrawing *tirailleur* battalion supported by one of the mounted companies was ambushed, leaving behind two officers and over 50 NCOs and men killed. Starved of replacements, the Legion in Morocco was down to an effective total strength of about six companies by the end of World War I.

Legionary in North Africa, c. 1914

Reorganization

Before reestablishing French control in northern Morocco the Legion was reorganized. In late November 1918, Colonel Rollet's glorious RMLE (Régiment de marche de la Légion étrangère) came back to North Africa; in July 1920 it became the Troisième Régiment étranger d'Infanterie (3rd REI) with two mounted companies attached to it. At the same time the remaining battalions of the existing and understrength 1st and 2nd Foreign Regiments were merged into a new unit designated Quatrième Régiment étranger d'Infanterie (4th REI). After World War I another period of great expansion began in the French Foreign Legion. Owing to postwar conditions, thousands of refugees, jobless professional soldiers and ex-servicemen, many of them nationless, were left stranded after the armistice. The Legion recruiting stations were crowded with new volunteers. Once again in the history of the Legion, men who a few months earlier fought each other on the battlefields of Europe donned the same uniform and white képi to become brothers-in-arms. By that time, the Legion became slightly more selective in accepting recruits, and as a precaution against enlisting well-known and wanted criminals, began to fingerprint recruits and to allow the police to vet them.

This influx facilitated the creation of new units. The Deuxième Régiment étranger d'Infanterie (2nd REI) was formed in December 1920. The Premier Régiment étranger d'Infanterie (1st REI) was raised in January 1921; based at Sidi-Bel-Abbes it became the Legion central depot. In 1921, another regiment was formed at Sousse (Tunisia), largely from defeated "White" Russians who, in the Wrangel and Denikin armies, had vainly fought against Trosky's Red Army; these men, most of them having recent military background and more particularly cavalry experience, were grouped at Saida into a mounted unit designated Premier Régiment étranger de Cavalerie (1st REC). Some of the Russian horsemen had to accept ranks far more humble than they had achieved in the tsar's imperial army. Despite misgivings over the increased opportunities for desertion offered by putting foreign legionaries on horses, the 1st REC fought with distinction in all North African campaigns. The combination of aristocratic attitudes of ex-imperial Russians, snobbish French cavalry officers' ethos, and the chivalric tradition attached to cavalry in general produced a strange elitist spirit and an arrogant collective pride; the horsemen of the 1st REC called their regiment Royal étranger (Royal Foreign Regiment), and demanded (and obtained) 19th-century-like luxurious and colorful equipment and uniforms, including white cross-belts, shoulder straps, together with mounted music.

Lyautey's caïds

When the war in Europe was over the French turned their attention to Morocco, particularly to the mountainous areas where tribesmen remained as firmly defiant and unruly as ever. Troops were moved in for pacification and it was decided to make full use of the Foreign Legion. The buildup in Morocco continued but the policy remained static until enough force became available. The French established a defensive line composed of blockhouses, fortified points and strongholds facing northward along the Rif Mountains, where the core of resistance lay and from where frequent raids came. The establishment of the defensive line was organized by Colonel Colombat, a mission sometimes compared to the Roman IIIrd Augusta Legion's task in constructing the *lime romanus* in Mauritania. Posts and forts had to be built in a hurry and material had to be brought in by mules. They were then supplied by road creeping up into the mountains, and tribes that had submitted to French rule had to be protected against raiders. Therefore the Legion was split into small detachments and garrisons and employed on local raids, patrolling, escort duty and building new strongholds. Life in these posts was depressing and dull, broken now and then by deadly ambushes and surprise attacks at night. The only distractions were the prostitutes of the Bordel Militaire de campagne (BMC, Military Field Brothel), strictly controlled by the Army Health Service, and drinking bouts; the men were paid the 16th and 30th of each month and all their money was spent on whores, wine and strong liquors.

Consumption of alcohol was one way to fight *cafard* (blues) and boredom. Alcoholism in the Legion was to remain an acute problem until World War II.

The period 1903–1934 found the Legion mainly occupied in Morocco and southwestern Algeria. Particularly in the 1920s popular films, novels and songs, against a background of palm trees, exotic Casbah, belly dancing girls, blazing sun and *sable chaud* ("Warm Sand" sung by Edith Piaf), contributed in giving the Corps a peculiar romanticism and mystery. Lyautey himself had a profound admiration for the Corps and later declared: "The Legion, during my time of command in south Oran and Morocco, has been my dearest troop."

The basic tactical element was the battalion, a self-contained and self-sufficient combat formation armed and manned to be fully able to maintain itself in combat without the support of other units. As battalions were scattered, sometimes isolated in huge and often barren territories, each *chef de bataillon* (major) was like a king in his sector. The autonomous officers instilled in their units a style, an attitude and rules of their own. The official designation was often replaced by a more personalized mark. They were called Nicolas's Battalion or Tscharner's Battalion or Kratzert's Mounted Battalion after the name of the commanding officer. Soldiers were glad and proud to be associated with their officers' personality and reputation, they thought in terms of the Legion battalion as their "home" and men of other French army formations were strangers to them. Pride and esprit de corps helped men to accept the hard Legion life made up of occasional danger, long exhausting marches, fatigues, discipline and punishments and—worst of all—the monotonous garrison duty. During this period there developed what was called Lyautey's *caïds* (big bosses, or local chiefs in Arabic), glamorous Foreign Legion officers such as Rollet, Maire, Corta, Aage of Denmark, Nicolas and several other legendary figures.

Prince Aage of Denmark, for example, was the son of Prince Waldemar, admiral in the Danish navy, and Princess Marie d'Orléans. From his mother's side he was a great grandson of King Louis-Philippe of France. In 1922, after the bankruptcy of the bank that managed his fortune, the penniless aristocrat volunteered to serve in the Legion. Soon back on his feet again through marriage with a rich American woman, Aage, however, stayed in the Corps and served in Morocco from 1922 to 1940 as *chef de bataillon* in the 3rd Foreign Regiment. The story went about that the snobbish and eccentric officer drank ice-cooled champagne and ate top-quality caviar on the battlefield. That was what the legend said, as the highly publicized prince was a colorful figurehead and a useful ambassador who had many influential acquaintances in the world of international politics as well as fruitful contacts among aristocratic circles throughout Europe. The extravagant prince was loved by his men, as he added to the Legion's glamour and prestige. He was a tall, strong, fearless Viking-like figure, a heavy drinker who played the drums in the Café de France at Ksar Es Souk, and who did not hesitate to brawl with drunken customers for fun. The legionary prince wrote a book in Danish in 1927 bearing the title *Tre Aars Kampe i Fremmed Legionen* (Three Years Fighting in the Foreign Legion). In 1936 he wrote another work, titled *Les Mémoires du Prince Aage* (Prince Aage's Memoirs), published by Payot Editeurs, Paris, in which he described rough and picturesque figures in curious situations. Aage reported that a legionary named Hoberg drank 10 liters of red wine during the day to quench his thirst, and one final bottle of white wine before going to bed at night in order to be able to say his prayers in Swedish. Tattoos were always popular among legionaries. Aage told of a man who had enlisted under the pseudonym of *Salaud* (literally "son of a bitch") who had his name tattooed across the palm of his right hand. That tattoo caused endless trouble in expressing his insulting opinion whenever he was saluting a superior and so he spent a lot of time on charges before it was decided to issue him a glove. Legionary "Son of a Bitch" was an alcoholic but also a brave soldier who made it to corporal. He was officially an orphan but when he was fatally wounded in combat he lay dying in the arms of a lieutenant who appeared to be none other than his own father!

Dozens of such fantastic stories, more or less true or heavily romanticized, were told in Aage's book. The courageous prince was granted the Légion d'honneur medal for bravery during the 1925 Rif War. Unfortunately for a man of war—whose fate it is to die a glorious death on the battlefield—Aage died in March 1940 from a heart attack like a common civilian. He was buried in the Legion cemetery at Sidi-Bel-Abbes. His body was brought back to France when the Legion left Algeria in 1962.

Another *caïd* was Colonel Maire. Born in 1876 into a strict conservative Catholic family, Maire was nicknamed the *Mousquetaire* (Musketeer). He had a contradictory character as a well-educated and cultured man with a passion for bridge, literature and music, and at the same time as a hot-tempered officer, systematically disrespectful toward the army authority and the French government. As Maire loudly and bluntly expressed his ideas, complaints and grievances, he never made it higher than the rank of colonel. Maire served in the Legion for 20 years, and, like the legendary Rollet, he was a legionnaire to the marrow. Despising anything that did not pertain to the Legion, he was highly popular with the troops. Like Aage of Denmark, Colonel Maire was a notorious drunkard, and like him he did not die in glorious battle, but from cirrhosis of the liver in 1951 at the military hospital of Val de Grâce in Paris.

Another famous legionary of that time was the writer Jean Genet (1910–1986) who enlisted in the Legion in 1928 and deserted in 1936, and who later wrote "Pompes Funèbres" and "Les Bonnes" in 1947 and "Notre-Dame des Fleurs" in 1948.

New technology

The tremendous boost given to military technology by World War I was inevitably felt in the colonial sphere. Before 1914, colonial military engagements broadly fell into two categories. The first type consisted of ill-equipped massed indigenous armies that took on generally smaller well-armed units of colonial troops in set-piece battles. The second category included formally organized colonial forces trying to deal with more mobile and elusive gangs of warriors whose familiarity with the terrain and superior ability to live off the country made them very difficult to pin down. This kind of guerrilla warfare already waged in the 19th century, increasingly characterized colonial campaigns after 1918, so that in the 20th century colonial warfare has become almost synonymous with guerrilla warfare or insurgency. The move away from pitched battles was principally due to technological advances in weaponry, and in term of firepower decisively in favor of colonial forces. Breech-loading rifles, reliable small mountain artillery guns with improved explosives and shells, armored cars and machine guns gave colonial administrations an edge in punitive power that could scarcely be matched by indigenous peoples. Legion units usually operated in all-arms columns including colonial artillery; in May 1925 an 80-mm mountain-gun Foreign Legion section was formed to serve in Morocco. Later full artillery battalions were created, and batteries were engaged in Syria (see below).

To these must be added speed, mobility and firepower provided by fighter and bomber aircraft, which although expensive and requiring considerable technical support, had become decisive weapons. Railways for transport of reinforcements and supplies as well as mechanization in general enhanced the mobility of colonial units,

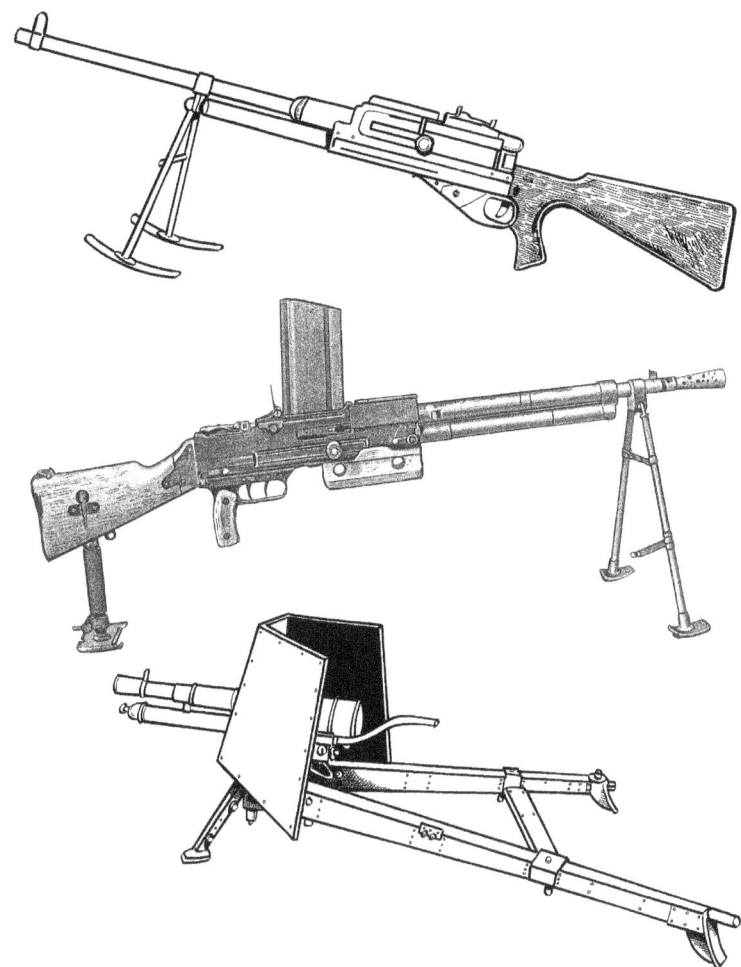

although trains, trucks, cars and armored vehicles were totally dependent on roads and tracks suitable for motor vehicles. In the late 1920s the "royal" 1st REC (Legion Cavalry Regiment) included *Escadrons motorisés* (motorized squadrons) equipped with cars, trucks and a few *automitrailleuses* (AM, armored cars). A gradual process of motorization began which by the mid–1930s would see mixed truck/armored cars units taking over the patrolling role of the old mule-mounted companies. Finally it is difficult to underestimate the growing importance of wireless in improving military communications. The scientific and techno-

Top: *Hotchkiss Fusil Mitrailleur 1922. The 7.5 mm Hotchkiss FM light machine gun, designed and issued to troops in the early 1920s, was gas-operated, weighed 8.8 kg, had a cyclic rate of fire of 685 rounds per minute, and was fed by magazines containing 25 rounds. This weapon was replaced by the light machine model 1924.* Middle: *FM Modèle 1924/29. France's effort after World War I to develop an effective light machine gun led to the design of the Fusil Mitrailleur modèle 1924 (automatic rifle), which was largely based on the U.S. Browning automatic rifle. Modified and improved in 1929 (notably the cartridge design), the FM 1924/29—also known as the Chatellerault from the manufacturing where it was built—was the standard French light machine gun of the 1940s and early 1950s until it was replaced by the AA52 machine gun. Rather similar to the British Bren gun, it could be used as an infantry platoon and squad light machine gun, or mounted on a vehicle, or on a fortress mounting in bunkers (notably in the Maginot Line). Weight was 8.93 kg (19.7 lbs.), overall length was 1.007 mm (39.6 in) and cyclic rate of fire was about 500 rpm. Caliber was 7.5 mm and feed was a 25-round detachable box magazine. The FM 24/29 had a bipod and two triggers: the fore for firing single shot, and the rear for automatic fire.* Bottom: *French infantry light gun. The 37 mm TRP model 1916 was designed to provide World War I trench frontline troops fire support for both attack and defense. It was a simple, light and handy weapon, weighing in action 108 kg (238 lbs.); it could break into three loads for pack transport: barrel, steel tripod and a pair of wheels which were removed in action. With a muzzle velocity of 367 m/s (1204 ft.), it could fire a shell weighing 0.55 kg (1.22 lbs.) to a maximum range of 2,400 m (2,625 yards). The 37 mm TRP ml. 1916 remained in service with the French army until 1939.*

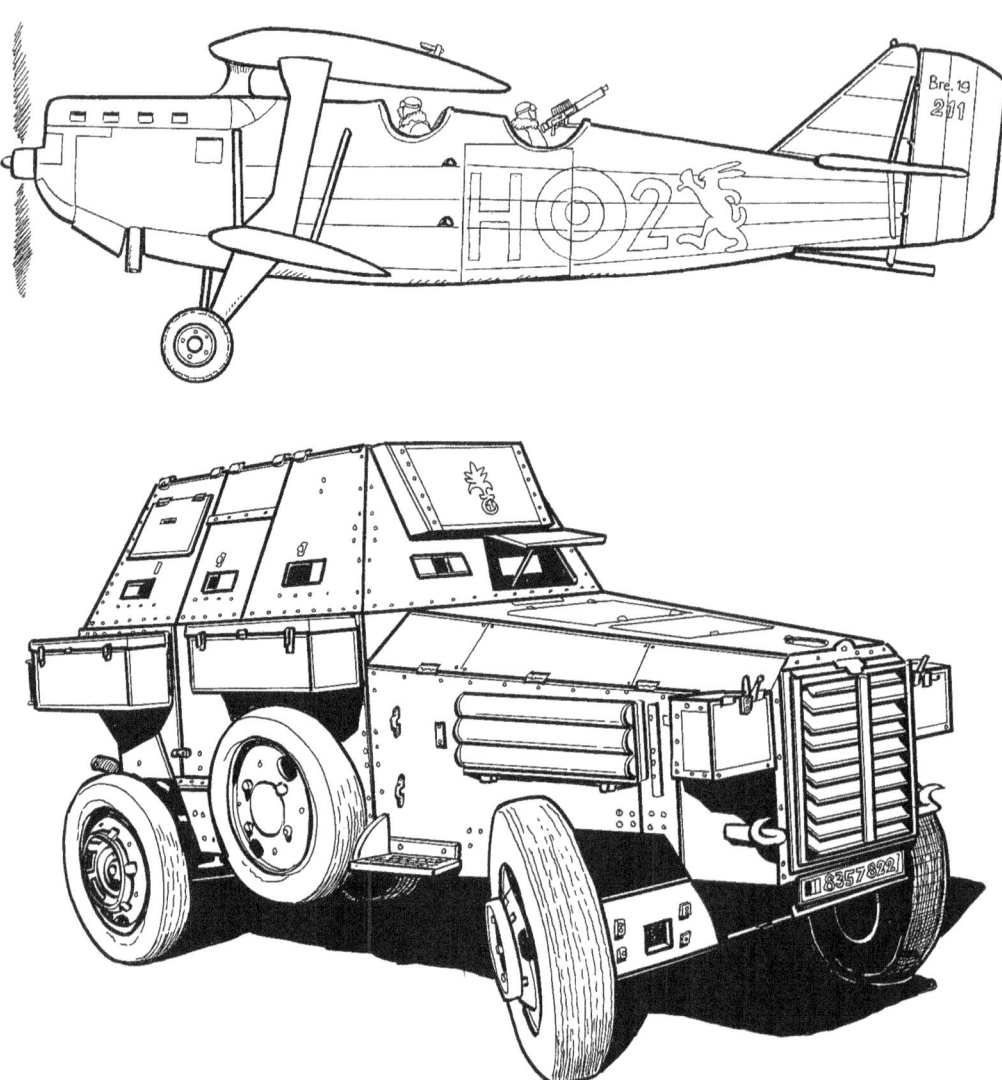

Top: *Breguet Bre.19.* Designed in 1921, the Breguet 19 was a two seat biplane used in various roles, including army support, reconnaissance and observation, and as a light bomber. About 1,900 Bre.19s were produced. The airplane was powered by a 513 hp Renault 12K 12 cylinder V-engine. Maximum speed was 235 km/h (146 mph), range was 1,200 km (746 miles), and weight (empty) was 1,722 kg (3,796 lbs.). The machine could climb to 5,000 m (16,405 ft.) in 29 minutes. The armed version had one fixed machine gun in the front fuselage, and one rearward-firing machine gun in the rear cockpit. A bomb load of 800 kg (1,764 lbs.) could be carried. Bottom: *Automitrailleuse Berliet VUDB.* The 4 × 4 Berliet VUDB armored car weighed 5 metric tons, length was 4 m and speed was 50 km/h on road. With a 40hp engine the vehicle was grossly underpowered and the chassis too weak for the weight of the armor. It had a crew of three (driver, gunner and commander) and was armed with one or two FM24/29 light machine guns. The motorized 6th Squadron of the 1st Legion Cavalry Regiment, raised in 1929 at Colomb Bechar in the Sahara, had 15 of these armored cars. Additional Legion motorized equipment included Renault and Citroen reconnaissance cars, White-Laffy armored cars, troop-carrying trucks, tankers and signal vehicles equipped with radio. Legion mounted units took to these primitive uncomfortable vehicles with great reluctance; they were less mobile, more fragile, and more demanding than horses and mules.

logical developments of warfare contributed substantially to the destructive power that colonial armies could bring to bear on indigenous forces. Constraints such as these proved too great even for Abd-El-Krim, the famous Moroccan leader during the Rif War.

The Rif War 1925–1926

Abd-El-Krim

Lyautey's advanced methods never completely succeeded in pacifying Morocco, and a shadow was cast over his waning years in service as resident-general by the outbreak of a violent rebellion. In April 1925 Abd-El-Krim (1882–1963), the Moroccan leader, proclaimed an independent republic in the mineral-rich Rif region of Spanish-held Morocco. Although the rebellion was undoubtedly encouraged by the incompetence of the European administration in Spanish Morocco, the wholesale defection of tribes in the French sector to Abd-El-Krim's side demonstrated Lyautey's failure to persuade significant numbers of Moroccans of the virtues of French rule. The so-called Rif War and the continued pacification of Morocco to the mid–1930s served as a forerunner of colonial wars to come.

Abd-El-Krim was a far-sighted, well-educated and astute man who had been employed in the Spanish administration. Disillusioned with the way the colonial power treated his people, he became a political agitator. Dismissed from office by the Spaniards he became the most influential nationalist leader. Krim was well connected in Europe, had gained sympathy there and had a clear understanding of the importance of world opinion. As early as July 1921 Krim launched a powerful attack and succeeded in defeating neglected and ill-led Spanish garrisons in the region between Melilla and Anoual. His dazzling victory inspired a pantribal war of independence. At Anoual, Krim seized important booty including 20,000 German-made Mauser rifles, 400 Hotchkiss machine guns and about 120 artillery pieces. He turned his volatile coalition of clans and tribes into a well-organized army with units, ranks, paid officers, specialists and basic logistic supporters. Krim hired European mercenaries and instructors, including a few Legion deserters, to train his army. One of the latter was a certain Josef Klems. Klems, a former NCO in the German army, had joined the Legion in 1922 and quickly rose to sergeant through his bravery and leadership capacity. For unknown reasons he deserted in 1923, fled to the mountains and offered his service to Krim. Soldiers experienced with modern weapons and artillery were eagerly sought and Klems was appointed grand master of artillery and called *El-Hadj-Aliman* (German chief). After the defeat of Krim, Josef Klems hid in the mountains until his native mistress betrayed him for money; caught by the French he was arrested, tried and condemned to death. For unknown reasons again, the German authorities acted in his favor and his sentenced was commuted to seven years of hard labor.

The Spanish authorities could not stop Krim, who grew in popularity, gained wider support, kept up the initiative, inflicted local defeats and casualties and won ground. By early 1924 Krim had consolidated his force and felt strong enough to free Morocco of all foreign invaders. Lyautey knew that the rising in Spanish Morocco would inevitably spill into French Morocco as Krim's goal was to expel both the French and the Spanish from his country. In this he was ill-advised; had he concentrated on the Spanish and used his contacts to reassure the French authorities, his scheme might have succeeded. As it was he took on two powerful enemies at once.

At first Abd-El-Krim achieved remarkable successes. In April–May 1924 Krim's force began to advance, and, in a preliminary display of force, crushed tribes such as the

Beni-Zeroual, Senadja, Branes and Tsouls who had accepted French domination. Krim's forces applied heavy pressure on the border between French and Spanish Morocco. The French were obliged to fight a defensive war centered around a line of fortified posts in the Taza Corridor near the frontier. At first the French did not fully realize the strength of the rebels and many forts were captured or evacuated. Although they wavered the defenses held and Krim was brought temporarily to a halt. However, this did not mean the end of the war.

The operations

A lull in major operations followed, but a year later, after further consolidation and preparation, Krim launched a second offensive along the northern edge of the Taza Corridor. The French forces (mainly composed of Legion units) were overwhelmed and, again, many forts were abandoned and evacuated. Fez the capital was threatened. It must be said that Abd-El-Krim's victory resulted in part because of poor coordination of French and the Spanish forces and in part because governments and military authorities both in Madrid and Paris greatly underestimated the situation and refused to send reinforcements. Quite surprised by his swift success, Krim, who had no real strategy, paused for a while. His hesitation allowed the French to recover and react. Lyautey expected the worst and asked for reinforcements. At last his call was heard. Troops were rushed to Morocco and Marshal Philippe Pétain—the victor of Verdun—was sent in August 1925 to command the punitive forces. Pétain was able to persuade the

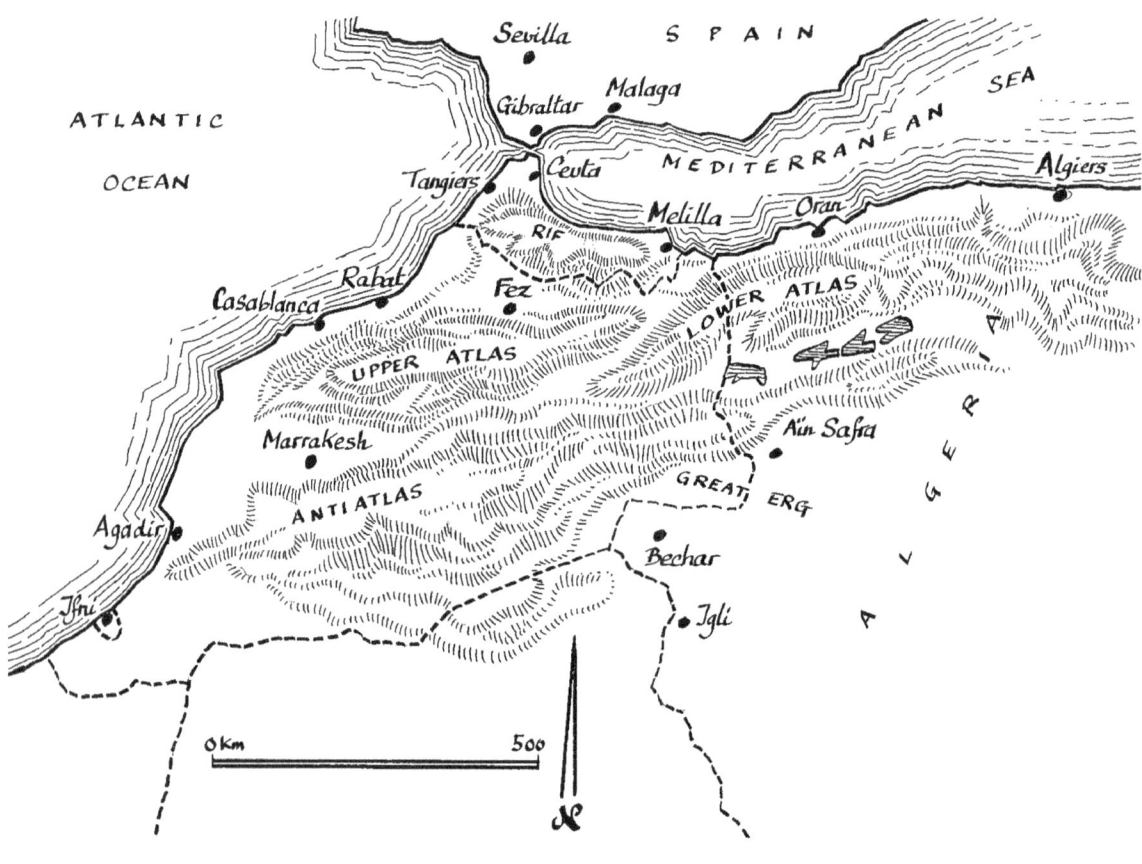

Sketch map of Morocco

Moroccan mounted rebel, 1925

new modern weapon systems; including light tanks, armored cars and reconnaissance and bomber airplanes. Both the Spanish and the French were alleged to have used poison combat gas during the Rif War. Attacks were followed by formal occupation by regular troops. The final, massive, and well-planned combined Franco-Spanish offensive was a success. Adb-el-Krim had hoped that other European countries would support him, and when no help materialized, he realized the hopelessness of the struggle. After a last battle at Targuist, he surrendered on May 23, 1926. Abd-El-Krim was deported to the Reunion Island, from which he escaped in 1947. He went to Cairo, Egypt, where he kept up his nationalist activities for Moroccan independence until his death in 1963.

The capture of Krim officially marked the end of the Rif War. The French could now turn to the reduction of the Atlas Mountains. Without a charismatic leader, organized resistance soon ceased, all lost territory was recaptured, and by Christmas 1926 the northern part of Morocco was considered pacified. But sporadic fighting with elusive rebels continued for several years. During the Rif War the French suffered some 12,000 casualties, a record not officially admitted for 20 years.

The Legion in the Rif War

The Foreign Legion was active in both fighting and working in Morocco: the con-

Spanish General Staff to a joint collaborative effort so that now the war involved both the French and the Spanish armies working together and preparing major military operations. In May 1926, Pétain launched a large expedition with about 300,000 troops in pursuit of the rebel leader with the Spanish forces making a wide pincer movement in conjunction with his own troops. Units were supplied from carefully prepared bases. The initial advance into the Taza Corridor and the mountainous rebel-held territory was effected by mobile auxiliary and Foreign Legion units supported by artillery and by

quest, the Rif War and the consolidation of French rule must always be closely associated with it. The legionaries took part not only in all battles of major importance but also in countless skirmishes, defensive actions and raids against the Moroccan rebels. To cite all the names of obscure, desolate, barren spots and inhospitable places—many of them hardly marked on the map—to describe all the actions in which legionaries fought, were wounded, suffered and died would be pointless. Let us add a few words about the nature of the Rif War, and mention a few selective engagements to suggest the Legion's role.

The Foreign Legion and the Franco-Spanish forces fought in difficult terrain; the coastal Rif Mountains are ice cold in winter, very hot in summer and not easily penetrable, the highest point is Djebel Tidighine (2,452 m). The Moroccan opposition and resistance were stiff. The rebels had good intelligence and could live off the country as they enjoyed the support of the semi-nomadic pastoral population. They had good leadership and a degree of modern firepower; they had a proud tradition of marksmanship, and they used with skill and courage all sorts of weapons, particularly a long curved razor-sharp sword known as a scimitar in close-range combat. Some rebels were convinced nationalists, other were fanatical Muslims waging jihad (holy war) but all of them fought, and did not hesitate to die, for their country or for their faith. The tribesmen were highly mobile, masters of ambush and concealed approach, often attacking at night, and legionaries could never relax. Hard-hitting in combat, they were ruthless and barbarous when victorious. Capture was dreaded more than death as it invariably meant bad treatment, sometimes torture and perhaps a lingering death. All legionaries kept one bullet aside to use on themselves in

Legionary 1st REI Morocco, c. 1925. This legionary at the time of the Rif War wears the blue képi with unbleached cover, the model 1920 khaki greatcoat over the model 1901 colonial khaki drill uniform, and a **boudin** *containing blanket and spare clothing rolled in the tent section carried across the breast. The rifle is a Berthier M1906/15 with needle bayonet.*

an emergency. Even dead bodies were mutilated as retaliation and to deter the enemy. The weather conditions—blazing sun and choking summer heat and icy winter rain and mud—were daunting. In the period 1921–1923 the 2nd, 3rd and 4th Foreign Regiments took part in numerous actions in attempting to pacify the Taza Corridor. For this purpose the Legion established and garrisoned fortified points in the Middle Atlas along the line Oudja-Taza-Fez. The legionaries were generally scattered in small and vulnerable posts in desolate and isolated places. Most of these posts did not constitute substantial forts proper but rather blockhouses made of wooden beams enclosed by a *murette* (or *sangar*, a breast-high piled rock wall over which the defenders could fire) or gravel-filled oil drums. When available, the position was protected with a barbed wire fence. The posts were often cut off, sometimes heavily shelled and often stormed with ferocity. They needed frequent resupply by vulnerable convoys which were easily ambushed along snaking mountain tracks.

Dozen of heroic stands and ghastly massacres passed into the Foreign Legion's history. One of the toughest engagements was fought near a place called Tichoukt. A Legion detachment, acting as an escort to a supply convoy, was ambushed. After a desperate fight to try to break through, the unit was completely annihilated. As in Camerone the legionaries fought till the last round and the last man. At a place called Tseghouchen, a Legion battalion fought for 12 hours against superior odds, before launching an offensive to drive the rebels back. At Astar, the Legion was ordered to withdraw but disliking this move, entirely on their own initiative they retook the hill and successfully repulsed several Muslim attacks. At Mediouna, a hill held by the rebels, a Legion battalion advanced guard (about 60 men) attacked at night using bayonets and grenades. Only three legionaries survived. During the Franco-Spanish operation of

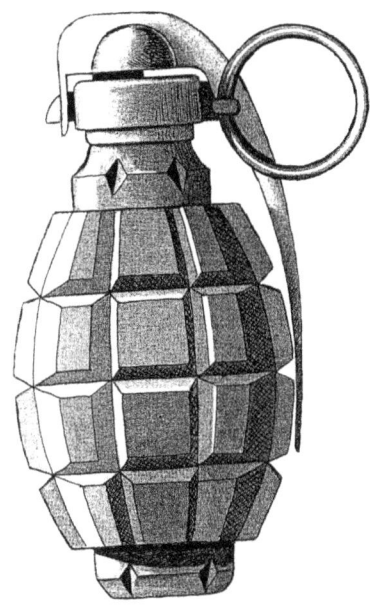

French defensive "ananas" grenade. Using a finger lever to start the fuse so as to burn only as the device left the thrower's hand, the grenade exploded in dangerous splinters four seconds after the safety pin was pulled and as the grenade was being thrown.

May 1926, the 2nd Foreign Regiment distinguished itself at Djebel Iskritten. The fort of Bibane changed hands four times. Lost and retaken, seized and recaptured with grenades and bayonet charges like a Verdun in miniature, it cost more than 400 French casualties. The post of Beni-Derkoul held by 30 Senegalese *tirailleurs* headed by Lieutenant Pol resisted for seven weeks; overwhelmed in a final assault, the survivors were all killed. After the surrender of Krim, the war was over but unruly raiders continued to make a nuisance of themselves in the desert regions on the southern border of Algeria and Morocco. Several Legion units, including the 1st Cavalry Regiment, the mounted companies and the 4th Infantry Regiment were deployed in the Atlas highlands to hunt the last rebels until the mid–1930s. Skirmishes took place at Djihani, El-Bordj and Ait-Yakoub.

The 1st Foreign Regiment returned to Algeria, while the 2nd, 3rd and 4th remained in Morocco for the rest of the interwar period. They participated in the final pacification of Morocco, which was completed by a series of expeditions through the southwestern Atlas Mountains in the years 1932–1934. Altogether between 1914 and 1935, the Moroccan campaigns cost the Legion 78 officers, 198 NCOs and 1,568 legionaries killed.

Syria, 1925

French protectorate

Syria, situated between the Mediterranean Sea and the valley of the Euphrates River in the Near East, is one of the countries where ancient civilizations first appeared. After World War I the defeated Ottoman Empire was dismembered and the two former Turkish provinces of Syria and Lebanon were placed under a French protectorate. The Syrians did not welcome French suzerainty, even under a mandate established by the League of Nations. In March 1920 a Syrian congress in Damascus proclaimed the independence and integrity of Greater Syria—including the Lebanon—as a constitutional monarchy under the Sharifian king Faisal. Paris decided to eliminate this challenge and ordered General Gouraud with a force of 70,000 under his command to move against the Sharifians in July 1920. The French using overwhelming force, including the use of airplanes, occupied Damascus and forced the government and monarch to flee. Gouraud's administration thereafter, like that of his successors, Weygand and Sarrail, was based on strict martial law with a few concessions made to Syrian opinion. However, the insensitivity of the French administration in Syria and Lebanon provoked a number of minor revolts after 1920 and a major Druse rebellion in 1925, when the entire French presence in the mandate seemed threatened. General Sarrail's response was draconian. In October 1925, after insurgents had infiltrated Damascus, Sarrail ordered the rebel-held districts to be bombarded by artillery and airplanes continuously for 24 hours. An estimated 5,000 Arabs were killed or wounded, with 137 French people killed and 500 neutrals killed or wounded. In the face of domestic and international outrage, Sarrail was recalled. The following May, his civilian successor, Henri de Jouvenel, also ordered bombardment of residential areas of Damascus, this time after a warning had been given. The governor later achieved a kind of pacification by political accommodation. Syria and Lebanon remained French protectorates until 1946.

The Legion in Syria

Among the French troops sent to occupy Syria in 1922 was a battalion of the newly created 4th Foreign Infantry Regiment (4th REI) with a mounted company. A few months later the 5th Battalion was sent as reinforcement. After three years of policing duties, the 4th Battalion was sent back home to Algeria, and the 5th Battalion remained in garrison supported by the 4th Squadron of the 1st Foreign Cavalry Regiment (1st REC). The first years were rather quiet, and posts held by the Legion were not seriously attacked. The legionaries built the camp of Dreir-ez-Zor, the post of Hassetche and the 300-kilometer-long road connecting that post to Aleppo.

In July 1925 the Druses, led by their chief Soltan-el-Attrache, rose en masse against the French administration. The Druses, from the hinterland in the Hawran Mountains in Syria, were an Ismailian sect originating in the Fatimid dynasty. An offshoot of Islam, they were fanatical, brave, warlike and had always been difficult to handle. Until 1918, when Syria had been a province of the Ottoman Empire, the Turks had left them alone as much as possible. Now, infuriated by the French occupation, the fierce Druses were out for blood and all who stood in their way were slaughtered. Two Legion battles remain associated with the operation in Syria during the major uprising of 1925.

Moussiefre

In July 1925 the fanatical Druse tribesmen rose in rebellion and streamed down from their hills moving toward Damascus and the coastal plains. The small French garrisons were alerted and the occupiers made an attempt to prevent them from moving forward. The French objective was the capture of Soueida, the main Druse base. At first the rebels were successful, notably at Kafer on July 22, 1925, where a Legion unit, led by Captain Normand, lost eight officers and 107 men. The French being too few, the Druses too many and the country too difficult, the French forces had to hurriedly withdraw. The revolt spread, and soon a large part of Syria was in open rebellion. In August 1925 the French had difficulty in maintaining control. By that time, the Legion was moved quickly to block the Druse advance. In September 1925, the 5th Battalion of the 5th REI (headed by Major Kratzert), the 4th Squadron of the 1st REC and several armored cars (led by Captain Landriau) were engaged in a battle at a small place called Moussiefre, a village near the mountain approaches. Ironically the newly created Cavalry Regiment of the Foreign Legion did not gain its first laurels in a heroic mounted charge under the African sun but in casual infantry operations in narrow streets in Syria where horses played no role at all. On September 16, attacked and surrounded by waves of some 3,000 fanatical Druse warriors, the legionaries were able to repulse them with machine-gun fire. Successive attacks were beaten off and the Legion units defended themselves with calm and determination for 10 hours in hand-to-hand fighting. At night the Druses attacked again, while infiltrators ambushed the defenders in the narrow streets of the village. The next afternoon French airplanes came to their rescue. Bombed and strafed from the air the tribesmen withdrew. That evening a rescue column—a battalion of the 16th Tirailleurs supported with armored cars—arrived. Sporadic firing and fighting continued but after midnight the attackers disappeared. The engagement, which could have become a disaster, cost the mounted Foreign Legion 47 dead, 83 wounded, and all its horses. Over 500 Druses lay dead on the battlefield and another 500 wounded were captured. This was the first French victory and it paved the way for the seizure of Soueida, which fell on September 24, 1925.

Rachaya

On November 20, 1925, Captain Landriau's 4th Squadron of the 1st Cavalry Regiment nearly had its own "Camerone." This action, which lasted four days, was one of the major epics of the short Syrian campaign. Again it was not a cavalry action, but a defensive battle on foot. The squadron, totaling some 100 horsemen headed by Captain Landriau, was stationed in the small hill-fort of Rachaya. On November 20, the stronghold, which was another old labyrinthine village, was attacked by some 3,000 Druses, who broke the defenses and infiltrated the fort. After desperate fighting the Legion horsemen were obliged to abandon parts of the fortified village. Close combat with hand-to-hand fighting and desperate bayonet charges went on for three days inside the shattered perimeter littered with dead horses and camels and with dying men from both sides. In the meantime carrier pigeons were sent off with appeals for help, the only means of communication the legionaries had. The Druses made frequent assaults, all were repulsed, but the Squadron suffered about 40 percent casualties. When the thoroughly exhausted survivors had thrown their last grenades and had only a few rounds left, Captain Landriau decided to *faire Camerone*, that is, fix bayonets and advance into the middle of the swarming enemy in a last wild charge. Each man had kept one last round for himself as none meant to be captured; it was known that the Druse, particularly the women, practiced fiendish torture on captured enemies. Fortunately a relief column of the 6th Spahis supported by airplanes pushed its way through—just in time. The rebels withdrew and faded away into their mountains. Rachaya, like Camerone in Mexico had been a magnificent defensive battle, but the squadron had suffered heavy casualties: 58 dead and wounded.

Aftermath

Until the end of 1925, the Foreign Legion searched for the Druse rebels, and other minor engagements took place at Massadi and El Chem. By the spring of 1926 the rebellion had been broken and the partly defeated Druse refrained from breaking into open revolt again. By the end of 1926 life in Syria had returned to normal.

After this campaign two Legion battalions, a mounted company and a cavalry squadron remained in Syria for occupa-

Left: *Legionary, 1st REC, Syria, 1925. The depicted Foreign Legion cavalryman, equipped for desert warfare, wears a uniform based on that of the* **Chasseurs d'Afrique** *and Spahis. He wears the Model 1886 colonial helmet and the roomy* **gandourah** *(loose light simple linen coat based on North African native clothing) over the khaki colonial tunic with matching* **seroual** *(Arabian baggy trousers). He has a pale khaki* **chèche** *(a Arabian-styled large desert scarf) worn in different ways: either looped round the neck, or crossed on the chest or wrapped all round the head and neck. He also wears leather gaiters and boots fitted with spurs. Equipment is standard French army with belts, haversack and ammunition pouches for the M1892/16 Berthier* **mousqueton** *(carbine).* **Right:** *Legionary, Syria, 1925. This legionary of the REI in Syria in 1925 wears the Model 1886 colonial helmet and the light khaki drill version of the Model 1914 uniform. Equipment is standard French army with leather belts and ammunition pouches, water bottle, and haversack.*

tion duties. These units were grouped together into a single formation designated Régiment de Légion du Proche Orient (RLPO, Near East Legion Regiment). Another battalion was sent in 1936 and the name RLPO was abandoned. The Legion units in Syria were amalgamated and became the Sixième Régiment étranger d'Infanterie (6th REI, 6th Legion Infantry Regiment).

The Legion, 1926–1939

Between the two world wars Algeria was quiet and the Legion's activities were reduced to training recruits intended for Morocco. The Legion's home base, Sidi-Bel-Abbes, still continued in this role, although when the 2nd Foreign Regiment had been created it was stationed at Saida, which became its depot. In October 1933 Sidi-Bel-Abbes officially became the *Dépot*

Left: *Moroccan Spahi, Syria, 1925. This spahi (auxiliary mounted man) wears the* **chèche** *wrapped round the head and neck, a* **gandourah, seroual** *(trousers of fairly ample cut), leggings, and boots with spurs. Equipment consists of a Saharan-type cartridge belt and bandolier/bayonet carrier made of leather. The weapon is the M1892/16 Berthier carbine.* Right: *Legionary, Morocco, c. 1930. From 1927 onward, though with a slight holdover of older uniforms due to administrative delays, the French Foreign legion wore a summer and a winter uniform of identical cut but different weight and warmth. The summer dress was of light sand-colored drill, the winter uniform of thick khaki serge. Both included a képi or a forage cap, a single-breasted tunic closing with a single row of six buttons; it had a falling collar of wide outline, no breast pocket, and skirt pockets with an external straight flap. The trousers were the same color as the tunics, of semi-breech cut, worn with puttees.*

commun de Régiments étrangers (General Depot of the Legion), where all recruits were initially sent for training and posting. The home depot came directly under the control of the General Inspection of the Legion, headed by the legendary Rollet, who served in the position of Legion inspector-general until his retirement in December 1935.

Curiously, the Legion still held a some-

Left: *Corporal, 2nd REI, Morocco, 1934. On the occasion of the commemoration of the Legion's hundred anniversary in 1931, Colonel Rollet wished to enhance the Legion's image. For parade and walking-out fringed shoulder straps with red crescents were reintroduced. Ceremonial appearances were encouraged and unit commanders introduced special uniforms for their* têtes de colonne; *handsome banners were produced for musicians in red and green which the Legion had made its traditional colors. Enameled breast badges as well as metal regimental, battalion and even company badges appeared, worn pinned to the right breast of the tunic. The grenade (with seven flames, the outer pair horizontal or recurved) was confirmed as a special Legion badge. The blue sash was worn at the waist under the leather belt and pouches, and the tunic skirts were often tucked into the trousers. The képi, still rather low and crumpled in profile, retained its white or pale fawn cover but neck cloths were discarded. The two gold chevrons of rank are worn on both forearms; the single gold serving stripe, denoting that this NCO is in his second five-year enlistment, is displayed on the upper sleeve.* Right: *Captain, 3rd REI, Morocco, c. 1936. This captain wears the model 1931 officer's képi, khaki tunic, pale mastic breeches and brown leather riding boots. He wears the 3rd REI double* fourragère *(lanyard).*

what undefined status, and until 1931 it was not included on the French army list of regiments, being regarded as a sort of irregular corps of vague standing. It was not until 1931 that it was formally included on the army list, and then it was placed just below the *Bataillons d'Afrique* (penal units), and just above the native colonial units and levies of different sorts.

On March 10, 1931, the Legion marked 100 years in existence. The centenary of the French Foreign Legion was delayed a little and celebrated on April 30, 1931, to coincide with Camerone Day. After a century of fighting and building, several times disbanded or destroyed in war, the Legion had survived a century of vissicitudes. Little help was given by the French authorities, but as usual the legionaries, spurred by General-Inspector Rollet and organized by Lieutenant-Colonel Forey, provided and improvised for themselves. Jealous of its traditions and proud of its uniqueness, the Legion organized a magnificent commem-

Left: *Corporal, 5th REI, Indochina, 1937. This corporal in walking-out dress wears the white M1931 colonial helmet, and the white colonial cut parade uniform with fringed shoulder straps and blue sash around the waist.* Right: *Legionary, 5th REI, Indochina, 1938. This legionary in full marching order wears the M1931 colonial helmet, the M1921 khaki drill uniform and full marching pack. In practice, in the exhausting heat and humidity of tropical Indochina, the* barda *(equipment and pack) were carried when in the field by coolies (hired indigenous porters).*

oration. Invitations were send out to ex-legionnaires to attend and many were able to come. Commemorations and banquets lasted for a whole week. General Rollet had a book published titled *Le Livre d'or de la Légion étrangère*. All regiments had their own imposing bands with drums, and grandiose parades and ceremonies were held in the presence of General Rollet, Marshal Louis-Felix Franchet d'Espèray, General-Governor of Algeria Cardes, Prince Louis II of Monaco (ex-legionary), Generals Guillaumat, George, Vandenberg, Thévenay and Colombat (who had commanded the Legion), as well as many foreign officers including General Stanley-Ford (U.S. military attaché in France), just to cite a few of the guests of honor. One of the greatest events was the inauguration of a Legion monument in the middle of the Court d'Honneur of the Quartier Viénot (Legion's barracks) at Sidi-Bel-Abbes. Designed by the sculptor Charles Pourquet, it was built by the legionaries themselves; the onyx stones were excavated from the quarry of Sidi-Hamza (75 km from Sidi-Bel-Abbes), shaped, polished, transported and assembled by volunteers who had a background in masonry. The monument is 9 meters in length, 7 meters in width and 6 meters in height. It consists of a stone pedestal supporting a large metal terrestrial globe indicating in gold the places were the Legion had fought and a special star for Mexico in honor of the battle of Camerone in 1863. At each side of the monument there are four life-size bronze statues of legionaries recalling the history of the Corps: conquest of Algeria; campaigns of the Second Empire; operations in Tonkin; and battlefields of World War I. At the front of the stone base is carved *La Légion à ses Morts, 1831–1931* (The Legion to Its Dead); at the back is the inscription *Honneur et Fidélité* (Honor and Fidelity). When the Legion had to leave Algeria in 1962, the monument was carefully dismantled, transported to France and reassembled by the Engineering Company of the 1st Foreign Regiment at the new Quartier Viénot at Aubagne near Marseilles; today the monument is located at the end of what the Legion calls *La Voie sacrée* (Holy Path). On September 14, 1932, a troop train carrying some 500 legionaries from Sidi-Bel-Abbes to Morocco derailed near a place called Turenne and plunged down a ravine; 56 men were killed and 217 injured.

When World War II broke out the French Foreign Legion included the 1st REI (Foreign Infantry Regiment) based in Algeria; the 2nd, 3rd and 4th REI stationed in Morocco; the 5th REI posted in Indochina; the 6th REI in Syria; the 1st REC (Foreign Cavalry Regiment) in Tunisia; and a second Cavalry Regiment (2nd REC) newly formed in 1939 in Morocco.

6

The Foreign Legion in World War II, 1939–1945

The Foreign Legion in 1939

The prewar Legion garrisons remained in North Africa, Syria and Indochina, but they provided staff officers and drafts for a number of new units. When World War II broke out the issue again arose of Germans serving in the Legion. In the years immediately before World War II the Nazis made use of the traditionally high recruitment of legionaries among Germans to infiltrate sympathisers and agents of Hitler's National Socialism into the Legion. These individuals had been deliberately sent to play on the patriotic feelings of their German comrades, and to exploit any favorable opportunity. The French army authorities recognized this, and hundreds of suspects were interned immediately after war broke out. In spite of the Legion's impressive record in World War I and in Morocco, Algeria and Syria, there was a natural reluctance to employ the Legion in Europe. Some 6,000 "duration only" foreign volunteers were enrolled, most of them living in France who joined for idealistic motives, thus watering down the potential subversive elements. At the beginning of World War II, there were also a number of celebrities serving in the Legion. The Count of Paris, the pretender to the French throne, not permitted to serve in a French unit, enlisted in the Legion's 1st RE as an ordinary legionnaire under the name Orlac. Prince Napoléon (descendant of Jérome Bonaparte, Emperor Napoléon I's brother) enlisted in 1939 in the 1st RE under the name Blanchard. Prince Sisowath Monireth from Cambodia enlisted for the duration of the war and served in the 5th RE in the northern Vietnamese province of Tonkin.

The "duration only" foreign volunteers were posted to three new task regiments in France for training. The 21st and 22nd Régiments de marche de Volontaires étrangers (RMVL, Task Regiments of Foreign Volunteers) were created in October 1939 and the 23rd RMVL in May 1940. Each regiment consisted of three battalions headed by French reserve officers. There was a large contingent of anti–Franco Republican Spaniards, as the outcome of the Spanish Civil War (1936–1939) had left many antifascist fighters idle. There were also young anti–Nazi Poles whose country had been crushed by Hitler in September 1939. To these were added a number of German Jews, Socialists, Communists, and other political opponents who had been forced into exile after Hitler's seizure of power in January 1933. All these men were eager to fight and defeat the Nazi regime. The quality of the three regiments (echoing that of their ancestors of 1914, the 2nd RM/1st RE, 2nd RM/2nd RE, 3rd RM/1st RE and 4th RM/1st RE) was, however, not that high as standards of discipline, equipment and leadership were poor, and they bore no real relation to the North African Foreign Legion proper. A camp was set up at Barcarès in the Pyrenees, and carefully screened staff and instructors were sent over from North Africa. The 21st RMVL was commanded by Lieutenant-Colonel Debuissy; the 22nd RMVL by Lieutenant-Colonel Villiers-Mor, and the 23rd RMVL by Lieutenant-Colonel Autmoitte. In North Africa the disappointed French Legion officers made representations to be employed in France. In the winter of 1939–1940, during the Phony War, two further units were created consisting of French reservists and volunteers, and drafts of reliable African veterans. These units were designated Onzième Régiment étranger d'Infanterie and Douzième Régiment étranger d'Infanterie (11th REI and 12th REI, Foreign Infantry Regiments). As in the case in 1914, the various groups of legionaries (roughly speaking divided into French reservists and African veterans) did not mix happily in the 11th REI and 12th REI, the former objecting to have to serve in the Foreign Legion and the latter dis-

Senegalese tirailleur, *1939. As had been the case in World War I, colonial troops were also engaged in 1939.*

trusting amateurs. German Stukas and Panzers soon united all of them. The recruiting mechanism was slowed down, perhaps deliberately, and the "half foreign" regiments filled up only slowly. The 11th REI, placed under the leadership of the famous *caïd* Colonel Maire, was trained at the camp of Valbonne near Lyon. The 12th REI, commanded by Colonel Besson was trained in the *département* of Ain.

Another formation was raised in February 1940 for service in France; formed with drafts from the two Régiments étranger de Cavalerie (REC, foreign cavalry regiments) this was a true Legion unit, a light armored reconnaissance battalion (comprising two squadrons of armored cars and motorcyclists) designated Groupe de Reconnaissance divisionaire *97* (GRD 97, Division Recce Group). The GRD 97 was attached to the Septième Division d'Infanterie Nord-Africaine (7th DINA, North African Infantry Division) and trained at the camp of Valdahon in France.

Lastly but most famous of all, the Treiz-

French Foreign Legion infantryman, 1940. At the outbreak of World War II the French Foreign Legion (and the French army) was using the same basic uniform pattern with which it had fought in World War I, although the color had changed from horizon blue to khaki/olive drab.

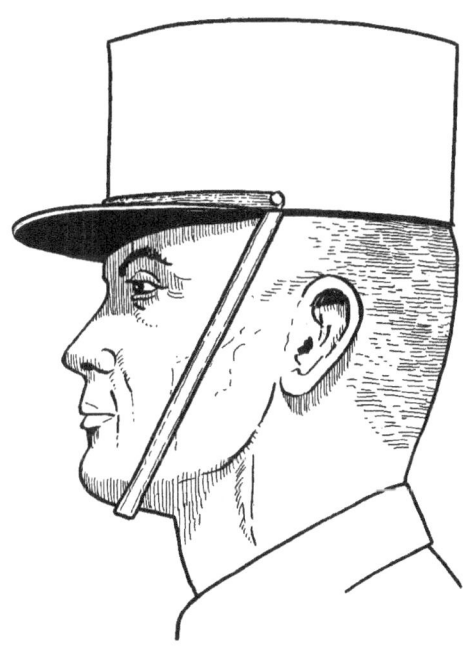

White képi. The white képi, indisputably the most recognizable feature of the Foreign Legion's uniform, was officially introduced in 1939. Its origin was a khaki képi cover created for wear by units participating in the pacification and conquest of Morocco in 1907. Bleached by sun and washing, the tissue became white, and experienced legionnaires took pride in the color.

ième Demi-Brigade de la Légion étrangère (13th DBLE, Half-Brigade of the Foreign Legion) was formed in February 1940 at Sidi-Bel-Abbes and Fez from legionaries posted in Algeria and Morocco. Totaling some 2,000 volunteers attracted by the prospect of an exotic campaign in polar regions, it was composed of two mountain-trained battalions commanded by Lieutenant-Colonel Raoul Magrin-Verneret. Lieutenant-Colonel Magrin-Verneret (later in World War II better known as General Monclar) gave the 13th DBLE a motto: *More Majorem* (In the Veterans' Fashion). Magrin-Verneret was born in February 1892 at Budapest, Hungary; between the wars he graduated from the Military Academy of Saint Cyr and joined the Legion in 1940. He took the name Ralph Monclar as nom de guerre. He died in June 1964 and was buried in the Hôtel des Invalides in Paris.

The 13th DBLE, which was destined to become one of the best-known regiments on the Allied side, was originally intended for an intervention to assist Finland. On November 30, 1939, Soviet Russia invaded Finland starting what became known as the "Winter War." By the middle of February 1940, a Russian breakthrough had been achieved and the Finns were forced to surrender.

The Norwegian Campaign

The 13th Half-Brigade was shipped to France and regrouped at the camp of Lanzac to receive weapons, equipment and training required for an expedition to the polar North. It was intended to embark and sail to the Finnish port of Petsamo when it became known that the Finnish had signed the Treaty of Moscow with the Russians on March 14, 1940.

Since Finland fell before the 13th Demi-Brigade could be deployed, the unit completed its Arctic and mountain training in France, and was send to Narvik as part of the Allied landing force in Norway in May 1940. Attached to the 1st Light Mountain Division headed by General Béthouart, the 13th DBLE embarked at Brest, Brittany, on March 24, 1940. After a short stay at Greenock in northern Britain, the unit landed in the fjord of Sjannland on May 6. A week later, Colonel Magrin-Verneret's Demi-Brigade went into action and assaulted the German-held village of Bjervick, which opened the way to the objective of Narvik. On May 28, the attack on Narvik was launched. Supported by a Norwegian battalion and an artillery battery, plus a group of French colonial artillery, the 13th DBLE engaged in one whole day of hard fighting to seize the city. The unit was badly battered with about 60 dead and wounded, but its morale was high as the legionaries had performed very well in the sharp encounter with the enemy. Without a respite, the Germans were repulsed at the border with Sweden, but in the meantime very bad news came from France. The country was invaded and the Germans were fast advancing. On June 2, 1940, the Norwegian government was informed that the Franco-British expeditionary force was badly needed in France and that the campaign had to be terminated. The 13th DBLE was ordered to withdraw. The legionaries left Norway and returned to Brest. Ordered to march to Rennes to defend the capital of Brittany, the unit came too late to play a role. Threatened with capture by the advancing Germans, the 13th DBLE was promptly shipped back to Britain with weapons, ammunition and equipment. On June 30, 1940, near Stoke-on-Trent, General Charles de Gaulle—then the almost unknown leader of the Free French—freely gave them the choice: either return to France or stay in Britain with him to continue the war against Nazi Germany. Half the troops opted to remain and fight with him alongside the British, the other half was repatriated back to Morocco. The rump Demi-Brigade, stationed at the camp of

*Legionary, 13th DBLE, Norway, May 1940. For the campaign in Norway, the legionaries of the 13th DBLE were issued various kind of warm battle dress, either a **canadienne** (sheepskin tunic) or a white pull-over quilted anorak with attached hood. Warm overtrousers were worn over the standard uniform. Snowshoes, overboots, puttees, thick oversocks, woolen trigger-mittens and tinted goggles were also issued. Armament included the standard M1892/16 carbine, the Mas 36 rifle and the M1924/29 light machine gun.*

Aldershot, was redesignated 14th DBLE until November 2, 1940, when it was known that the Vichy government had decided to disband the remnants of the 13th DBLE in Morocco. So the Free French troops of the Legion readopted figure 13. After re-forming and reequipping, the 13th DBLE was shipped to Africa and celebrated Christmas at Douala (Cameroon). It continued its journey, disembarking at Port Sudan in February 1941. The story of the 13th DBLE in Africa was about to begin.

The Battle of France

During the Phony War all the new Legion units were either sent into the front line or placed in immediate reserve. The hard winter of 1939-1940 weeded out many of the formations. At first neglected, the Foreign Volunteers Task Regiments (RMVE) received better clothing in April 1940; although adequately armed, equipment was uneven. The 22nd RMVE, for example, was nicknamed the "string regiment" as almost complete lack of equipment straps forced the legionaries to improvise all their slings from cord. The men had only a few antitank guns to resist the German Panzers, and no antiaircraft guns to use against the formidable Stukas. The only advantage enjoyed by the Legion was the presence in its ranks of veterans of the Spanish Civil War, who were more or less experienced with modern warfare and German tactics.

On May 10, 1940, while the 13th DBLE was fighting in Norway, the German attack was launched on France and all the Legion regiments were heavily engaged in the subsequent fighting. The general pattern of the war (*Blitzkrieg* = Lightning War) was marked by German air attacks, followed by heavy artillery shelling, by engineers who cleared obstacles and wire and finally by a strong push by armored vehicles and infantry. The 11th REI, headed by Colonel Maire and after December 24, 1939, by Colonel Robert, was attached to the 6th North African Division, and moved to Stenay between the Meuse and the Chiers rivers. The unit was deployed in a blocking position at the foreposts of the Maginot Line. It was involved in hard fighting between May 27 and June 11 at Inor Wood in the part of the Maginot Line known as *Tête de Pont de Montmédy* (Montmédy Bridgehead) between Sedan and Longuyon. Under repeated assaults, the regiment stood and fought back, losing half its strength until it was ordered to retreat. The legionaries moved back to Verdun; on June 18, the remnants of the 11th REI were pocketed at Saint-Germain-sur-Meuse and virtually wiped out. After burning their colors rather than allow them to fall into German hands, survivors kept up their discipline, retreated to Toul, and continued to fight delaying actions in the chaos of the general retreat until the armistice of June 22. The regiment suffered 75 percent casualties. The 12th REI, commanded by Colonel Besson, had a short and unfortunate fate. It was attached to the 8th Infantry Division, and engaged near Soissons. On June 6, the Third Battalion of the 12th REI was decimated by heavy enemy artillery fire and air strikes after 36 hours of hard fighting. The day after, by nightfall the rest of the regiment was encircled and only about 500 men managed to break through. In the general retreat, the survivors fought delaying but hopeless skirmishes at Berzy-le-Sec, Neuilly-Saint-Front and Villaret-Bussières. The defense of the bridge at Bonshommes near Limoges by some 300 surviving legionaries of the 12th REI, on the armistice day on June 22, 1940, marked the last fighting by this unit in the ill-fated Battle of France. The 21st RMVE, headed by Lieutenant-Colonel Debuissy, was deployed in the Ardennes. Subjected to repeated heavy attacks on June 9 and 10 at Buzancy and La Grange-au-Bois, the legionaries were unable to hold their positions. Forced to withdraw they were taken out of the front and not used again in battle.

The 22nd RMVE, under the leadership of Lieutenant-Colonel Villiers-Mor, was engaged at Peronne. It made vigorous assaults, taking the village of Villiers-Carbonnel on May 24. Counterattacked by the Germans, the legionaries put up a stubborn and impressive resistance before being reduced to half strength and eventually being overrun by German infantry supported by armored forces in a ferocious three-day battle.

The 23rd RMVE, commanded by Lieutenant-Colonel Aumoitte, deployed near Soissons, poorly armed and lacking training, succeeded nevertheless in holding enemy tanks for two days at the village of Pont-sur-Yonne before being forced to retreat on June 17. They joined in the general withdrawal and helped gather together the scattered men from broken units. At the end of the war the 23rd Regiment was regrouped at Châteauponsac in Haute-Vienne.

The GRD 97 made contact with the Germans on the Somme on May 18, and they fought with distinction and courage for the next three weeks in a series of delaying actions against superior forces at Epinancourt, Béthencourt, Barleux, and Belloy-en-Santerre, places reminiscent of the actions of the RMLE in July 1916. On June 9 the Reconnaissance Group 97 was tasked to cover the retreat of the 7th North African Infantry Division. They stubbornly defended the village of Quesnel and launched a furious counterattack—in true Legion style—on German armor in the forests of Noroy and Ravenel. Outgunned and outmanoeuvred by the enemy, the results were disastrous and within minutes half the group's vehicles were destroyed. Instead of retreating the legionaries re-formed and

Motorcyclist GRD 97 in 1940. The motorcyclist wears a leather crash helmet, with goggles, and the densely woven and waterproof khaki canvas double-breasted jacket of 1938 vintage. Riding gloves, cartridge pouches and the 1892 M16 carbine complete the equipment.

charged again, suffering heavy casualties. Counting 23 officers and 650 legionaries at the beginning of the campaign, the GRD 97 was reduced to 12 officers and 250 men by the end of June 1940.

The Foreign Legion and the Vichy Regime

The armistice of June 1940 and the establishment of Marshal Pétain's Vichy regime put the French Foreign Legion in a perilous position. The fate of the legionaries depended to some extent upon where they were at the time of the armistice. If the men of the 13th DBLE, after the Norwegian campaign, were in the fortunate position of being able to choose whether to join General Charles de Gaulle's Free French forces in exile in London or return to occupied France, others had no choice at all. The German occupation forces put pressure on the Vichy government to disband the Foreign Legion, but this was resisted. For the time being the units posted in Algeria, Morocco, Tunisia, Syria and Indochina were left to carry on their garrison duties. For the next two years life in North Africa was one of humdrum garrison duty for the Legion; the men were left with small arms and equipment. There was little trouble from the inhabitants, but there were some ugly episodes involving the Vichy and German authorities.

Right after the armistice of June 1940 an embarrassing problem arose. About 6,000 volunteers had joined for the duration of the war, and, after France's defeat, they felt that their war was over, so they wished to be discharged. The Vichy government refused, mainly because most had nowhere to go and would probably remain in North Africa where they might become an uncontrollable liability. They grew discontented and mutinous. Efforts to persuade these "duration only" legionnaires to contract for a regular Legion enlistment generally failed, in spite of thinly disguised blackmail efforts. They were arrested, interned in camps, and press-ganged into working on extending the railroad track southward from Colomb Bechar in the Sahara. Working and living under harsh conditions, many of them died, and only a few of them managed to escape.

The German authorities posed another problem for the Legion. The Legion regiments in North Africa were harassed by inspections from German commissions anxious to check on personnel. The German army wanted all German legionaries back for draft in the Wehrmacht. About 1,000 legionaries from German origin were released from the Legion at their own request; they were not allowed to go home and instead were formed into a special battalion in the German army. The SS police services hunted German criminals, anti–Nazi political opponents, deviating artists, and Jews who had fled Germany after 1933. The most famous "wanted" men enlisted in the Legion included the composer Max Deutsch (1904–1982), the abstract painter Hans Hartung (1904–1989) and the journalist, novelist and social philosopher Arthur Koestler (1905–1983). Before long, however, the Legion became adept at posting men likely to attract the Gestapo's attention into the desert on long training exercises, until the danger was past. The 4th Foreign Infantry Regiment, newly designated Quatrième Demi Brigade de la Légion ètrangère (4th DBLE, Foreign Legion Half Brigade) was quietly filled out with such fugitives and "wanted" men who were transferred to Senegal where even the most officious Nazi SS policeman was unlikely to follow. Another trick, when an inspection was imminent, was to ship to Indochina legionaries liable to attract German interest. Despite the cat-and-mouse games with the Nazis some 2,000 men were combed out by the Germans. They were formed into a Wehrmacht regiment for desert service, known as the 361st Motorised Infantry Regiment, which served in the famous Afrika Korps's 90th Light Division.

Legionary, 13th DBLE, London, 1940. The legionary inspected by General Charles de Gaulle at Whitehall, London, on July 14, 1940 (Bastille Day), still wears the outfit issued for the expedition in Norway. This included the M 1926 Adrian steel helmet, a khaki shirt, baggy golf trousers, puttees, ski socks and heavy mountain boots. The chèche *around the neck and the blue woolen sash around the waist are Legion touches. The weapon is a MAS 36 rifle.*

After the fall of France, the Legion's strength dropped as recruiting sources dried up. The number of volunteers was very low, so low that some changes were made. Not only was the 4th REI transformed into the 4th DBLE, filled with men who did not wish to be handed over to the Germans, but the 2nd Foreign Infantry Regiment (2nd REI) was disbanded. The reduced 1st REI stayed at Sidi-Bel-Abbes and the 3rd REI remained in Morocco, both on garrison duties. The 2nd Foreign Cavalry Regiment (2nd REC) was so undermanned that it was disbanded, and its men who remained fit for duty were transferred into the sister unit, the 1st REC.

The 13th DBLE in East Africa

Until 1942, the 13th DBLE (Foreign Half-Brigade) was the only Legion unit to form part of the Free French forces, and during this period the formation fought several battles and won unique honors. After the snow of Norway and the London fog, the unit was brought up to a strength of two battalions and engaged, in December 1940, in winning over French Cameroon to the Gaullist cause. When this was done, the 13th DBLE was then sent on, round the Cape of Good Hope, to land at Port Sudan in February 1941, where it arrived just in time to participate in a campaign against the Italians in East Africa. The 13th DBLE, having reached the figure of about 2,000 legionnaires, always had difficulty in passing that number because there was a distinct shortage of recruits—many who might have volunteered had already committed themselves elsewhere.

In December 1940 the Italians were routed and driven back across the Western Desert to beyond Benghazi. In only 62 days, the Allies took 130,000 prisoners and captured 380 tanks and 845 field guns. Meanwhile, in January 1941, Allied forces invaded Eritrea and broke the Italian resistance by April.

At first the British were reluctant to use Monclar's French legionaries, but when they saw how the 13th DBLE fought, they changed their view about the Legion. Alongside British troops the 13th DBLE fought with distinction at Enghiahat and at Keren, an Italian stronghold that was taken on March 27, 1941, after a siege of seven weeks. At Massawa in early April, the legionaries assaulted the fort of Montecullo where some 15,000 prisoners were taken.

Italian Somaliland was overrun after an amazing advance of 1,054 miles in 35 days. This all but forgotten campaign, fought against odds of 7 to 1, over all but impassable terrain, was one of the most brilliant in military annals. The fall of East Africa to the British secured the southern flank of Egypt, but it also amounted to a crushing humiliation for the Italian dictator Mussolini, who had lost almost all of his empire as well as a significant diminution of his military strength. The legionaries of the 13th DBLE were soon needed for another mission, this time in Syria.

Syria

Strategic background

From May 27, 1941, the Vichy-held protectorate of Syria was considered by the Allies to be "enemy-occupied" territory. Syria and Lebanon had remained under the control of the Vichy government after the capitulation of June 1940, and their strategic situation made them highly desirable both to the British and to the Germans. The importance of this area can scarcely be exaggerated. If the Axis came to dominate Syria, Iraq and Iran they could secure for themselves the precious oilfields located in the latter two countries. Vichy worked hand-in-glove with the Germans, and Marshal Pétain was put under heavy pressure to enter the war on the German side, a thing he never did, but he was inclined—as a gesture of good will—to allow the Germans to operate their air force from Syria. At the same time Axis agents were planning and engineering pro–Nazi coups in the region. With German influence rife in Syria and further Axis expansion expected after the campaigns in Greece and Crete, it was decided to capture Syria before the Vichy protectorate could become a German outpost that could be fully exploited for the conquest of the Middle East.

A fratricidal campaign

On June 8, 1941, a joint force of British, Australian and Free French forces passed into Syria from Jordan and Iraq, which the British had also just occupied. The 13th DBLE was part of the column that advanced to Damascus. At first they met no opposition and it was hoped that Vichy resistance would only be token, but this was not so. Vichy troops, headed by General Dentz, manned strongholds along the line Chameh-Meryoun–Mount Hermon and fighting soon took on an emotionally painful cast since it entailed Frenchmen fighting Frenchmen. The main resistance to this Allied invasion was put up by the 6th Régiment ètranger d'Infanterie (6th REI). A tragic echo of Barbastro in Spain (June 2, 1837) was heard at a place called Damas in the Syrian hills when legionaries of the 6th REI—loyal to Vichy—and the Free French legionnaires of the 13th DBLE met in battle. The fratricidal combat lasted for two days. It was very fierce and casualties were significant, but, even in the heat of battle, Legion traditions bubbled up, both sides treated each other as comrades when it came to taking prisoners or picking up wounded. Legionaries of the 6th REI, for example, prevented the Senegalese troops from looting and ill-treatment of the 13th DBLE wounded, only to fire with machine guns at the oncoming men of that unit minutes later. Both sides gave full military honors to the dead, regardless of which side they fought on. In the end, the 13th DBLE won the day and brushed aside the remaining opposition. Sporadic skirmishing continued for another two weeks, during which time several units of Frenchmen from opposing camps violently clashed with each other. On June 21, 1941, Vichy resistance was over, the Free French entered Damascus and the Allies occupied Syria. The armistice of Saint-Jean-d'Acre ended the fratricidal war on July 14, 1941. Syria was turned over to the Gaullist Free French and a pro–British regime was put in place for the rest of the war.

Reorganization

After the defeat of General Dentz's Vichy troops, the 6th REI was disbanded, and its men, of whom there remained about 3,000, were given the choice either of being repatriated to Vichy-held territory or of joining the 13th DBLE. About 1,000 from the ranks joined the Free French Demi-Brigade, which formed a third battalion. Only two officers and a few NCOs accepted the offer to join the 13th DBLE, which illustrates the French cleavage of opinion at this period.

An able and popular officer took over the 13th DBLE. Lieutenant-Colonel Dimitri Amilakvari had a prestigious background. He was not only a White Russian refugee but also a Russian prince, hereditary titular holder of the charge of Grand Squire of the Crown of Georgia. The young Dimitri and his princely family were obliged to leave Russia after the 1917 Bolshevik Revolution and took refuge in Constantinople before settling in France. In 1924 Amilakvari graduated from the French Military Academy at Saint Cyr, served in the Rif War of 1925, joined the French Foreign Legion in 1926, and took part in the pacification of southern Morocco. Posted in the 4th Foreign Infantry Regiment, "Amilak" (so called by his soldiers who loved him) was a man of immense charm and character who did much to raise the morale and efficiency of his men. He distinguished himself by his personal bravery, leadership and organizational qualities, and he became another legendary figure of the Foreign Legion. In 1939, he obtained French nationality and was appointed head of the 2nd Battalion of the 13th DBLE, then commanded by Lieutenant-Colonel Monclar (Magrin-Verneret). He took part in all the campaigns of the 13th Half-Brigade: Norway, Dakar, Douala, Port Sudan, Eritrea and Syria. In August 1941, aged 36, "Amilak" was promoted to the rank of lieutenant-colonel and placed at the head of the 13th DBLE.

When the Syrian affair had been settled, it was decided that the Free French contingent and the 13th DBLE should join the British 8th Army in Libya.

Bir Hakeim

Military background

The Battle of Bir Hakeim was an episode of the Desert War, a fluctuating conflict between Axis and British forces fought for the control of Libya and Egypt in 1941–1942.

Early in 1941 the British had almost succeeded in ejecting the Italians from Libya but in February 1941 Hitler sent the Deutsche Afrika Korps (DAK) commanded by Lieutenant-General Erwin Rommel to help his defeated Italian ally. At the start of February 1942, the British 8th Army dug itself into position in a line between Gazala and Bir Hakeim, 30 miles west of Tobruk. The line was, of course not a continuous linear defense, but rather a network of strongholds known as "boxes," fortified areas surrounded by large minefields. It extended over some 50 miles from the Mediterranean Sea in the north to Bir Hakeim inland to the south. Across this line the two armies faced each other for the next four months while they built up their strength.

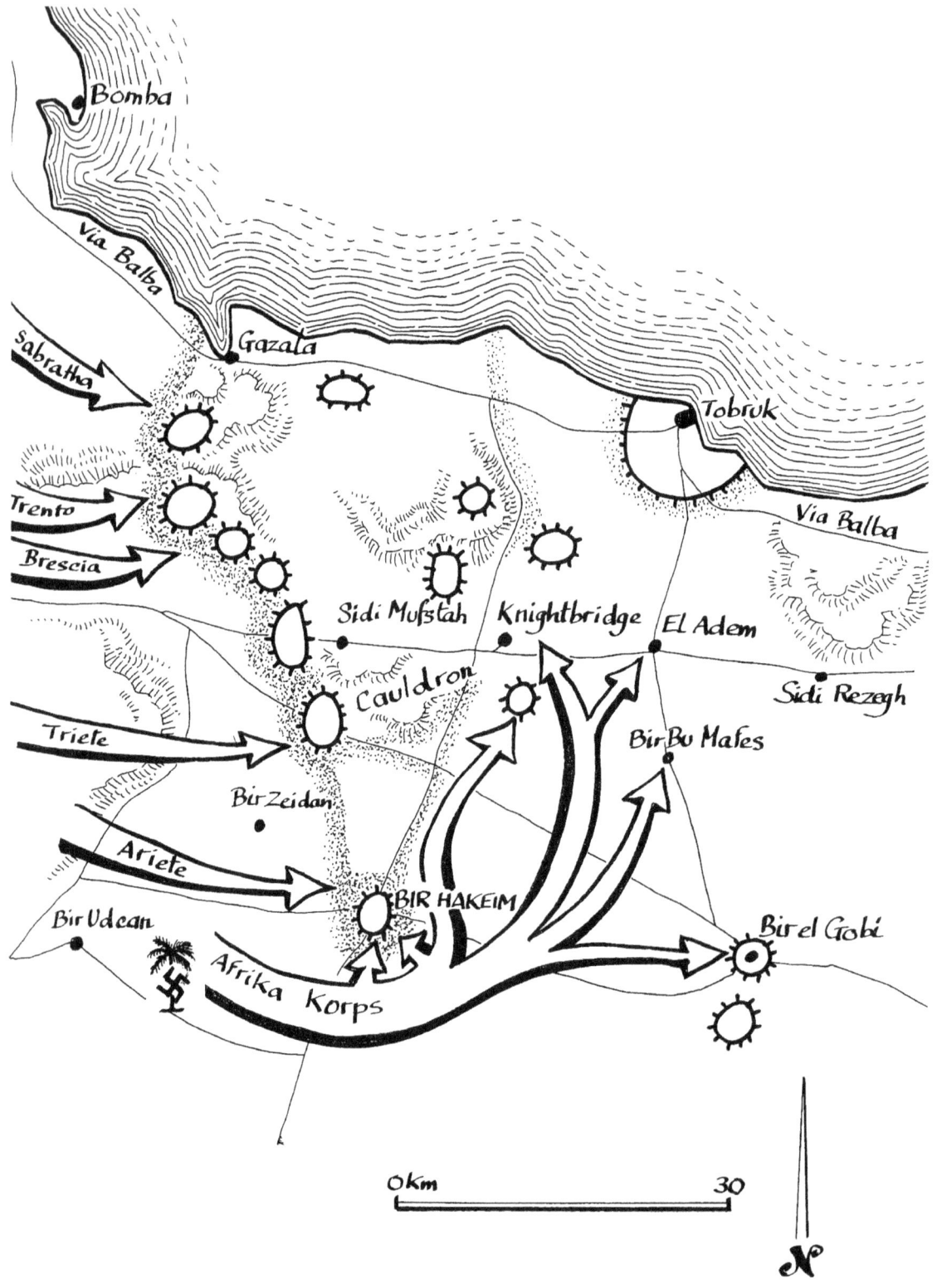

Sketch map of the Gazala line

The "box" of Bir Hakeim

The Free French-held "box" of Bir Hakeim (Old Man's Well) constituted the southernmost stronghold of the British Gazala defensive line. It had once been an Italian military post established at the crossing of two tracks to control that part of the desert. There was a ruined fort in the middle of barren empty flat ground. The "box" was an irregular circle, about 4 kilometers in width and 5 kilometers in length. In the months preceding the battle, the men had had time—in the broiling African sun—to dig a multitude of fox holes in the sand, along with combat trenches and communication saps, armed emplacements, underground kitchens, field infirmaries and dressing stations, dugouts, shelters and supply dumps in field fortification style. All these were leveled, well camouflaged and difficult to spot; the trenches were narrow, and, unless a bomb or a shell fell on them directly, little damage was done. Like all the other boxes of the line, the fortified position was surrounded by large V-shaped minefields composed of antitank mines (exploding under a pressure of 200 kg) and antipersonnel mines, making the terrain a death trap. In a flat and bare desert, deprived of natural obstacles and thus extremely favorable to mechanized warfare and broad tank movements, the minefields were essential obstacles: They constituted the actual ramparts of the positions. Those protecting Bir Hakeim were patrolled by a mobile detachment of the 3rd Legion Battalion, headed by Captain de Lamaze with 63 Bren Carriers divided into three squadrons, whose tasks were to make reconnaissance operations, launch local raids and ambushes, collect information, lay mines, detect and destroy infiltrators and obstruct enemy mine-clearing teams; for this purpose, there were gates and narrow patrolling lanes in the minefields, particularly in the northern direction so as to maintain contact with the neighboring "box" of Got el Ualeb held by the British 150th Brigade.

The heavy armament of Bir Hakeim was placed in open emplacements protected by entrenchments and sandbags, all of it covered by camouflage nets. It included 24 75 mm guns, 84 antitank guns (caliber 75 mm, 47 mm and 25 mm), 44 mortars, 72 Hotchkiss machine guns, 18 Bofors antiaircraft guns, and 8 heavy antiaircraft machine guns.

The garrison, totaling 3,500 men, was commanded by General Marie Pierre François Koenig (1898–1970), a veteran of the colonial wars and the Norway campaign, one of the few senior French officers to rally to de Gaulle in 1940. This force, designated 1st Free French Brigade, was composed of several formations, including the following.

- 2nd Colonial Half-Brigade composed of 2nd Task Oubanghi-Chari Battalion (Senegalese and African volunteers) commanded by Lieutenant-Colonel Roux; and 1st Pacific Battalion (formed with volunteers from Tahiti, New Caledonia and New Hebrides), headed by Lieutenant-Colonel Broche.
- 1st Colonial Infantry Battalion, commanded by Major Savey;
- 1st Battalion of Fusiliers-Marins (Marines) Half-Brigade, headed by Frigate-Captain Amyot d'Inville;
- 1st Colonial Artillery Regiment, headed by Major Laurent-Champrosay;
- 22nd North African Company, headed by Captain Lequesne;
- 2nd Antitank Artillery Company, commanded by Captain Jacquin;
- one engineering company;
- one signal company;
- one medical company;
- a British liaison and antiaircraft artillery detachment headed by Captain Tompkins;
- the 13th Foreign Legion Half-Brigade, which represented about half the force of Koenig's Brigade; it was divided into three battalions headed by Lieutenant-Colonel Amilakvari.

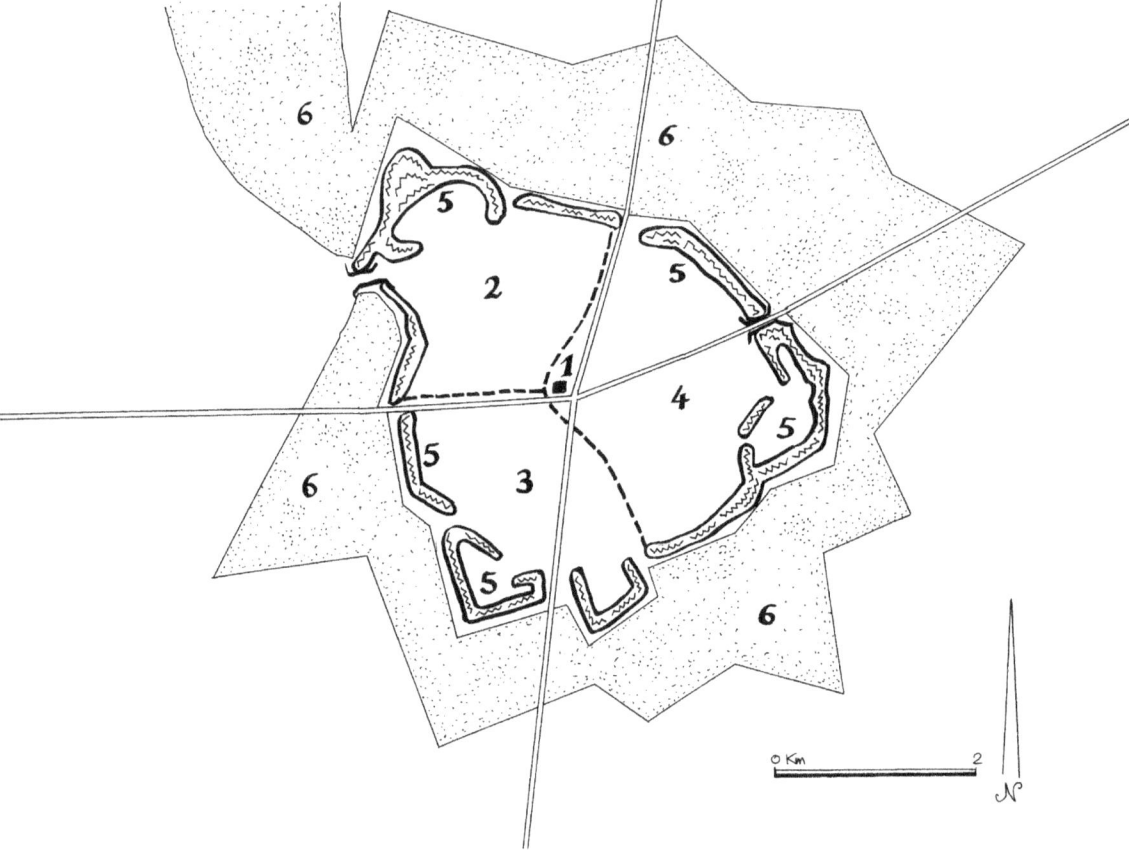

Sketch map of the box of Bir Hakeim. 1: General Koenig's Headquarters; 2: Northern Sector held by 1st Task Battalion; 3: Southwestern Sector held by 1st Pacific Battalion; 4: Eastern Sector held by Legion's 13th DBLE; 5: Front line combat trenches, artillery emplacements, dugouts and barbed wire; 6: AT and AP minefields.

Those fighting at Bir Hakeim included Pierre Mesmer, who later held several overseas posts and became French premier in 1972 under President Georges Pompidou. John F. Hasey (1916–2005), later to become a senior CIA officer, served in the Legion as staff officer of General Koenig. Worthy of mention is the exceptional fate of a courageous woman named Susan Travers (1909–2003) who had joined the 13th Demi-Brigade in London in 1940 as an ambulance driver, and stuck to it throughout the war. She accompanied the 13th DBLE on every step and served as General Koenig's driver at Bir Hakeim. For her bravery, gallantry and fidelity the highly regarded Miss Travers was made an informal member of the Legion. She stayed with the 13th DBLE, still a driver, to serve in the Indochina War after World War II.

The Battle

Rommel's forces included about 90,000 soldiers, including 50,000 DAK Germans and 525 tanks. The British opposed them with 100,000 men, 700 tanks and more artillery and planes than the DAK and Italian forces combined. The "Desert Fox" was not impressed, however, and needed to defeat the 8th Army entrenched in the Gazala Line if he wanted to capture Tobruk. He began with frontal diversion attacks on the line, launched by the Italian Divisions

Sabratha, Trento, Brescia and Trieste, supported by German tanks and planes. At the same time he launched an outflanking drive with the Afrika Korps and the Italian Division Ariete at and around the southern strongpoint of Bir Hakeim, where he concentrated most of his DAK forces. On May 26, the defenders of the southern pillar of the Gazala Line were attacked by German planes and Italian tanks of the Ariete Division. They held the assault, and counterattacked; the score at the end of the first day's fighting was 32 Italian tanks destroyed. In the meantime, Rommel's leading elements swung around at the back of the defensive line, his vanguard reaching El Adem. A bitter tank battle followed in the area between May 30 and June 2. Rommel's rearward communication and supply lines were, however, greatly threatened by the unbroken resistance of the French. On June 2, the Germans encircled the Bir Hakeim "box," and demanded the surrender of the defenders. This was refused and the Afrika Korps attacked with infantry and armor supported by Junkers 87 dive bombers. The fighting lasted for nine days, during which the legionaries and FFL troops stood firm, although water was rationed and food and ammunition dropped to a low level. When the Italians succeeded in breaching the British line to the north, Rommel decided to withdraw behind the gap his allies had created. While he resupplied his troops, the British advanced and eight days of bitter tank fighting took place in an area known as the "Cauldron."

In the meantime Bir Hakeim was still the target of heavy artillery and Stuka attacks. A second offer to capitulate was made by Rommel but this, too, was rejected. After June 5, Rommel engaged more numerous and powerful artillery (150 mm and 210 mm) to smash the French box; the defenders were subjected to a barrage such as had never previously been seen in the whole campaign. On June 6, the DAK engineers infiltrated and cleared lanes in the minefields, and infantry assaulted the position, but they were repulsed with heavy casualties. After a lull, the attacks, again prepared by artillery, Stuka dive bombers and Italian Caproni bombers, were resumed with yet more vigor. On June 9, the Germans had infiltrated en masse inside the minefields and the 90th Light Division's leading elements were only 200 meters from the defended perimeter. Bir Hakeim had become a burning inferno. Short of ammunition, and suffering more and more casualties, Koenig's Brigade was at the end of its tether, tortured by thirst, harassed by sandflies, exhausted by the heat and fighting, and soon to be overwhelmed. When it became obvious that holding Bir Hakeim was hopeless and militarily useless since the whole Gazala Line began to collapse, General Koenig considered a breakout.

The retreat

The withdrawal was planned for the night of June 10–11, 1942. At nightfall, a 150-meter wide path through the minefields was cleared, enabling the defenders to make their way through it into the open desert; the objective was to meet the 7th British Motorized Brigade at the rally point of Gars-el-Arid east of the position. The retreat was a total chaos, with vehicles driving out of the narrow corridor cleared of mines and exploding in the night, milling groups of backed up vehicles machine-gunned by the Germans, flanks of the chaotic columns lit by flares and bombarded by enemy artillery and countless individual and confused skirmishes in the dark, until Captain de Lamaze's legionaries, mounted in Bren Carriers, boldly charged their way through the encircling enemy. This sacrificial operation—marked by hand-to-hand fights with bayonets and grenades and Bren Carriers ramming enemy guns—allowed the rest of the garrison to escape. The next morning, the enemy bombarded and captured an empty position. The following days saw the remnants of the Bir Hakeim garrison scattered over some 8,000 square kilometers of desert and some stragglers did not rally at the planned point of regrouping before June 14 while others disappeared in the desert. The Free French garrison of Bir Hakeim lost about 900 men, and the 13th DBLE suffered so many casualties that on June 15, 1942, it was temporarily reduced to two battalions. Casualties on the German side are unknown, probably as many, but Rommel also lost 51 of his precious tanks, 20 armored cars and about seven planes.

But beyond this, the impact of Bir Hakeim was also psychological: It had been an impressive defensive battle, but it became also a symbol. The epic defense of Bir Hakeim was immediately turned into a great victory by the Free French propaganda service in London, and it announced to the world the rebirth of French honor. Actually Bir Hakeim was merely a delaying action. But with impressive resistance in true Legion style, it was a proud achievement, a defining moment for de Gaulle's cause. By holding out far longer than had been expected the 1st Free French Brigade had enabled the British 8th Army to withdraw in good order and so won precious time needed to prepare for a reversal of the situation at El Alamein. Bir Hakeim showed the Allies that the army of Free France had recovered its old valor.

Left: *British Bren LMG. The Bren light machine gun was reliable, robust, simple and accurate. It was widely used by British, Commonwealth and Allied forces from 1938 to 1956. About 300,000 were manufactured. The weapon was gas-operated and used a .303in SAA ball in a 30-round detachable curved box. With a length of 1,150 mm (45.25 in.), and a weight of 10.15 kg (22 lbs. 5 oz.), it could easily be carried and fired by one man; cyclic rate of fire was 500 rounds per minute.* **Right:** *Legionary, North Africa, 1942. Legionaries wore mostly British uniforms with a few remnants of French uniform, equipment and weapons being retained. The depicted legionary wears the basic British army desert uniform consisting of khaki drill shirt and shorts, long woolen socks, and canvas web gaiters. Greatcoats were issued to combat the severe drop in temperature at night. The white képi was a Legion touch. The weapon is the excellent British rifle No. 1 SMLE Lee Enfield. This bolt-action, self-loading rifle fired a 0.303 inch SAA cartridge, had a length of 1,132 mm (44.75 in.), a weight of 3.71 kg (8 lbs. 2 oz.), and a 10-round detachable box magazine.*

El Alamein

During the Battle of El Alamein, the Legion 13th DBLE, still a part of General Koenig's 1st Free French Brigade, was deployed on the extreme south of the front near the impassable Qattara Depression. The Free French, attached to General Horrocks's XIII Corps, were ordered to conquer a steep ridge called Qaret El Himeimat, strongly defended by the Italian Folgore Division and elements of the Afrika Korps.

Left: *Legion NCO, Libya, 1941. Due to the requirements of desert warfare, the wearing of official apparel and the strict observance of military regulations were largely a matter between the men and their commanding officers. Frontline men often had no other choice than to mix different styles of uniform, equipment and headgear together. A common practice was to wear articles of clothing based more on personal choice and comfort than on rules and regulations. Arab sandals, British shorts, Legion képi and chèche (scarf) were popular.*
Below: *Armored Dodge 3-ton truck. The 3-t Dodge D15 medium 4 × 2 truck had a maximum speed of 85 km/h, and a payload of 3,300 kg. The military 3-t Dodge underwent several conversions, including into cargo carrier, ambulance and bus. The depicted truck (called "Tanake") was an improvised armored version designed in 1941. It had a varied crew, basically a driver, a gunner and a commander plus several infantrymen riding along. Armament was mixed, generally one 37 mm gun, or one French* **fusil-mitrailleur** *FM24/29 or a British Bren light machine gun. The vehicle was underpowered and the chassis too weak for the weight of the armor but the Free French forces had to make do with whatever material they could lay their hands on. The Dodge Tanake became particularly famous owing to the 13th DBLE at Bir Hakeim, which was equipped with 16 of them.*

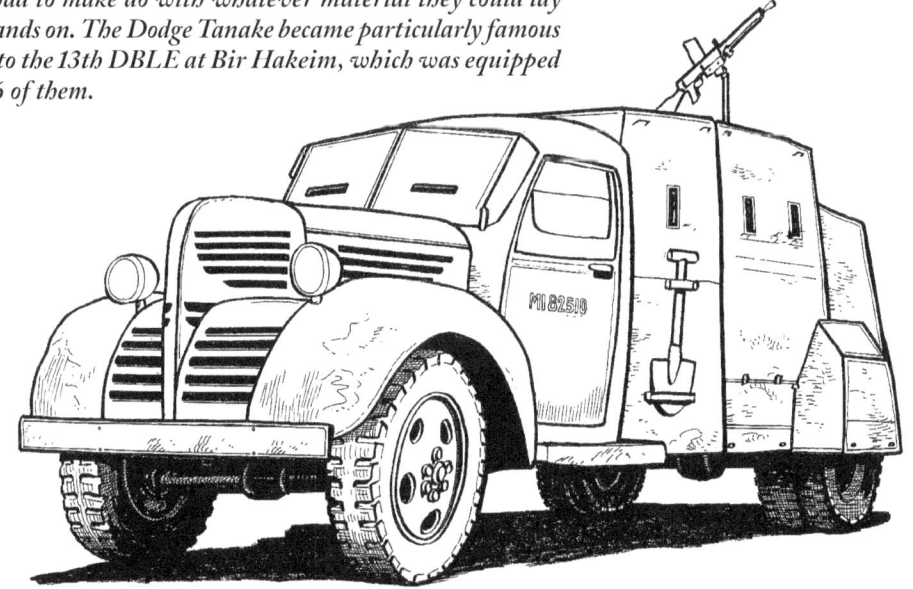

Legionary with FM model 1924/29. The light machine gun model 1924/29, quite similar to the British Bren, was the standard French LMG during World War II and in the 1950s.

This was a diversion attack in the south while the main offensive would be launched to the north. The French forces were poorly equipped and badly armed for undertaking such an operation against such a strong enemy. The British had not provided them with tanks, and this oversight might be explained by quarrels at the top as, by that time, the relationship between de Gaulle and Churchill was particularly strained.

On October 24, 1942, lanes in the minefields were cleared and the 1st Legion Battalion assaulted across open ground. While it was vulnerable out in the open, the enemy launched a strong counterattack with tanks, which badly hit the flank of the unit. The 2nd Legion Battalion, which had been posted in reserve, went out to counterattack the Axis counterattack. Outflanked and subjected to heavy artillery and mortar fire, the legionaries could not advance. In his efforts to get his men moving forward again, Lieutenant-Colonel Dimitri Amilakvari stood up to urge them on, but minutes later, he was mortally hit by a mortar shell splinter. He was yet another Legion commander to be killed at the head of his legionnaires. The much admired "Amilak" was greatly mourned by his men. He was replaced at the head of the 13th DBLE by Colonel Bablon. The attack on El Himeimat was brought to a halt and only captured when the Axis retreated.

After this costly failure, the 1st Free French Brigade and the 13th DBLE were sent for a short rest to Tobruk. The 1st Free French Brigade was upgraded to divisional status, and became the Première Division de la France libre (1ère DFL, 1st Free French Division). After re-forming and rest, the 1st DFL and the 13th DBLE continued with the British 8th Army until it reached Tunisia.

Tunisia

On November 8, 1942, the Allied invasion of Vichy French North Africa, codenamed Operation Torch, began. Three main task forces, under the command of General Eisenhower, set troops ashore at Casablanca (Morocco), and Oran and Algiers (Algeria). The Allies had made great diplomatic efforts to secure at least a passive response by the Vichy garrisons to their projected invasion. The main landings began in muddle and confusion as might be expected from a first attempt at combined operations. Before landing successfully, attacks on the harbors of Algiers and Oran met with Vichy resistance. The overall military situation remained uncertain and confused for a few days, until a cease-fire was negotiated and the half-hearted fighting ceased on November 11. The political situation was extremely complex, though, as the American government still hoped to cooperate with the Vichy authorities in North Africa, if not with Pétain himself. De Gaulle was excluded from the operation and not even informed of Operation Torch. After complicated political moves General de Gaulle was reluctantly recognized by the Americans as sole Free French leader. While political quarrels and plots raged among the Allied top leadership, the invasion of Tunisia began in late 1942.

After a difficult campaign, the defeated Axis forces capitulated unconditionally on May 13, 1943. A few hundred men escaped by air to Sicily, but in all 275,000 prisoners were taken. Operations in Tunisia ended in total victory and marked the end of the desert war in North Africa.

In the period from June 22, 1940, to November 8, 1942, the French Foreign Legion in North Africa was not involved in military actions, but it was not idle. The troops continued to build and train and they still constituted a small but hard-hitting force, but they unfortunately lacked modern weapons. When the Anglo-American forces landed at Oran, the 1st Foreign Infantry Regiment was ordered to resist. One battalion was moved from Sidi-Bel-Abbes northward to

U.S. M1 steel helmet

U.S. 0.30 in. Browning machine gun M 1019A4

repulse what Vichy considered enemy forces invading part of France. While the rank and file and NCOs were accustomed to doing what they were ordered to do without complaint, officers suffered from agonizing choices. In the confused situation many no longer knew where their duty lay. Should they fire at the Allies who obviously came to liberate France or should they disobey their legal government's orders? Was it their duty to repeat the tragical and fratricidal fighting of Syria? For a few days there was dilemma, confusion and hesitation, and the Legion leadership deliberately dragged its feet. The troop was halted when it came into contact with the Allies, and although there were a few scuffles, the Corps's leadership remained prudently passive until the

U.S. M4A1 Sherman medium tank

U.S. White Scout Car M3

Vichy authorities and forces capitulated. When the French forces stationed in North Africa went over totally to the Allied side, the choice was clear. When the Americans landed at Casablanca, some German legionaries made an attempt to seize the Colomb-Bechar radio station. This was forestalled but it showed that a small element of unreliable Nazi sympathizers lingered on in the Foreign Legion. This might explain why the Americans were, at first, extremely reluctant to provide the Legion with modern weapons.

When the final battle against the Tunisian Axis-held bridgehead started, the Legion did not intend to be led out, and

Armored car driver, 1st REC. The legionary depicted here wears the U.S. tankman uniform. Headgear included a crash helmet with pierced hard leather skull without chinstrap; earphones—omitted here—would be inserted under the snap-fastened diamond of leather on the cheekpieces; headgear could also be the French model 1935 tank helmet, or the standard U.S. M1 steel helmet for crews of open-topped vehicles. The man wears a two-front-pocketed windbreaker jacket deprived of shoulder straps; and a one-piece light grey-green overall, replaced by thickly padded overtrousers and tunic in winter. Goggles, scarf and gloves were general issues.

prepared for fighting along the Anglo-American Allies. The Corps was waking up and making ready for war again. The mood was all cheerful bustle and enthusiasm. The 4th Foreign Legion Half Brigade (formed as we know of Germans "wanted" by the Nazis) was hastily returned from Senegal. The North African units of the Foreign Legion raised two Régiments étrangers d'Infanterie de marche (REIM, Task Regiments), designated 1st Foreign Infantry Task Regiment and 3rd Foreign Infantry Task Regiment. Although handicapped by their old-fashioned equipment, outdated weapons and unsuited transport, the Legion units were hurriedly thrown into action against the still formidable Axis forces.

The 3rd REIM was committed with the American forces in the fighting at Kasserine Pass. They advanced and met the Germans at a height called Djebel Mansour. Being too eager and pushing too far forward, forgetting that their obsolete small arms were no match for modern German weapons, they got into difficulties. The 3rd REIM was almost encircled, and only succeeded in getting clear with the assistance given by the Allied air force.

The 1st REIM was engaged alongside the British 1st Army to contain Rommel's offensive. The regiment suffered some 300 casualties but held on to its main defensive position. They were able to force the Germans back to regain all the lost ground. In early May 1943, now issued with modern American weapons, uniforms, equipment and vehicles, the 1st REIM took part with notable spirit at the successful attack on Pont du Fahs in northern Tunisia. They pushed on to the town of Zaghouan where they were halted by strong enemy artillery fire.

The 1st REC (Foreign Legion Cavalry Regiment) mustered a small mobile mechanized combat group, which became known as the Groupe Autonome (GA, Autonomous Group). The GA distinguished itself at Foum el Gouafel on January 11, 1943, when a strong German position was captured at the cost of only five wounded.

The Free French 13th DBLE, advancing from Libya with the British 8th Army, came up against the German-held fortified Mareth Line. Deployed on the southern flank of the front, the 13th DBLE was committed in a two-day battle against the famous Afrika Korps 90th Light Division in the mountainous area of Djebel Garci. The legionaries assaulted the defended positions and were able to push the Germans out, but they suffered heavy casualties.

After the Axis defeat in Tunisia, a number of German legionaries, who had been drafted in the Wehrmacht Afrika Korps 361st Infantry Regiment, were captured. Most of them wished to rejoin their comrades in the Legion, but for the moment this was not allowed. It was only later, in 1945, that many were permitted to reenlist in the French Foreign Legion.

During the battles of Tunisia, the French Foreign Legion had recovered its reputation as a reliable and excellent fighting force. The Free French forces, now increased in strength by the addition of Vichy troops, and the Legion were organized and trained along U.S. lines, and reequipped with U.S. materials, which transformed the units into a modern army. Comfortable battledresses, smart uniforms, and well-designed equipment, modern small arms and powerful heavy weapons with plentiful ammunition were issued.

By June 1943, the strength of the Foreign Legion had decreased well below 10,000 and some reorganization was obviously necessary. All existing task regiments, including both 1st and 3rd REIMs, were disbanded and the best men, equipped and uniformed by the U.S. Army, were formed into the second Régiment de marche de la Légion étrangère (2nd RMLE, Task Regiment of the Foreign Legion) to appear in 30 years—the first one being the RMLE commanded by Colonel Rollet during World War I. The RMLE was officially created on July 1, 1943, as a motorized unit with men transported in excellent GMC and Dodge military trucks and officers in command cars and Jeeps. The 1st REC (1st Foreign Cavalry Regiment) was maintained, brought up to strength, and reorganized into a light armored support unit equipped with a variety of modern U.S. military vehicles including Jeeps, all-wheel drive trucks, scout cars, halftracks, armored cars, and light tanks. The historical, illustrious and heroic 13th DBLE was, of course, maintained as a motorized regiment equipped with trucks and halftracks. Its men regarded themselves as "true" Free French, Gaullist from the first hour, and between them and the ex–Vichy legionaries there was mutual wariness. The Legion units were attached to the 5th Moroccan Division, and, for six months, all formations were given extensive training and instruction for employing their new materiel with maximum efficiency. Once the war in Africa was won, all thoughts and efforts turned to the invasion of Europe. The next target was Italy.

Italy

The French Foreign Legion played a modest role in the campaign in Italy. In late April 1944, the 13th DBLE, after a period of hard training in Tunisia, was shipped off to Italy where it joined the 5th U.S. Army. Fighting their way slowly northward in the face of heavy enemy resistance, the legionaries, commanded by Colonel de Sairigné, took part in the fighting at the Garigliano River, at Monte Pencio, and at the capture of Rome. After the fall of the capital of Italy, the 13th Foreign Half-Brigade continued its advance in a northerly direction. They fought a small, local, but brilliant engagement at a place called Radicorfani in Tuscany on June 18, 1944. This was a natural defensive position on top of a steep hill with a Renaissance castle, which the Germans had heavily fortified. The garrison included three officers and 90 soldiers well armed with machine guns and other weapons. At the foot of the hill were deployed two 75 mm antitank guns and

Legionary with U.S. Thompson submachine gun, Italy, 1943.

U.S. Thompson submachine gun. The Thompson was rather heavy, about 5 kg (10 lbs. 9 oz.), 813 mm (32 in.) in length with its fixed wooden butt, and rather expensive to manufacture, but it was a remarkable weapon using a form of retarded blowback operation. It used the 0.45 in. M1911 cartridge and had a cyclic rate of fire of 700 rpm. A grand total of 1,400,000 classic "Tommy Guns" were built in the period 1940–1945.

three formidable Jagd-Panther self-propelled AT guns. Held off by incessant fire the legionaries were unable to launch a frontal assault. Instead, they split up into small groups. While a detachment attacked the SPGs, destroying two of them and forcing the third one to withdraw, the others groups diverted the defenders by sustained fire, allowing a small party to climb up the sides of the escarpment. Using surprise and speed they attacked the castle from the rear with grenades, and obtained the surrender of the defenders after a short and fierce assault. After taking the castle, the legionaries seized the small town of Radicofani, opening the way to Tuscany.

The End of the War

While the Allies waged a hard-fought struggle for the liberation of Italy, a huge Allied task force landed in Normandy on June 6, 1944. The successful landing, Operation Overlord, was followed by a hard struggle known as the Battle of Normandy.

In August 1944, Paris was liberated and another Allied army landed in southern France as a follow-up to the Normandy landing. The 13th DBLE, the first Legion unit to set foot in France since 1940, landed at Cavalaire on August 16, 1944, and was immediately committed into battle. After hard fighting at Toulon and Marseilles, troops quickly moved northward and the operation devolved into a pursuit of the retreating Germans by the Allies up the Rhône River valley through Avignon, Montélimar, Lyon and Dijon. The 13th Legion Half-Brigade was involved in several battles on the way; casualties caused the Half-Brigade again to be reduced to two battalions. By the autumn of 1944, most of France was liberated, but many German troops had escaped and regrouped in defensive positions in Alsace.

The newly formed Foreign Legion Task Regiment (RMLE, headed by Colonel Tritschler) and the Foreign Cavalry Regiment (1st REC, commanded by Colonel Miquel), attached to the 5th Moroccan Division, landed in southern France in September 1944. Both units were engaged in the Vosges Mountains and upper Alsace to

Legionary in Provence, August 1944

Legionary, RMLE, Alsace, 1944. The legionary depicted here wears the U.S. M1 steel helmet, and the U.S. Army long wool overcoat well suited for low temperatures encountered in the last winter of World War II in northern Europe. His weapon is the U.S. self-loading semi-automatic M1 Garand rifle. Introduced in the U.S. Army in 1937, this rifle became standard issue until the 1950s. Both simple and robust, with a quite massive construction, it was a conventional gas-operated rifle firing the 0.30 in. cartridge. It had an 8-round integral box magazine, a weight (unloaded) of 4.37 kg (9 lbs. 8 oz.), and a length of 1,103 mm (43.5 in.), the 10-in. bayonet not included.

force the key pass of Belfort between Colmar and the border with Switzerland, where strong German defenses barred the way. The campaign, fought in extremely bad weather with cold, rain and snow, started on November 2, 1944, by capturing a number of villages stubbornly held by the Germans. The 13th DBLE was brought from reserve to assist. Now the entire Free French Foreign Legion was engaged in action. On November 22, an attack on the city of Montbéliard was launched, where the legionaries destroyed half a dozen Panther tanks. They kept advancing and succeeded in breaching the German defenses, facilitating the capture of Belfort. In December, the enemy did not limit its operation to defensive actions but also launched a limited attack, which was intended to support a yet more ambitious offensive in the Ardennes in Belgium known as the Battle of the Bulge. Hitler used his last reserves for this powerful offensive, which in the end, but with heavy losses, was won by the Allies. After the failure of the Ardennes offensive, ultimate defeat was inevitable and the scene was set for the final act, the conquest and defeat of Nazi Germany. In January 1945, at high cost, the Legion seized several bridges on the Rhine. The RMLE crossed the river, took a village named Gamsheim, but, deprived of armored support, two of its companies were wiped out by a powerful German counterstroke. This was followed by a series of small battles and bloody skirmishes as the French resumed their advance. The much depleted 13th Half-Brigade and the RMLE, after a difficult infantry battle fought in cold and snow, seized Colmar on February 2, 1945. This was the last action of World War II for the 13th DBLE; the unit, now counting less than 1,000 survivors of the battle of Alsace, was withdraw from frontline service and put into reserve.

The fall of Germany

The role played by the Legion in the last offensives which led to the fall of Nazi Germany, of course, was minimal compared to the millions of Russian, American, British and Commonwealth, French, Poles and all the other nations present in the Allied forces. At the local level, however, the operations in which the 13th DBLE, RMLE and 1st REC were committed, were not insignificant.

After the capture of Colmar, the RMLE entered Germany and moved toward Stuttgart, where, on February 15, 1945, it participated in a series of battles which led to a breakthrough. On February 19, the regiment fought a hard battle at a place named Lautenburg; grimly defended by the Germans, the city was taken after costly hand-to-hand street fighting. Colonel Tritschler died of sickness, and he was replaced by Colonel Olié at the head of the RMLE. After a short break, the regiment continued its advance and, after another series of hard-fought encounters from April 4 to April 21, entered the ruins of Stuttgart. After the capture of the capital of Bade-Württemberg Province, remnants of the RMLE and legionaries of the depleted 1st REC were deployed in the Black Forest to crush the last fanatical Nazi defenders of this forested mountain region. They hunted skirmishers and snipers and fought a particularly hard battle at Friedrichshafen. By that time Hitler's Third Reich was collapsing.

On May 7, 1945, Germany unconditionally surrendered. The cease-fire that ended World War II in Europe found the legionaries of the RMLE at Arlberg in the Tyrolian Alps in Austria. The war against Nazi Germany was over.

In June 1945, a victory parade was held in Paris, and detachments of the RMLE, 1st REC and 13th DBLE were present. The latter particularly had been through a long and heroic odyssey. It had fought with distinction in Norway, Africa, Syria, the Western Desert, Tunisia, Italy and France. It had come out of the war very well and had become one of the best-known French units in the world. Together with other Free French formations (such as General Leclerc's 2nd Armored Division, and Generals de Lattre de Tassigny and Juin's armies), it had become the symbol of the Gaullist Forces françaises libres and the epitome of France's military rebirth and renewed honor. Today the 13th Demi Brigade de la Légion étrangère still exists. Its colors are inscribed with the following battle honors: Douala, Cheren, Massaoua, Bir Hakeim, El Himeimat, Djebel Garci, Rome, Radicoffani, Toulon, Lyon, and Belfort. Curiously, Narvik is not included, although the unit had performed very well there.

French Indochina in World War II

In 1930, the three battalions of the Legion which had occupied the province of Tonkin since the beginning of the 20th century were merged into one unit called Cinquième Régiment étranger d'Infanterie (5th REI, Foreign Infantry Regiment). A post in the 5th Foreign Legion Regiment in comparatively peaceful Indochina meant a life of pleasure and comfort with generous pay, good allowances, little hard physical work, charming women and infrequent military activities, limited only to occasional skirmishes with local smugglers, bandits, and river pirates. This life of luxury (also shared by the 9th and 11th Colonial Infantry Regiments) came to an abrupt end in September 1940 when Japanese forces launched a surprise attack on French posts in the region of Lang Son, near the Chinese border, and at the border of Tonkin and Cambodia. Elements of the 5th Regiment fought the powerful Japanese "Canton Division." Headed by Colonel de Cadoudal, they held the Dong-Mo Pass until diplomatic action led by Admiral Decoux, general-governor of Indochina, brought an end to the conflict. These were the only military actions undertaken by the Legion during that period.

On March 9, 1945, the general Japanese attack came as a total surprise. At Tong, Hanoi, Lang-Son, and other places, many Frenchmen and legionaries were arrested and interned, some murdered by the Japanese. Colonel Alessandri regrouped what was left of the Legion (infantrymen and artillery groups of the 5th Regiment, as well as local auxiliaries, etc.) and decided to take to the mountainous jungles to start guerrilla operations. After hard battles at Tien-Cuong and Tien-Zien, the improvised task force reached the Black River on March 10, 1945. They were forced to withdraw and began an epic march of 800 kilometers to China, which lasted for 52 days. Harassed by Japanese commandos, lacking food, water and ammunition, the remnants of the 5th Foreign Regiment reached the Chinese border on May 2, 1945. They marched yet another 450 kilometers to reach Montzeu in Yunnan where they awaited the defeat of Japan. In February 1946, the 5th Foreign Regiment—reduced to one battalion—left their quarters at Tsao-Pa and returned to Indochina, after which the regiment was disbanded.

7

The Foreign Legion in Indochina, 1945–1954

Historical Background

After World War II the major colonial powers (Great Britain, France, the Netherlands, Belgium and Portugal) faced growing opposition in their overseas possessions. Colonial empires were contested both by the local nationalist elites who wanted to take control of their own countries' destinies, and by the two superpowers, the United States and the Soviet Union, who sought allies in their global rivalry.

From the start, the Vietnamese only grudgingly accepted French overlordship. By the early 20th century French-educated intellectuals in Vietnam included rabid nationalists prepared to challenge France on its own terms. In 1925, a Vietnamese nationalist party, seeking independence of a unified Annam, Tonkin and Cochin China, was founded by left-wing exiles, attracting revolutionaries like Ho Chi Minh. France's military collapse of June 1940 and the occupation of Indochina by Japan had greatly stimulated this strong desire for liberty. Throughout Asia the European white man was no longer regarded as invincible, and the indigenous people now knew that he could be defeated in battle.

In August 1940, Indochina had been occupied by Japan but had remained a Vichyite pocket, as Admiral Decoux, Pétain's governor-general in the region, had manoeuvred adroitly to preserve all that was possible of the French "presence." The scattered and ill-equipped French troops stationed in Indochina spent much of World War II in enforced idleness, controlled by the Japanese. In March 1945 the Japanese violently eliminated the Vichy French authorities and massacred their troops with characteristic savagery, as they considered the new Fourth Republic put in place by General Charles de Gaulle to be at war with them. At the same time the Communist-dominated Viet Minh proclaimed a united front against both the Japanese and the French. The post–World War II resistance against the French was dominated by the figure of its great leader, Ho Chi Minh (1890–1969), "the Enlightened." As a young man Ho had traveled to Europe and had become a militant member of the Communist Party. In the 1920s and 1930s, he continued his Marxist education by working for the Comintern (International communist organization) in Moscow and China. He was a convinced Communist but remained a fervid nationalist too. During World War II, Ho Chi Minh succeeded in integrating communism into the nationalist cause, and he set up a united resistance front called Viet Nam Doc Lap Dong Minh Hoi (Independence Front for Vietnam), or Viet Minh in popular parlance. By 1944 Ho Chi Minh had organized the Viet Minh into a nationwide political party with a military branch headed by a former school teacher named Vo Nguyen Giap.

After the capitulation of Japan on August 10, 1945, the Allied leaders at the Potsdam Conference had settled the temporary disposition of French Indochina. The southern part of the country was to be administered by British forces, and North Vietnam was occupied by Chinese nationalist forces headed by Chiang Kai-shek. However, this temporary arrangement did little good apart from providing a semblance of law and order.

Against the confused background of Japanese defeat, future Chinese aspirations and a motley of Vietnamese nationalist groups, the French naively thought to readily resume their prewar role as colonial rulers. In October 1945, a French task force under command of General Leclerc landed at Saigon to participate in operations against the Japanese and vigorously reestablish France's claim. In Tonkin (the northern part of the country) the situation was confused. Reluctantly the Chinese gradually withdrew, but, profiting from the vacuum of power, the Viet Minh set up an independent Republic of Vietnam in Hanoi in September 1945. The French government, still smarting from the trauma of World War II, was in no mood to compromise, but it was forced to negotiate since its presence in the region remained weak. Contacts were made with the Viet Minh, and an unsatisfactory and fragile modus vivendi

Legionnaire, RMLE-EO (2nd REI), Indochina, 1946. Until c. 1950, the French army and the Legion were heavily dependent on British and U.S. supplies. The depicted legionnaire wears complete British battledress uniform and webbing equipment with the white-covered képi, and he is armed with a British rifle No4.

(agreement) was signed in July 1946. The talks were doomed from the start, and the political situation deteriorated swiftly and drastically. Tensions rose sharply, incidents multiplied, and in November 1946, grave troubles and fighting broke out in the port city of Haiphong with French properties looted and civilians murdered. The French counterattacked with all they had, including naval batteries, causing indiscriminate carnage to the civilians. The large-scale insurrection spread to Hanoi in December 1946. The Indochina War was beginning.

After fierce and savage combat the French succeeded in reconquering Hanoi and gained effective military control of the sur-

Legionnaire, 3rd REI, Indochina, 1948. The man wears a mixture of U.S. and British uniforms and equipment, and he is armed with a Sten submachine gun.

cities and along the lines of communication. Ho Chi Minh and Giap activated their organization throughout the Indochinese Peninsula. At first the Viet Minh made use of guerrilla tactics, but Ho Chi Minh's liberation movement began to get Communist Chinese military aid after the latter's victory in 1949, enabling the creation of a conventional army. Hitherto, the United States had taken a decidedly hostile position toward French attempts to reestablish their colony in Indochina, but soon the French colonial war served as one of the anticommunist front lines in the emerging Cold War. With the Korean War in progress in 1950, the United States, in its turn, provided substantial military aid to the French. A terrible war of attrition quickly escalated into a large conventional conflict.

In the course of this war, which was to last until 1954, the French troops, all of them regular volunteer and professional soldiers, including units of the Foreign Legion, were doggedly engaged in a war of "pacification" in which they had neither allies, the active sympathy of many among the French people nor the support of the Vietnamese population. Public opinion in France was indeed little interested in this difficult, complex, expensive and unpopular conflict in a very distant land. The successive and unstable governments of the Fourth Republic ordered the army to fight and win, but it furnished neither the military means nor the desperately needed firm political direction. Thwarted in its mission, confused, ill-supported and misunderstood,

rounding delta area (the flat land at the mouths of the Black/Day River, Red/Clear River and Song Cau River). This extremely violent episode left each side with a legacy of mistrust and hatred. Ho Chi Minh called for a revolutionary war, and he went underground, withdrawing his fighting forces to the jungles of northern Tonkin while holding control of several small towns. The French were strongest in the south, in the

the French army achieved a few victories, but suffered many setbacks until it was badly defeated at Dien Bien Phu in 1954.

Sergeant, 2nd REI, Indochina, c. 1950. The legionnaire wears a French colonial helmet, U.S. khaki shirt, British shorts, and pataugas *(canvas and rubber ankle boots). Equipment consists of British/U.S. webbing and a Sten submachine gun.*

Warfare in Indochina

Revolutionary guerrilla

Despite the apparent ease with which the French had reasserted their hold over the major centers of population in 1946 and 1947, they suffered under severe handicaps from the start. The key element in Maoist revolutionary warfare (defined by the Communist leader Mao Tse-tung) was the passive or active support enjoyed by the Viet Minh, which brought them a constant flow of intelligence, and this priceless advantage allowed them to orchestrate their subversive activity. The Viet Minh soon fought a vitiating series of guerrilla operations which would exhaust, and, in the end, defeat the French army by conventional warfare. Given the size of Vietnam, its varied geography, which includes both highlands covered with tropical jungles and lowlands consisting of vast plains with rice paddies and marshes, and given the importance of its population, the French could occupy and hold only the most important places (towns and communication lines), so a familiar pattern soon emerged. Communications and contacts were controlled by the French during the day, by the Viets at night. The French were lords of the town and the main *routes coloniales* (highways), the Viets of the hinterland, the isolated villages and the footpaths. Even in the southern province of Cochin China, where Ho Chi Minh's auxiliary Nguyen Binh entered the fray with his forces, the situation was not materially different. The French, limited by the ineffective size and insufficient mobility of their forces, were compelled to choose between alternatives: mopping up operations in Cochin China or major attacks in northern Tonkin. The latter alternative meant destroying the Viet Minh by luring it into battle or pacification of the vital strategic regions such as the Red River delta around Hanoi and Haiphong. With correct foresight the French chose to force the issue in Tonkin, and they assigned a high priority to guarding their security within the delta area and along the crucial highways to Hanoi. However, seven years of war were to see them meet defeat in both objectives.

Advancing in paddy field

Anti-guerrilla warfare

On the whole the French were powerless against the growing Viet Minh guerrilla activities. They responded to guerrilla warfare and terrorism by blind retaliation and acts of anti-terrorism based on collective responsibility. Large-scale and local mopping up operations were launched, suspects were taken hostage, roughly handled, imprisoned or shot and villages serving as bases for the Viets were burnt. Far from being a deterrent, retaliation, use of blind terror and indiscriminate destruction only increased hatred. Atrocities were committed by both sides in a dramatic and bloody spiral of violence in which the civilian population paid the highest price. The French army intelligence service manipulated and tried to use local rivalries, religious struggles, popular resentments, regional frustrations, individual and collective greed, and political opposition. To increase their existing strength the French raised additional local troops. Without scruple, they engaged their fellow countrymen against each other by raising native antiterrorist units, self-defense militias, guard and escort formations, auxiliary police forces and even special antiguerrilla commando units composed of former Viets who had turned coat. In strictly military terms the local formations' value was on the whole rather limited but the consequences were disastrous. They only reactivated ancient hatreds, which degenerated into civil war, religious conflict, blind retaliation, uncontrolled criminality and sterile battles over local issues.

On the whole, the French frontline soldiers had a high respect for the Viet Minh enemy, but the top leadership persisted for some years in considering them to be mere bandits. Even when the early guerrilla gangs from 1946 had become a well-equipped, well-armed and highly disciplined regular army in the early 1950s, the top leadership

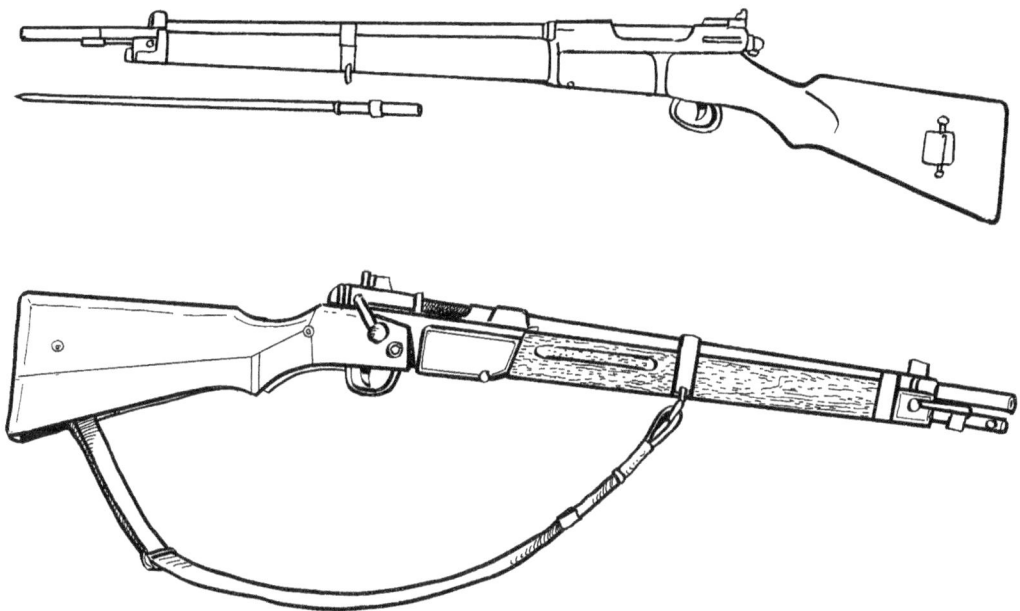

French MAS 36. **Top:** *The MAS rifle model 1936 with bayonet, developed by the Manufacture d'Armes de Saint Etienne in 1936, was intended to replace the older Lebel and Berthier designs. It was the last bolt-action rifle adopted by the French army. After World War II the MAS 36 became France's standard rifle. The spike bayonet was carried reversed in a tube under the barrel. Length was 1,020 mm (40.15 in.), weight unloaded was 3.78 kg (8 lbs. 5 oz.), and the magazine was a 5-round integral box. It was a tough, reliable and reasonably effective weapon, but it was considerably outclassed by contemporary rifles like the American M1 Garand.* **Bottom:** *The MAS 36 existed in a shortened version with light aluminum* crosse repliable *(CR folding butt), which was standard issue for paratroopers.*

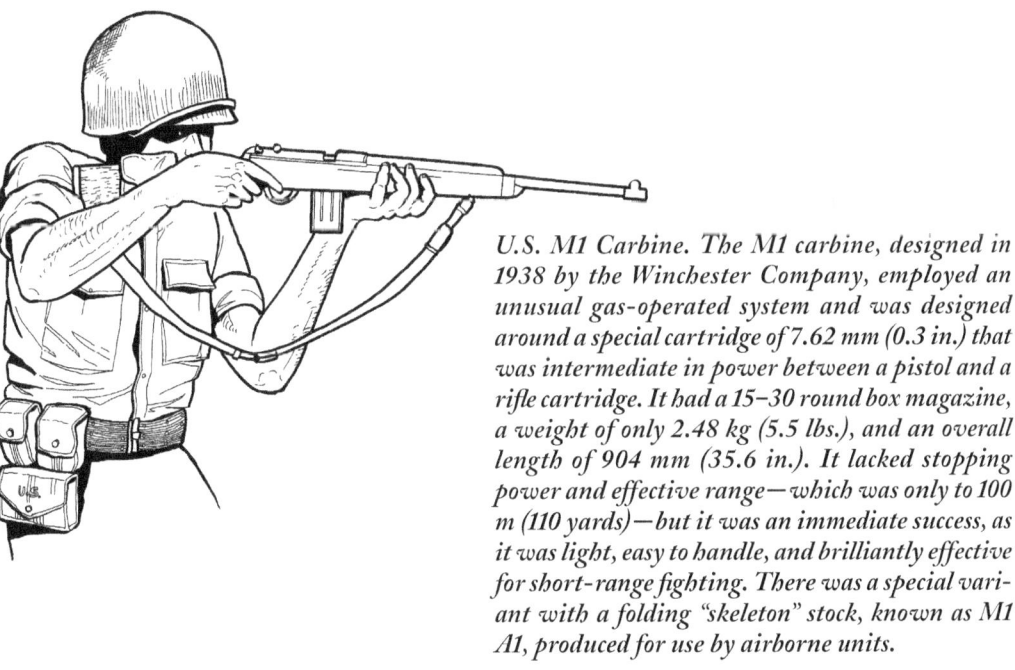

U.S. M1 Carbine. The M1 carbine, designed in 1938 by the Winchester Company, employed an unusual gas-operated system and was designed around a special cartridge of 7.62 mm (0.3 in.) that was intermediate in power between a pistol and a rifle cartridge. It had a 15–30 round box magazine, a weight of only 2.48 kg (5.5 lbs.), and an overall length of 904 mm (35.6 in.). It lacked stopping power and effective range—which was only to 100 m (110 yards)—but it was an immediate success, as it was light, easy to handle, and brilliantly effective for short-range fighting. There was a special variant with a folding "skeleton" stock, known as M1 A1, produced for use by airborne units.

and the French authorities still felt contempt for the Viets' military abilities.

The Foreign Legion in the Indochina War

French Expeditionary Corps

The strength of the CEFEO (French Expeditionary Corps in the Far East) varied between about 115,000 and 185,000 soldiers. Of this total only 50,000 were French nationals. Legally, it was forbidden to send conscripts to oversea theaters of operation. Draftees of the Service Militaire National served in France or for occupation duties in Germany. So the Expeditionary corps was exclusively formed of volunteers and professionals of the Colonial army. The staff officers were French, who led some 25,000 volunteers from North and West Africa and some 20,000 men provided by the Foreign Legion. The CEFEO, and the Legion as well, always suffered from a shortage of manpower, and this was aggravated by the system of tour of duty, which meant that neither top command, officers, NCOs nor ranks had time to grow into the job. From 1950 onward a serious effort was made to constitute a loyal and effective anti-communist Vietnamese National Army. This *jaunissement* ("yellowing") had variable results. At various times locally enlisted Vietnamese (between 50,000 and 90,000) served as lightly armed *supplétifs* (auxiliaries).

Tirailleur *Algérien, Indochina, c. 1949. French fatigues, bush hat and a mixture of U.S. and French webbing gave a typical appearance to colonial troops.*

Legion infantry and cavalry

After World War II the ranks of the French Foreign Legion were greatly increased by thousands of postwar refugees and displaced persons. There were large numbers of demobilized professional soldiers from about 50 nations. The Legion also discreetly recruited in German POWs camps, so the German element was strong, although the popular legend of Waffen SS and ex–Nazis veterans has been enormously exaggerated. By that time the French Foreign Legion totaled a unprecedented strength of 30,000. In 1950 the status of the Legion was improved, with creation by decree of the

Legion headgear in Indochina. 1: USMC camouflage hat; 2: Japanese cap; 3: Bush hat; 4: U.S. baseball-style cap

Groupement de la Légion étrangère (GALE), which made the Legion virtually an independent corps within the framework of the French army, giving it a somewhat similar status to that enjoyed by the U.S. Marine Corps. The Legion was now controlled by the Inspection technique de la Légion étrangère in Paris, an inspectorate headed by a general officer with a small staff. The men of the Legion had always kept very much aloof and to themselves, seldom mixing freely with soldiers of the French army. It was not until the Indochina War that this barrier broke down to some extent.

The first Foreign Legion unit to arrive in Indochina was the hastily formed Régiment de marche d'Extrême-Orient (RMEO, Far East Task Regiment). This early unit was made up of the first combat-ready formations of depot troops and new recruits in North Africa; it was shipped out to South Annam in February 1946. The RMOE was soon redesignated Deuxième Régiment étranger d'Infanterie (2nd REI Foreign Infantry Regiment). The 2nd REI was immediately engaged in hard fighting and suffered 300 dead in its first few months of operation.

The glorious World War II Treizième Demi-Brigade de la Légion étrangère (13th DBLE, Half-Brigade of the Foreign Legion), which had distinguished itself at Narvik and Bir Hakeim, arrived in March 1946; its separated battalions saw action for two years in the southern province of Cochin China.

In June 1946, the Régiment de marche de la Légion étrangère (RMLE, Task Regiment of the Foreign Legion) arrived; it was redesignated 3rd Regiment of the Foreign Legion (3rd REI). It was engaged in Annam, and later saw extensive combat in northern Tonkin.

The 4th REI was reconstituted in 1946; it remained in Morocco. The 1st REI remained in Algeria. Both 4th and 1st REI became depot regiments, intended for training and sending out recruits for the combat units to Indochina, and for receiving veterans returning from that theater of operation.

The 6th REI was briefly reconstituted in 1946 in Tunisia, and served mainly as a reserve force for Indochina. Recruits from the 6th REI and 4th REI were united to constitute the reborn 5th REI, which was sent to Indochina in 1947, and operated in northwest Tonkin on the Chinese and Laotian borders.

The Premier Régiment étranger de Cavalerie (1st REC, Cavalry Regiment), equipped with light-armored vehicles in early 1947 was divided into units for road security duties. From September 1951, part of the 1st REC became an autonomous group with a special mission: hunting the elusive Viet

Left: *Legionnaire infantryman, Indochina, c. 1951. The man wears a bush hat, the standard French green drab fatigues with four-pocket jacket, French* **pataugas**, *U.S. webbing and ammo pouches. His rifle is the French MAS 36.* **Right:** *Legion NCO, Indochina, c. 1950*

guerrilla groups through the swamps and flooded paddy fields of Cochin China. Equipped with so-called *Crabs* and *Alligators* (armored amphibious vehicles) provided by the U.S. Marines Corps, the 1st REC was organized in mobile groups which proved very effective in the field.

The second Régiment étranger de Cavalerie (2nd REC, Cavalry Regiment) remained in Morocco; it became a depot regiment, intended for training and sending out recruits for the fighting 1st REC in Indochina.

Badge of 13th DBLE (Demi Brigade de la Légion étrangère) in 1946.

Legion Paratroopers

The Indochina War saw the appearance of a new Legion soldier: the paratrooper. In spring 1948, it was decided to form a French Foreign Legion paratrooper force to enlarge the existing airborne troops in the Far East. Initially, however, the High Command had serious doubt concerning the ability of the Legion to form an elite paratrooper force. The Foreign Legion soldiers were unanimously recognized as a highly effective in-

Paratroop Badge

fantry force, but senior para officers believed the Legion lacked the agility and flexibility demanded by airborne operations. In the Legion itself many officers were apprehensive of a clash between the well-known exclusive self-consciousness of the paratrooper, and the Legion's own esprit de corps. Soon the bloody experience of the Indochina War made all misgivings vanish.

In April 1948 at Hanoi, the first operational Foreign Legion unit was formed with volunteers raised from the 2nd and 3rd Foreign Infantry Regiment and from the 13th Foreign Legion Half-Brigade. This first unit—called Compagnie parachutiste du Troisième Régiment étranger d'Infanterie (CP 3e. REI, Airborne Company of the 3rd REI)—was placed under the leadership of Lieutenant Jacques Morin, and for administrative and operational purposes attached to the 3rd Battalion of 1st Chasseurs parachutistes Régiment (III/1 RPC). Meanwhile, in French North Africa, the formation of new Legion Airborne troops proceeded. In May 1948 a training center was created at Khamisis near Sidi-Bel-Abbes, the Legion headquarters city in Algeria. In July 1948 the 1er Bataillon étranger parachutiste (1st BEP, Airborne Foreign Battalion) was formed, under command of Capitaine/Chef de Bataillon Pierre Segrétain. After intensive training the 1st BEP was sent to Indochina and arrived at Haiphong (North Vietnam) in November 1948. A second airborne battalion (2nd BEP)

Legion paratrooper, Indochina, c. 1949. The man wears a bush hat, a British camouflage smock, U.S. fatigue trousers and U.S. webbing, and is armed with a U.S. Thompson submachine gun.

French MAT 49 Submachine gun. The French-made MAT 49 developed by the Manufacture d'Armes de Tulle and adopted by the army in November 1949. The Pistolet-Mitrailleur de 9 mm modèle MAT 49 had a simple and orthodox blow-back design, and it was a very sturdy, solid and ingeniously designed weapon: when not in use the magazine it could be folded forward, and the wire stock could be telescoped into the receiver. It fired the 9 mm Parabellum cartridge held in a box magazine of either 32 rounds or 20 rounds. Cyclic rate of fire was 600 rpm and effective range was about 100 m. The MAT 49 was a reliable, excellent and popular weapon, but relatively heavy: weight (empty) was 3.50 kg (8 lbs.), which, however, helped subdue recoil. The MAT 49 became the standard French army submachine gun, universally used in Indochina and Algeria. It remained in service until 1979. The bottom illustration shows the MAT 49 in folded position.

was constituted at Sétif (Algeria) in October 1948, mainly with Legion volunteers from Morocco; it arrived at Saigon in February 1949. In November 1949 a third battalion was formed from volunteers from the 1st REI. This unit, remaining at Sétif, was a training and transit formation intended to provide replacements for both fighting BEPs in Indochina. The administrative staff, officers and NCOs of the three BEPs were mainly drawn from the French army airborne force. The soldiers came from the Legion infantry and cavalry, and many of those volunteers had already had parachute experience in other World War II armies.

French regular and Foreign Legion parachutist units played a central role in the Indochina War. Until 1954, they formed a mobile striking force which was rushed as needed from one end of the country to the other. They saw action and suffered heavy losses in numerous security operations, offensive and defensive battles and countless rescue actions.

Main Legion Battles in Indochina

Characteristic features of the war

Shortage of space naturally prevents more than the briefest note on the long and complex French Indochina war, characterized by constant ambushes, attacks on posts, hit-and-run raids, counteroffensives and mopping up operations of infiltrated regions. The Viet Minh waged typical Maoist guerrilla warfare. Their spies were everywhere, their armed groups were invisible among the mass of the population. These irregulars carried on an underground struggle behind the French lines. Living off the countryside, usually recruited from the local populace and merging with the population, they hid in dense forests, mountains and swamps, terrains they knew well. Their activities were both political and military. During the day they behaved like ordinary local peasants. At night they blew up roads and bridges, attacked isolated posts and sabotaged and interrupted communication lines by pulling down telegraph wires. They launched quick attacks, hit-and-run raids and skirmishes. They sniped at lone vehicles or ambushed and looted small convoys. They infiltrated the local peasants not only by using propaganda and persuasion, but also by using intimidation, terrorism and coercive bombing, and by torturing and murdering pro–French authorities, assaulting enemy individuals and liquidating collaborationists. The Viet guerrilla often delayed and disorganized supply lines, hindered the use of particular routes or even took control of more or less extended zones. Psychologically, Viet guerrilla warfare created a climate of insecurity, permanent stress, nervousness, hidden threat and lurking danger for the French occupiers and their local accomplices. To counter this, all important points, such as administrative offices, supply dumps, logistic depots, roads, railway lines, bridges and other key positions, had to be militarily guarded. The countryside was patrolled, jungles, marshes, rice paddies and bushes were combed and rail and road convoys were protected by armed escorts.

Worthy of mention is a Legion *train blindé* (armored train), code-named *La Rafale* (Burst), which was built by the legionaries themselves. The train was operated by units of the 2nd REI in the years 1948–1950. Intended to secure the region between Ninh Hoa, Phan Thiet and Na Trang in South Annam, the train included two armored locomotives, eight armored combat, five troop quarter cars, one headquarter car, one

*Vietnamese militiaman, c. 1951. Armed with a MAT 49 with magazine pouches, this auxiliary wears his civilian clothes including a black peasant blouse (*cao ao*), trousers (*cai quan*), and sandals.*

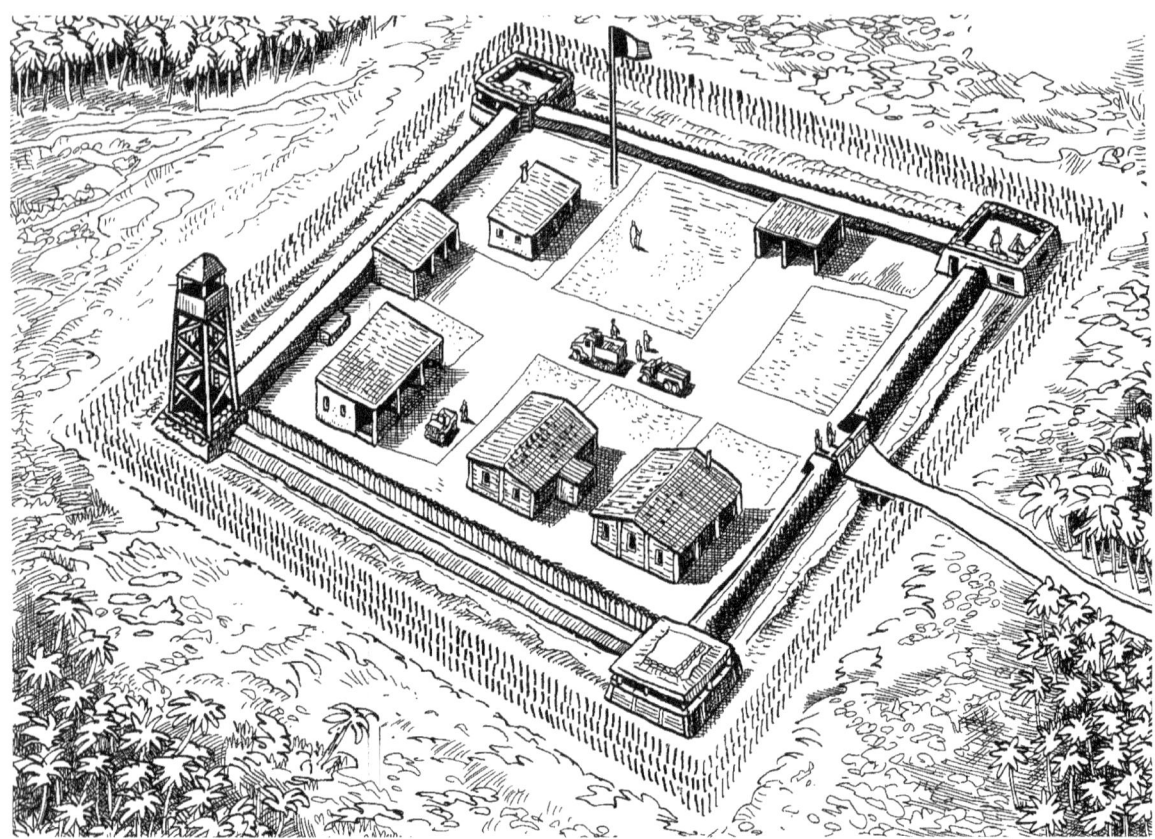

A "post" in Indochina, c. 1947. With earth and timber walls, flimsy wooden or local brick buildings, sandbag blockhouses with marginal overhead protection, inadequate barbed wire (often supplemented by sharpened bamboo), the posts were more suitable to 19th-century police duty than to 20th-century modern warfare.

infirmary car, one kitchen car, and two cars loaded with rail repair material. The *Rafale*, manned with about 100 officers, NCOs and legionaries under the leadership of Captain Raphanaud, was armed with eight twin Reibel machine guns, one 40 mm Bofort gun mounted in turret, one 20 mm gun, one 81 mortar and one 60 mortar. The train was several times ambushed, notably in April and July 1949, but it was never destroyed; its garrison launched counterattacks, rescued encircled posts, and intercepted Viet troops in the jungle along the track almost until the end of the war.

The available troops had thus to be split up into hundreds of small company-sized garrisons, entrenched in small fortified "posts." These posts generally consisted of a rectangular earthwork hemmed with sharpened bamboo or barbed wire, and defended by bunkers armed with machine guns at the corners; the middle of the post was occupied by primitive hutments and a watchtower. The posts were comparable to isolated islands surrounded by waters infested by sharks. After dark the Viets controlled the whole country except in the large cities. The post garrison's influence rarely extended beyond rifle-range in daylight and beyond the barbed wire of their post at night. The unsafe areas were so vast and the communication lines so extended that "pacification" often proved an impossible task.

Gradually the Viet Minh guerrilla groups grew stronger, better armed, and more confident. Ambushes and raids were constant,

M29C Weasel. The U.S. Weasel, known in the French army as the **Crabe**, *was an amphibious tracked light carrier. Length was 5 m and weight was 5 tons. Its feather tread pressure of 150 gram/square cm (2 lbs./sq. in.) meant that it was the ideal vehicle for use in the muddy ground encountered in the lowlands, rice paddies and marshes of Indochina. The vehicle could carry six men, including the driver, and various arms; either a 12.7 or a 7.62 machine gun, sometimes a recoilless 75 mm SR gun. The amphibious armored LVT was also used by the Legion REC under the name Alligator.*

and became more and more deadly for the isolated garrisons. Remote areas became unsafe for all but convoys with strong escort. Consequently the French reacted with a series of violent antiguerrilla countermeasures. Intelligence was gathered from the population using guile, blackmail, threat and intimidation. Suspects were beaten and tortured. Agents and paid informers tried to infiltrate the Viet units. Despite resorting to harsh methods, the French were always two jumps behind the elusive Viet guerrillas. Patrols and "search-and-destroy" raids were launched against concentrations of guerrilla fighters. Columns invested villages, searching for weapons and propaganda materials. Anyone caught red-handed was brutaly interrogated and then shot. Large mopping up operations were also launched with important military means including local static units reinforced with navy, colonial infantry, air force, armored vehicles, artillery and mobile strike forces of which the best were made up of Foreign Legion BEP and battalions of *chasseurs-parachutistes* (BCP paratroopers). These operations aimed at anticipating the Viet Minh manoeuvres, searching and destroying supply dumps and pursuing, capturing or destroying the groups of guerrilla fighters. But armored and motorized forces, as well as artillery, were limited to the roads and mobile reserves were never sufficiently numerous to fully exploit local successes. Paratrooper forces were effectively engaged as quick reaction troops, but too often they were sent in to retrieve losing battles, and inevitably they suffered tremendous losses. The use of inappropriate, conventional warfare methods against an elusive enemy gave poor results; brutalities against the civil population became routine and only hardened hostility toward the French, thus increasing the Viet Minh's base of support. Large-scale military offensive operations often resulted only in troops returning to their base with an empty bag, tired, thirsty and thoroughly frustrated. Decisive victory was never achieved. In spite of considerable local successes the overall picture of "pacification" was totally discouraging.

Operations in Tonkin, 1947–1949

The establishment of the Communist Chinese People's Republic on the northern border of Indochina had immense repercussions on the strategy of the war. Mao Tse-tung's arrival in power in October 1949 created for the French forces an undisguised military threat that overturned all predictions and expectations for a rational conduct of the war. Communist China became a potent supply base and ideological citadel that the Communist Viet Minh could draw on inexhaustibly. The French did not yield the opening of the Chinese frontier to the Viet Minh without a struggle, but the war proved costly, chastening, and in the end disastrous.

The terrain of Tonkin perfectly suited guerrilla operations, and geography gave the Viets nearly always the initiative. If the French firmly held the huge southern delta around Hanoi, the virtually unexplored thinly populated northern Upper Tonkin (or High Region, the hinterland composed of thickly jungled mountains traversed by only a few narrow, winding and vulnerable *routes coloniales* (RC, colonial roads) was virtually held by the Viet Minh. During the period between 1946 and 1949, the Viet Minh fought a limited guerrilla war, inflicting a steady drain on French manpower while building up their own conventional forces. In Upper Tonkin, the French controlled only the immediate vicinity of their main towns and roads, which were reinforced by *postes kilométriques* (PK, fortified posts). At night there was no such thing as a "safe road" in the High Region.

A typical "post" was generally placed on a hilltop dominating the road; the forest around it was cleared to give a field of fire; it was held by a garrison of between 20 to 120 men; it was composed of a variably large perimeter with a few permanent hutments, supply stores, and garages for the vehicles; the post was enclosed by a low earth wall, combat emplacements and trenches reinforced with sandbags, dugouts and shelters covered with earth, and concrete armed bunkers at the corners; armament consisted of machine guns and mortars, sometimes light artillery pieces. Around the position, obstacles included a ditch, barbed wire, and, when this was not available, sharpened bamboo. Some small posts were only concrete bunkers. All of them were totally dependent on roads for supply. Some posts were so isolated that ammunition and supplies had to be assured by parachute drops. The PKs which guarded the roads and river highways were extremely vulnerable. They were constantly watched by Viet Minh spies who gathered valuable intelligence. These informants could be "innocent" traders or workers from a neighboring village who offered their service to the garrison; occasionally they were local women who became the mistresses of the soldiers; or they were *ralliés*, former Viets who pretended to have turned coat. A tragic, subtle, complex and confusing cat-and-mouse game in and around the post was played out; survival or horrible death often depended on psychological talent detecting in time who was a

Patrol in the jungle

Kilometer post on the RC4

traitor and who could be trusted. After careful planning and an in-depth rehearsal, which could last for months, the French position was attacked by suicidal assaulting waves of Viet soldiers. Attacks that combined professional excellence with suicidal motivation often left the defenders unnerved. Describing all operations would be pointless but the few examples that follow might illustrate the way the Legion waged the war.

Phu Tong Hoa

Occasionally some garrisons managed to hold out. In July 1948, the small post of Phu Tong Hoa, held by a single company (104 legionaries) of the 3rd REI (Régiment étranger d'Infanterie), was attacked at night by no less than three Viet Minh battalions. After a massive mortar bombardment, the post was assaulted by human waves. The garrison repulsed them at the cost of 23 dead and 48 wounded. When the relief column came the next day they were greeted by a perfectly aligned honor guard of survivors all of them more or less wounded, but all of them impeccably clean, fresh shaven, and in their faultless parade dress amidst the ruins of the post-typical Foreign Legion glamour.

But often the post was overwhelmed, the soldiers were massacred, wounded dispatched, weapons and supplies captured and the smoking ruins quickly abandoned by the Viets, who withdrew to their invisible bases in the jungle.

Loung Phai Pass

The Tonkin war was characterized throughout by the frequent effort of the French to try to fight their way to the rescue of a besieged position, as an attacked garrison could always call for help by radio.

Above: *Emblem 1st BEP (Batallion étranger parachutiste)*. Right: *Badge 4th Régiment étranger d'Infanterie*.

The Viets adopted an opposite attitude: units which got into difficulties were not reinforced, but ruthlessly abandoned. Giap's tactical plans always took account of a rescue party. A motorised relief column could only approach along a single predictable road, easily blocked by the Viets. The rescue force was often ambushed and destroyed in its turn, and if it did get through to the besieged post, it was often too late to do anything but extinguish fires and bury the dead. Soon the post was rebuilt and another lonely garrison was left isolated in the misty mountains, until the next attack. In mid–October 1949, a Spahi (North African) motorised unit was ambushed near the Loung Phai Pass on the Route Coloniale No. 4 (RC4 Colonial Road), and the Loung Phai post was attacked. Rapidly Operation Thérèse was launched; the 1st BEP (1st Foreign Airborne Battalion), after a "blind" jump over an appalling DZ (Dropping Zone) among forested cliffs, found the burnt-out vehicles and the dead of the Spahi columns. The paratroopers were just in time to rescue the Legion garrison of Loung Phai Pass post who had desperately resisted.

Dong Khe

The post of Dong Khe—again on the RC4—was held in May 1950 by two companies of North African *tirailleurs* (riflemen). They were attacked and wiped out, and the post was retaken by two battalions of paratroopers. A new garrison—composed of the 8th *Tabor* (Moroccan Infantry)—was posted there until September 1950 when the 5th and 6th Companies of the 3rd Foreign Infantry Regiment took over. On September 16, the two companies were attacked by six Viet Minh battalions supported by artillery. After a devastating shelling, the post saw fierce fighting, a portion of it was taken by the Viets, trenches and bastions changing hands as furious close-range counterattacks alternated. The garrison called for help by radio, and the next day, while the legionaries still held out, suffering severe casualties, the 1st BEP (1st Foreign Airborne

Battalion) was dropped nearby. Anticipating that move, General Giap had deployed numerous troops in a security cordon around Dong Khe, and the Foreign Legion paratroopers encountered strong resistance, which prevented them from relieving the garrison. Dong Khe finally fell the next night, costing the French Foreign Legion 85 dead and 140 wounded and captured, many of whom died later in the Viet Minh prisoner-of-war camps. Only a handful of exhausted survivors managed to make it to the French lines. Dong Khe was not an isolated incident. The attack marked the start of a major Viet offensive on Colonial Road No 4.

Battle of Colonial Road No. 4 (1950)

In autumn 1950, General Giap—owing to massive Chinese support—had succeeded in creating well-equipped, well-armed, trained and disciplined regular divisions. With training camps, supply dumps and rest areas safe in the middle of the mountainous jungle border, and with a constant and substantial flow of modern materiel provided by his Communist neighbor, Giap was finally able to launch an ambitious offensive. The always inadequate French air force was not able to detect his preparation as the Viets were masters of concealed movement and camouflage; large columns of supply coolies with bicycles moved, unnoticed, enormous tonnage of ammunition, supply, and even heavy artillery while combat troops were deployed around the RC4. The Viet Minh commander-in-chief felt confident enough to unveil the potential of his regular force, and strong enough to drive the French army from Upper Tonkin. The so-called Battle of Route Coloniale No. 4 was begun.

Colonial Road No. 4 (RC4) ran along the mountainous border with China, connecting Cao Bang in the north to Lang Son via Dong Khe, the Luong Phai Pass, That Khe,

Legion Vietnamese Paratrooper, c. 1952. The Vietnamese volunteer wears a U.S. steel helmet, a USMC camouflage tunic, a French Bergam sac à dos (rucksack) mixed with U.S. webbing and equipment. His weapon is the MAS 36 rifle CR with folding butt.

Ananas Pass, Na Cham, and Dong Dang. The distance between Lang Son and Cao Bang is about 140 kilometers. Cao Bang and the small towns along the RC4 had been reoccupied by the French in mid–1947. The small towns linked by the RC4 were supposed to function as "anchors" and hedgehogs in the Viet-controlled High Region territory. Numerous fortified posts along the road were added, and the whole RC4 system was intended to constitute an interdiction line, firmly closing the frontier between northern Vietnam and southern China. Apparently the French were determined to permanently hold Cao Bang. When they captured the town it was in ruins. In the period 1947–1949, the town was completely rebuilt with everything a civilian community and a military garrison needed, including stone houses, shops, marketplaces, military quarters, and administrative offices as well as everything needed for leisure-time activities, including bars, nightclubs, restaurants, gambling halls, brothels and opium *fumeries* (dens).

The RC4, its strongholds, PKs and fortified posts were actually no "Maginot Line" but rather a poorly defensible and vulnerable road. The RC4 had been frequently ambushed in the period 1947–1949. The worst stretch was the last 70 kilometers between That Khe and Cao Bang. By August 1950 the pressure on supply convoys was so strong—disastrous ambushes occurred once or twice weekly—that the French High Command reluctantly decided to evacuate increasingly threatened Cao Bang.

The garrison of Cao Bang, placed under the command of Colonel Charton, totaling about 1,600 men, included the 3rd Battalion of the 3rd Legion Infantry Regiment (III/3 REI, headed by Commandant Forget), a Moroccan *tabor*, and a group of local Vietnamese *supplétifs*. The order of evacuation for Cao Bang, planned by General Revers from his Hanoi headquarters, specified that Charton was to destroy all supplies and sabotage his heavy materiel (artillery, vehicles, etc.), and—armed only with light weapons, food and water—to rapidly proceed by foot in a southerly direction to That Khe (on the RC4, 70 km away) where a relief force would wait for them. This partly motorised column—called *Groupement Bayard*—comprised two Moroccan *tabors* (battalions of Moroccan *tirailleurs*), and several other units, headed by an artillery officer, Commandant Lepage. The task force "Bayard" was reinforced by the 1st BEP (1st Foreign Airborne Battalion) which had jumped at That Khe on September 17, 1950. Lepage's force left Lang Son in the south, drove north to That Khe, and from there was to meet Charton's evacuees at Dong Khe. Between and around both French columns, in the thickly jungled mountains, General Giap had deployed Division 308, Brigade 209, 11 infantry battalions, and several artillery battalions, most of them freshly arrived from training camps in southern China.

The well-planned evacuation of Cao Bang, which began on October 1, 1950, went wrong from the start and quickly turned into a tragic disaster. First of all, Charton disregarded General Revers's order. He refused to abandon the panicked civilian population of Cao Bang and loaded them and their goods into the available vehicles. So instead of a combat-ready, light, mobile infantry task formation, Colonel Charton's column constituted a slow, conspicuous, heavy convoy encumbered by crowds of civilians. Regularly harassed by advance and reconnaissance Viet groups who destroyed the bridges and mined the road, Charton's cumbersome column proceeded much more slowly than planned. The day after departure the column was totally blocked and trapped. The vehicles, heavy equipment and civilian refugees were abandoned on the RC4. The disorganized and already demoralized military column continued by foot through the very difficult forested mountains, trying to reach Lepage at Dong Khe. Charton's group was soon hunted by the Viets in the jungle.

Meanwhile the progression of Lepage's *Groupement Bayard* was equally slow. On October 2 and 3, 1950, at hill 615 south of Dong Khe, the relief force was blocked, surrounded and heavily attacked. On October 4, the increasingly disorganized *Groupement Bayard* had to abandon its vehicles and artillery and move by foot to Na Pa where it lightly entrenched while waiting to meet the remnants of Charton's men. By that time Giap rushed his forces in to exploit the

Legion paratrooper headgear. **Left:** *Green Beret, 1st BEP.* **Right:** *U.S. M1C helmet with modified cloth chin harness.*

dislocation of the French columns. Unfortunately for the French, heavy rain and mist prevented support from their tactical air force based at Hanoi. Until October 6 the Bayard force fought their way though the hills over bad jungle paths at an agonizingly slow pace, carrying on their backs the increasing number of wounded. Frequently attacked, seriously short of food, water and ammunition, they moved to hill 765. On October 7 the dislocated and weakened French formation was surrounded and subjected to deadly Viet machine-gun and mortar fire in a wide natural chalk cliff amphitheater near the village of Coc Xa. The 1st Legion Airborne Battalion (1st BEP) was ordered to break the encirclement, which it did but at very high cost. By that time the Bayard column was broken up, dislocated, and many men were separated from their units, killed or taken prisoner. The 1st BEP, after the bloody combat of Coc Xa, was seriously depleted: It was reduced to 130 Legion paratroopers. In the evening of October 7, the Bayard survivors, at last, met with Charton's equally mauled force at hill 477. Under constant Viet pressure, it was hastily decided to disperse the remaining force in platoon-sized parties, each led by an officer or an NCO. The mission now was to withdraw, in a "March or Die" attempt to reach and reassemble at That Khe. The wounded were abandoned with volunteer medics, many of whom died later in captivity. On October 8, the High Command sent in a rescue force to the crumbling RC4. The 3rd BCCP (3rd Battalion of Colonial Paratroopers) and a replacement company of Legion paratroopers newly arrived from depot in Algeria were dropped at That Khe. They picked up stragglers, including 29 legionaries from the 1st BEP with the 2nd Company commander, Captain Jeanpierre; these were the only survivors of the BEP that only 10 days before counted 500 men.

In spite of the last-minute reinforcement, the situation soon deteriorated. On October 10, the totally confused High Command hastily ordered the evacuation of That Khe, while many stragglers from both the Lepage and Charton groups were still trying desperately to reach it through the enemy-infested

Paratroop badge worn on beret

jungle. The abandonment of That Khe announced the general retreat—in great disorder—down Colonial Road No. 4. By October 18, the confused withdrawal on Route 4 led to total disaster. This provoked defeatism and despair with, according to eyewitnesses, pitiable and deplorable scenes of panic comparable to those seen in France in June 1940. The posts and towns along the RC4—notably the vital stronghold of Lang Son—were hastily evacuated. Important centers far from direct threat such as Lao Kay and Hoa Binh were abandoned at the same time.

The Viet Minh's victory was total, and it astonished those who had underestimated its strength. General Giap had conquered large territories and important towns in northern Tonkin. The elimination of the threatening hedgehogs of Cao Bang and Lang Son secured complete access to the frontier with the Chinese allies. The Viet Minh forces had inflicted about 6,500 casualties, including some 4,800 dead and missing. They had captured about 1,300 tons of supplies and ammunition, including many small arms, crew-served weapons and artillery, enough to equip a complete division. The French army and the Foreign Legion were shocked by the evidence of the Viet Minh's strength and skills. The time of guerrilla warfare was over. Henceforth the Indochina "pacification" became a conventional war between two opposing regular armies.

De Lattre's Pacification

At the critical moment of the defeat on the RC4, General (posthumously Marshal) De Lattre de Tassigny was rushed to Indochina with the dual function of high commissioner and army commander-in-chief. Jean-Marie Gabriel De Lattre de Tassigny (1889–1952) was one of the genuinely prestigious figures of recent French military history. He had fought the Germans in 1940, and had remained in the Vichy French "Armistice" army. In 1942 he was taken prisoner for his opposition to the German occupation of the southern "Free Zone," escaped from a POW camp, and managed to join de Gaulle in London. He had distinguished himself during the Allied landing at Saint-Tropez in August 1944 at the head of the First Free French Army with which he had liberated Marseilles, Lyon, and Colmar before invading the Reich, and signing the capitulation of Germany on France's behalf on May 8, 1945. Appointed army general inspector in late 1945 he became chief of the French ground forces in 1948. De Lattre de Tassigny was popularly known as *le Roi Jean* ("King John") for his elegant manners and his aristocratic taste for luxury and pomp. Having both political authority and military power, he gave a new impulse to the Indochina War. In the period 1951–1952, De Lattre de Tassigny, whose tireless activity and skill as well as personal charm were legendary, endowed the reeling French army with an esprit de corps and sense of mission. "King John" became a traveling missionary for the cause of the Indochina War. His journeys took him to New York, London and Rome, where he succeeded in persuading the United Nations and France's Western allies that the situation in Indochina had worldwide implications. At this time of great intensification of the Korean War, American ears were alert to the anticommunist arguments that De Lattre de Tassigny put forward. U.S. aid and massive delivery of war material, particularly airplanes, to the Franco-Vietnamese armies dated from this time. De Lattre's superior initiatives—supported by U.S. war material—partially reestablished the military balance and almost succeeded in pacifying northern Vietnam. While leading his campaigns prudently, he placed great stress on the integration of air warfare in the total operation. He made the first serious attempts toward developing a loyal Vietnamese auxiliary force, the so-called *jaunissement* ("yellowing," that is, the creation of a Vietnamese anticommunist force).

De Lattre took personal command, assembled reinforcements, unleashed constant air attacks ordered the construction of a defensive belt of fortifications to defend the delta around Hanoi. Cooperating with local Catholic militias, it seemed that the French had retaken the initiative. In early 1951 De Lattre had, in a series of well-planned and well-executed offensives, broken the back of the first general attack the Viet Minh had seen fit to mount, pushing the enemy back from vital territory and assuring for the time being the protection of the delta. Overwhelmed by French firepower and De Lattre's first-class leadership, General Giap and his commanders were taught a grim lesson: They could not defeat the French in the open, at least not yet. For a while, the Viet Minh were obliged to return to guerrilla tactics, and the war became a stalemate. Observers felt that with the increase in U.S. military aid and the superior fighting techniques of the French and allied Vietnamese forces, Ho Chi Minh had henceforth lost all chance of winning a major military decision and that only a political settlement could take place. Unfortunately De Lattre de Tassigny's job had only begun when he became seriously ill at the end of 1951. He was repatriated to France and died on January 11, 1952. He was replaced as commander-in-chief by General Raoul Salan who continued offensive efforts.

In spite of encouraging successes (e.g., Na San in October 1952 and Phu Doan in November), the French position in Indochina was far from being stabilized. In fact it could be described as precarious. The whole of Upper Tonkin on the border with China, the coasts of Annam, and major enclaves in all parts of the country were held by the Viet Minh. Land communication links between Tonkin, Annam and Cochin China were extremely unreliable. Moreover, the neighboring states of Laos and Cambodia had been significantly infiltrated by the Communists. In early 1953, a considerable part of the French Expeditionary Force was diverted from its

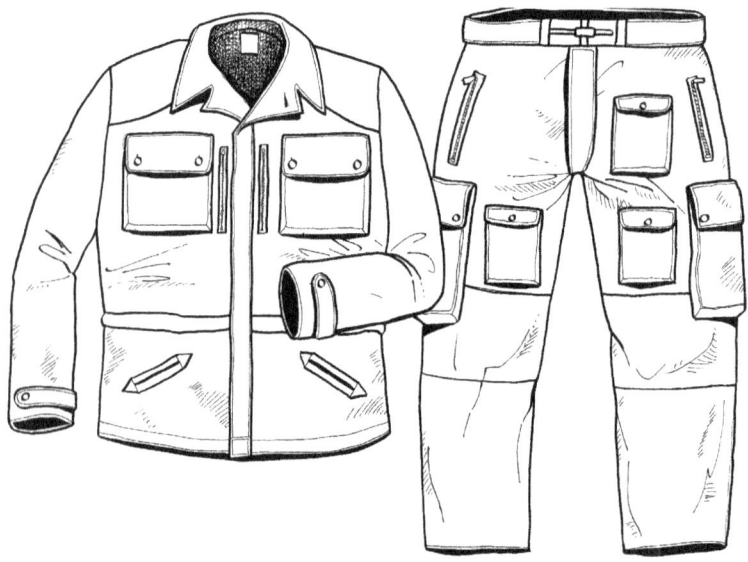

Paratrooper uniform type EO (c. 1950). The camouflaged combat suit type EO 47/52 reached units in late 1953.

primary area of action and would henceforth have to guard against the threat to Laos, which, as the only Indochinese country favorable to the political solution embodied in the establishment of the newly created French Union, merited protection. The diversion of troops permitted the rapid infiltration of the delta area by small Viet groups, who proceeded to gain the support of the local population.

In June 1953 General Salan was replaced as commander-in-chief by General Navarre. The French continued to launch sweeps to catch and destroy Viet forces where their firepower and training would prevail, but operations mostly proved ineffective, as the Viets fought only when it was to their advantage. This stalemate held as long as the Korean War continued; but when that conflict ended in 1953, the Chinese were able to provide increasing military support to Giap.

Dien Bien Phu

Strategic and political background

To forestall a worsening situation, the French baited a trap for the Viet Minh. They challenged Ho Chi Minh and Vo Nguyen Giap's armies into the open by throwing a force into Dien Bien Phu, across their communication and supply lines from China to northern Laos. The aim was to pull the Viet Minh in strength into an open battle where superior French firepower would tell, and French elite paratroopers could deal them a devastating blow. In November 1952, such an operation had been a success at Na San in the Thai Highlands, and had bred among the French High Command a dangerous optimism about operations based on these advanced air-supplied bases. This high-risk strategy was also instituted with a political purpose in mind. The "Big Four" foreign ministers had met in Berlin and agreed to promote a Geneva conference in April which would attempt to tidy up some of the loose ends left by the Korean War and deal incidentally with Indochina. The French

Legion paratrooper Indochina 1954. The man wears the jump/combat suit model 1947/53. He is armed with a U.S. M1A1 carbine with "skeleton" folding stock.

position at Geneva called for "bargaining from strength." Luring Giap into an eventual and, hopefully, decisive battle was part of this plan. A military victory at Dien Bien Phu would create political conditions favorable to maintaining a hard line at the negotiating table.

The campaign in Laos and the battle of Dien Bien Phu amply demonstrated the recovery of the Viet Minh after De Lattre and Salan's short and partial successes. By early 1953 Giap had had time to forge a manoeuvrable and well-balanced regular army, led by officers of talent and high morale, accustomed to exacting marches and showing great logistical ingenuity. Dien Bien Phu also showed that the French military top leadership had totally underestimated the sophistication, dedication and capabilities of their opponents.

The fortress

There is little point in attempting a complete history of the complex battle of Dien Bien Phu, and the following section will only briefly present the role played by the Legion.

Preparations started in November 1953 with French parachute troops dropped by, including the 1st BEP (1st Legion Parachutist Battalion), to secure the basin of Dien Bien Phu populated by small villages of Meos tribesmen in the Thai Highlands. At this place, the valley of the Nam Youm River is about two and a half miles wide and nine and a half miles long. In this large "bowl," or enclave, fringed by wooded hills which overlook it on all sides, Dien Bien Phu constitutes a crossroads hub connecting Laos, Thailand, Burma and China. As Dien Bien Phu was no less than 280 kilometers northwest of Hanoi, and as it lay in hostile territory infested with Viet guerrillas, it could be supplied only by air, so an ancient airstrip built in 1920 was repaired and extended to enable troops and supplies to be flown in. Nothing and no one could get either in or out, except by air; Dien Bien Phu was virtually an "island." In the following weeks the force was built up to include some 12 battalions totaling over 14,000 men, including legionnaires, paratroopers, North African *tirailleurs* and local Vietnamese troops, all placed under the command of General Christian de la Croix de Castries (1902–1991). Small hills in the basin were lightly fortified and developed into a huge sprawling entrenched camp. The fortress consisted of a central position with headquarters, underground shelters and stores, field hospital, airstrip and dispersals for U.S.-made Bearcat bomber-fighter aircraft, emplacements for 28 heavy guns, and 12 U.S. medium Chaffee tanks. Striking air force, artillery and mobile armor were considered sufficient to silent all opposition. Around this core, *centres de résistance* (CR, hedgehog-type strongholds incongruously given girls' names) were established. The CRs were divided into *points d'appui* (PA, support points composed of trenches, machine-gun and mortar posts), arranged for all-round defense, placed to cover one another, and hemmed in with barbed wire and sharp-pointed bamboo poles. The base was intended to serve as an anchor for offensive raids and sorties by French-led commando groups into the Laotian border country.

By December 1953 four Legion battalions were flown in, and another arrived in January 1954. One battalion of the 3rd REI (3rd Foreign Infantry Regiment) was deployed in a position detached to the south, known as Isabelle. One battalion of the 13th DBLE (Half-Brigade of the Foreign Legion) held a position to the southwest of Dien Bien Phu known as Claudine, and another battalion of the same regiment held a stronghold to the northeast of the perimeter known as Béatrice. One battalion of the 2nd REI defended Huguette in the northwestern part of the camp. A battalion of the 3rd REI with its heavy mortar company arrived later and was deployed in a

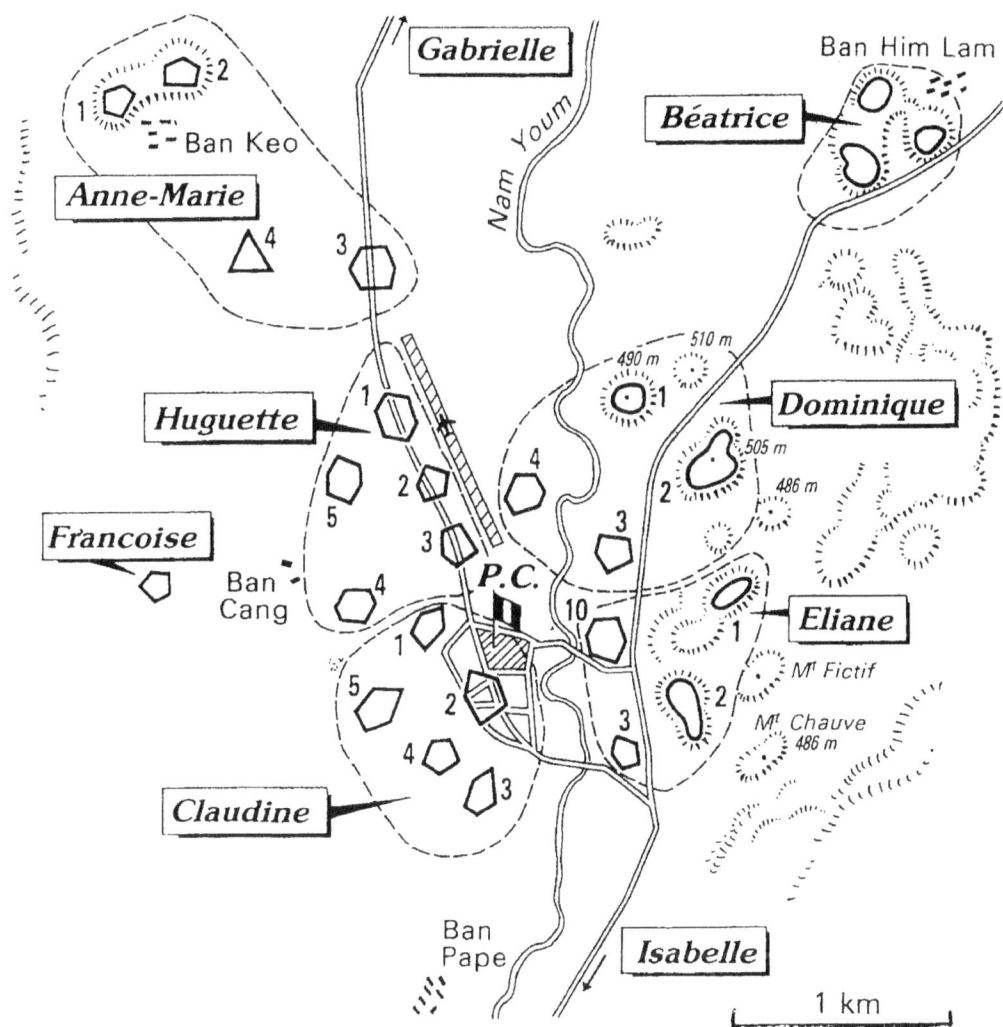

Map of the entrenched camp of Dien Bien Phu. The northeastern advanced position of Béatrice was defended by the 3rd Battalion of the Legion 13th DBLE. The 3rd Battalion of the 3rd REI was posted at position Isabelle, located 4 kilometers south of the main core. The 1st Battalion of the 13th DBLE and the parachute 1st BEP were posted at Claudine, south and west of the P.C. (Command Post). The 1st Battalion of the 2nd REI defended the western position Huguette flanking the airstrip.

position on the western perimeter known as Eliane. As for the paratroopers of the 1st BEP, they were held in mobile strike reserve.

It all seemed impressive but what the French High Command in Hanoi did not know was that Giap had accepted the provocative challenge and made massive preparations. The chief of the Viet Minh army had gathered important forces including four well-trained infantry divisions totaling about 50,000 men equipped and armed by the Chinese. These troops converged in secret on Dien Bien Phu and took up positions in the surrounding wooded hills where they were under cover from the air. At the same time, about 200 support artillery pieces and a huge supply of ammunition were carried by 75,000 coolies and installed in well-camouflaged positions in the mountains dominating the French-held hills. The Viet Minh had neither a tank force nor aviation but they had accumulated a massive and powerful antiaircraft artillery.

At first the French launched reconnaissance patrols around their base, but it soon appeared that these skirmishes were extremely costly. In early December 1953 the Legion's 1st BEP had already lost 52 paratroopers in sorties north of the valley. In fact it became clear by January 1954, that they were totally encircled. The foolishness of placing so many troops in such a position was obvious, but it was now the High Command's view that the camp would serve as the anvil on which the French garrison would smash Giap's army. In fact, what the French had flamboyantly built to serve as a secure offensive base for a test of strength had become a trap. The expected quick battle of movement became a lengthy and bloody siege.

The siege

On March 13, 1954, the first serious Viet attack was launched. A heavy artillery barrage opened, which surprised the French by its strength and accuracy. The Viet guns rapidly exposed the inadequacy of the light fortifications. Simple trenches, flimsy bunkers, wooden dugouts, open gun-pits and sandbag breastworks could not withstand the enemy's heavy 105 mm projectiles. The French battery proved hopelessly unable to silence the Viet artillery, and the officer in charge, Colonel Piroth, committed suicide the next day. Air force strikes on the Viet artillery positions in the hills with napalm bombs and saturation bombing were unsuccessful. The stronghold Béatrice, attacked by a mass infantry assault pressed forward regardless of casualties, was conquered within two days and the defenders, the 3rd battalion of the 13th DBLE, were almost wiped out with 326 dead, missing and wounded. Similar tactics and methods were tried at the same time against Gabrielle and Isabelle but both held fast. After these first massive attacks, which had dented the French defenses, the Viet Minh resorted to sapping, while their artillery kept on pounding at the defenders. Rapidly the military position worsened. The hedgehog Gabrielle, much too isolated by the loss

Legion paratrooper, Dien Bien Phu, 1954. The 1st BEP parachutist wears a U.S. steel helmet, the U.S. 43 pattern field combat tunic and British trousers. The weapon is a U.S. M1 carbine.

Shaffee tank. The U.S.-made M24 medium tank Shaffee had a crew of five, a range of 280 km (174 miles), and a maximum speed of 42 km/h (25 mph). It was armed with one 75 mm gun, two .3 mm machine guns, and one .5 inch AA machine gun.

of Béatrice, was evacuated on March 15 after fierce fighting. A few days later, Anne-Marie, held by disheartened Thai partisans, was abandoned too. Costly counterattacks launched by paratrooper reserves failed to recapture them. Fierce fighting took place on the position Eliane and parts of the stronghold changed hands as many as six times. Because of Viet flak installed ever closer to the fortress, many French aircraft were destroyed, the remainder left for safety, and the defenders were penned inside the camp. The bravery and sacrifice of the besieged failed to prevent the tightening of the circle and the successive capture of several strongholds. By March 27, the airstrip—the umbilical cord with Hanoi—was under constant fire and unusable. This meant that the shrinking perimeter of Dien Bien Phu was completely isolated: henceforth, casualties could no longer be evacuated and all supplies and reinforcements had to be airdropped, usually at night by aircraft running the gauntlet of heavy AA fire. In spite of enemy Flak fire that precluded accuracy, many men volunteered to come to the rescue of their trapped comrades, and to die with them right up to the eve of the final collapse. For example, the 2nd BEP and untrained volunteers from the 3rd and 5th REI jumped under enemy fire into the besieged camp in early April. Constant enemy artillery fire and massive infantry assaults slowly but surely reduced the number of French positions. Savage attacks fell on the defenders of the eastern positions code-named Eliane and Dominique, and on Huguette in the northwest. Furious counterattacks by reserve units and the few remaining tanks were whittled down until their strength was inadequate to achieve any lasting success at any point. The courage of the defenders and their officers was prodigious but their suffering was appalling. In addition, their miserable situation was worsened by the heavy spring monsoon rains which transformed Dien Bien Phu into a gigantic and filthy mud pool. Because of the Viet anti-aircraft fire and rainy weather, it became difficult, soon impossible, to supply the camp. Food, medical supplies and, most important, ammunition ran critically short. The Viet Minh seemed careless of casualties, and the battle became a repetition of the trench warfare of 1914–1918. In the inadequate trenches and dugouts, which began to melt into a sea of mud, the garrison, reeling from fatigue and short of every necessity, nevertheless defended themselves untiringly. In sacrificial fighting, they held, lost, retook and lost again a series of holes in the mud. On April 30, 1954, under Viet bombardment, the anniversary of Camerone was celebrated at the 13th DBLE command post where Lieutenant-Colonel Lemeunier read the traditional proclamation over a radio hook-up that could be heard throughout the camp.

In early May, the final assaults came. On all sides waves of Viet infantry pressed relentlessly forward, fierce fighting took place in the trenches with hand grenades, bayonets and knives. One by one the few positions still held by the French were overrun, but it took the Viets several days to reduce the last isolated pockets of desperate and stubborn resistance. On May 7, 1954, at 1700 hours General de Castries ordered a cease-fire.

The southern position Isabelle, held by

Viet Minh regular infantryman, 1954. The man wears a flat bamboo and fiber woven helmet with cloth and net cover, a khaki drill uniform, captured French belt pouches, and Chinese canteen and knapsack. He is armed with a Mauser rifle.

the 3rd battalion of the 3rd REI, held on a little longer. The légionnaires formed up to break out in an attempt to fight their way southward; less than 100 of them ever reached French lines.

The garrison at Dien Bien Phu totaled some 15,709 men. By the end of the siege the number of able-bodied men stood at 5,864. The surviving defenders, about 11,720 men, after a long and appalling "death" march through the jungle, went into a harsh captivity in Communist "reeducation" camps.

Dien Bien Phu cost the French Foreign Legion about 1,500 dead and 4,000 wounded. It cost France Indochina, and it gave Giap and the Viet Minh an aura of invincibility.

Aftermath

The defeat at Dien Bien Phu brought the Indochina War to a grinding halt. Military operations stopped on July 20, 1954. The immediate evacuation of Tonkin began. This meant the sad, unfortunate abandonment of the population who had been loyal, including sympathizers, military auxiliaries, local militiamen and the pro–French population of the Catholic bishoprics. Well in advance of the military decision to evacuate, a huge flight of refugees had started spontaneously.

The defeat at Dien Bien Phu sealed the fate of French colonization in Southeast Asia. It also caused a grave governmental crisis at home. Pierre Mendès-France (1907–1982), a Radical-Socialist who had been part of the World War II Free French group in London, was appointed president of the Republic because he had, for a long time, been seeking to end the war. The Geneva Agreement of July 21, 1954, partitioned Vietnam along the 17th parallel. Laos and Cambodia were made independent and neutralized. Communist North Vietnam was ruled by the Viet Minh under its president Ho Chi Minh, while the southern republic was governed for a while by Emperor Bao Dai. At that time nobody guessed that another 20 years of warfare lay ahead.

The French army had suffered a crushing defeat in Indochina, and some officers thought they had gained the benefit of a cruel lesson. Analyzing their defeat, they henceforth believed they had a clear understanding of how to defeat a popular revolutionary army in the future. In some army circles and messes, embittered professional officers were determined never ever again to lose a war.

The French Indochina War had lasted nine years, and the Legion had been in it right from the start and had stayed right to the bitter end. Four Legion infantry regiments (2nd REI, 3rd REI, 5th REI and the 13th DBLE), as well as the cavalry regiment (1st REC), and the two airborne BEPs had been involved, plus the numerous companies of specialists, engineers, builders and air supply and transport staff which had supported them. The war had been a great—probably the greatest—challenge to the Foreign Legion. According to the French historian Paul Bonnecarrère the total casualties suffered by the Legion in Indochina were 309 officers, 1,082 NCOs and 9,092 soldiers. Over three times as many had been wounded and some 1,100 were listed as missing.

No sooner had the humiliated and defeated French army ended the confusing and traumatic Indochina War than a serious insurrection broke out in Algeria, on November 1, 1954.

8

The Foreign Legion in the Algerian War, 1954–1962

Historical and Political Background

FLN and ALN

France's defeat in 1940 and the disastrous war in Indochina had fundamentally altered the relationship between France and the Algerian Muslim people, resulting in a dramatical lowering of French prestige. French imperialism came under increasing criticism.

About one million Europeans lived in Algeria. Called curiously, and no one knows why, *Pieds-Noirs* ("Black Feet") they formed a mixed population of French, Spanish, Maltese, Italian and Jewish origin. Despite their various origins they were strongly determined to stay as their fathers and grandfathers had brought the rudiments of civilization, built the infrastructure, and made the land prosperous. Most of them had never been to France; they regarded Algeria as their own land where they felt totally at home. Forming a small privileged minority amidst an overwhelming and feared majority of Muslims, they did not intend to leave their country and also refused to share their wealth, their privileges, and their status as "real Frenchmen" with the Muslims. The *Pieds-Noirs* were, on the whole, conservatives who were opposed to any change and any movement toward integration with the Arab population. They owned modern farms and they trained the urban middle classes. A few were extremely wealthy, either large landowners or business, transport or industrial tycoons. The Muslim population, some 9 million, were second-class citizens with limited civic rights ("Frenchmen of North African stock" in the official jargon), poorer, less educated, barred from holding any important offices, and on the whole treated with paternalist condescension. The majority among them demanded only social reforms and equality, but a small radical fringe favored total independence and creation of a sovereign Algerian nation.

On May 8, 1945, the celebration of victory over Nazi Germany turned into a horrific event in the northeastern city of Sètif. A spontaneous anti–French demonstration got out of hand and, in the panic, shots were fired and mobs ran amok, spreading out to murder more than one hundred European civilians. This massacre was followed by a

8. The Legion in the Algerian War, 1954–1962

Left: *Djoundi ALN, c. 1956.* After the outbreak of the Algerian War, the ALN was organized into 11-man **faoudj** *(squad)* and 350-man **failek** *(battalion)*, but in practice, due to a shortage of weapons and French surveillance, the most frequent combat unit was the 110-man **katiba** *(company)*. Desperately poor in the early years of the insurrection, equipment consisted of captured arms, hunting rifles, British, American and German World War II stocks supplied by Egypt, and various weapons purchased from illegal dealers. Until the end of the war, the ALN suffered from a shortage of heavy weapons such as machine guns, mortars, and bazookas. Unlike the Viet Minh in Indochina, they could never build up a well-structured military force. Algeria was divided into Wilayas (autonomous politico–military commands), each responsible for regional activities including mobilizing, training, arming and commanding the ALN, indoctrinating and taxing the civil population by persuasion or terror: Wilaya 1 (Aures mountains); Wilaya 2 (Region of Constantine); Wilaya 3 (Kabylia); Wilaya 4 (region of Algiers); Wilaya 5 (region of Oran); Wilaya 6 (Sahara Desert); and Wilaya 7 (France) where the FLN levied revolutionary taxes from Algerian émigrés.

The depicted **djoundi** *(private)* wears civilian dress and is armed with a vintage World War II German MG 34 general-purpose machine gun.

Right: *Fellagha, c. 1958.* ALN fighters were called by the French rebels, **fellaghas**, **fellouzes** *(in slang)* or more officially HLL *(Hors-la-loi = outlaws)*. The depicted **fellouze** wears a World War II Afrika Korps-styled high-fronted peaked cap, an American khaki field jacket provided by Egypt, captured French khaki trousers, and traditional sandals. He is armed with a World War II German MP 40 submachine gun and carries his ammo magazines in a captured French gas mask bag.

ruthless repression over the following weeks. French police and troops, as well as improvised *Pieds-Noirs* militia and spontaneous lynching parties killed about 6,000 Algerian Arabs more or less at random—the exact figures have never been known. The massacre of Sétif marked a turning point in Algerian nationalism as it discredited moderate voices and increased the call for outright armed insurrection.

For the time being nationalist sympathizers and independence-seeking leaders were forced underground and began to work secretly to build up a subversive movement. In spite of changing attitudes and the fact that an irresistible wave of nationalism was sweeping over Africa and Indochina, the French authorities in Paris and the European *Pieds-Noirs* in Algeria still looked over the heads of the Muslim Algerians. During the early 1950s, while colonial war raged in Indochina, Algeria seemed calm and quiet; however, a handful of radical nationalist leaders slowly built up a new underground movement, which became known as the Front National de Libération (FNL, National Liberation Front) whose goal was total national independence within a loose Islamist framework. The subversive political FNL, which interestingly had neither connections with nor sympathy for international communism orchestrated from Moscow during the Cold War, soon developed an underground military branch known as Armée de Libération Nationale (ALN, Army for National Liberation).

General characteristics of the war

On November 1, 1954, the FNL orchestrated a series of attacks on police stations and official buildings. The totally surprised French government responded by condemning the rebellion, reasserting Algeria's colonial status, declaring a state of emergency and—in an attempt to win hearts and minds—instituting a few ineffective social reforms. Later attempts to soften this position clashed with the reality on the ground where misunderstanding, fanatism and cruelty were sharpened by a ferocious racism that drove many Algerian moderates into the camp of the radical FNL. Terrorism and massacres on the part of the rebels were answered by terrorism and massacres on the part of the French. Of all France's colonial conflicts, the war in Algeria was the most savage. It provoked tragic crises, enormous human suffering, caused the fall of the Fourth Republic and profound constitutional change, and brought France to the brink of civil war. The conflict has left deep scars which are still felt today between the French and the Muslim community living in France; in many respects, the Algerian War is not yet over even as these lines are written in 2007.

As in the case in Indochina, successive, unstable governments of the Fourth Republic ordered the army to fight and win, but it furnished neither military means nor desperately needed firm political direction. The cost to France—human, moral and financial—steadily turned the tide of public opinion, both national and international. Under pressure from European *Pieds-Noirs* in Algiers supported by the French army, General Charles de Gaulle returned to power in May 1958. The new president did not tie himself up with promises, and he simply but firmly asked the army to do its duty: win the war in the field. In the back of his mind even an incomplete military victory over the FNL rebellion would place France in a strong position when the ineluctable negotiations with the Algerian nationalists took place. With insight de Gaulle was convinced that the war could never be won by arms, and that it was foolish and contrary to France's interests to continue it since the Algerian crisis deeply undermined national unity and international prestige, both crucial to his plans for a new, strong and modern France. De Gaulle knew that nothing could prevent Algeria from becoming a free and independent state, but given the blind passion, political short-sightedness, fanatism and virulent stubbornness of the radical supporters of *Algérie française* (French Algeria), he made at first no overt declaration stating his intentions.

The war in Algeria was indeed far more complex than simply a struggle between communist nationalism and Western colonialism, as had been the case in Indochina. The very term "war" was not even used. The French called it *Opérations de maintien de l'ordre en Afrique du Nord* (operation to maintain order in North Africa). The issues were complex and fervently supported; passions ran high; on every side, resentment and bitterness were so ingrained that fighting grew ruthless, stubborn and protracted. The war was in fact a complex amalgam of several civil wars, conflicts and struggles, all equally passionate. There was a war on the ground between the French army and the ALN and a battle in the wider world (notably at the United Nations) for international support; a civil war among Muslim Algerians themselves (FNL versus the rival party called Mouvement National Algérien [MLN]); a ferocious dispute between Berber Kabyles and Muslim Arabs; personal enmities within the FNL's leadership; and a struggle for influence between the political FNL and the military ALN.

The war profoundly divided the French themselves: A majority at home grew increasingly in favor of stopping the war, and a fanatical minority opposed any changes, determined at all costs to keep *Algérie française*. In its closing phase, the conflict also induced elements of the French army (and Foreign Legion) and a hastily created extreme right-wing Organisation Armée Secrète (OAS Secret Armed Organization) to oppose and engage in violent rebellion against de Gaulle's government. The Algerian tragedy cost many thousands of lives and ran like a stain through the political life of France.

Expected to follow a hard line against the FLN, de Gaulle recognized that history and the interest of France demanded decolonization in Africa and independence for Algeria. In spite of attempts on his life and a terrible terrorist campaign launched by the OAS, de Gaulle backed with foresight a difficult but well-conducted policy of firmness that led to a referendum which, on July 1, 1962, confirmed Algerian independence.

Military Aspects of the Algerian War

ALN guerrillas in the early years

The Algerian War, in which politics and passion played a role equally as important as military operations, does not lend itself to a detailed description. Despite superficial similarities it differed completely from the Indochina War, which saw both guerrilla warfare and a few conventional pitched battles. The pattern in Algeria was one of constant dreary patrolling, occasional sweeps against the ANL in the mountainous areas and maintenance of urban security.

The French won the war militarily while they lost it politically and diplomatically. In a feat unique in modern history, they defeated the ALN's revolutionary guerrilla war on the ground owing to intelligent offensives.

After the surprise attacks of November 1, 1954, the Algerian nationalists were able to more or less strike where they pleased. They quickly broadened the scope of their operations to include the whole of northern and central Algeria putting the French much on the defensive. They used low-intensity guerrilla tactics against widely dispersed soft targets, concentrating upon ambushing small parties of French troops and upon acts of terrorism such as attacking isolated farms. At the same time the FLN developed a ruthless campaign of indoctrination by intimidation, assassination, torture and mutilation to prevent their Muslim compatriots from collaborating with the French. In 1955 the authorities created the Specialized Administrative Sections (SAS) tasked with an ambitious and generously funded "hearts-and-minds" program. Teams of devoted and courageous volunteers led by Arab-speaking officers were sent to remote villages to provide the population with practical help and a visible French presence. They offered public health, education, building and agriculture assistance, but they also gathered intelligence and acted as liaison with the armed force. The SAS were rather popular with villagers but also prime targets of the FLN. On the whole, counterinsurgency operations produced poor results and large sections of the country became unsafe, especially at night, both for the French and for peaceful inhabitants who were not in full sympathy and agreement with the FLN's goals, ideals and methods. In 1957, due to an alarmingly high number of "incidents" both in towns (particularly in Algiers) and in the countryside, French reservists and *contingents* (draftees) were sent to Algeria, where the number of occupation troops rose to 400,000. The bulk of the French forces in Algeria consisted thus of conscripts who were unsympathetic to the aims of the war, and who could be relied upon to carry out only routine security duties. The main burden of aggressive warfare therefore fell upon a small number of professional soldiers, including the Legion and the parachute regiments. These men battled ruthless methods used by the FLN and the ALN to swing a largely apathetic Muslim civilian population behind their cause. Opposed by a determined ALN rural guerrilla force and a ruthless FNL urban terrorist network that used intimidation, threat, atrocity, torture, and physical terror to cow civilians and tempt the French into retaliation, the Foreign Legion and the para regiments were compelled to make a difficult choice: use the methods of the enemy and win, but, by doing so, damned by national and world public opinion. The Algerian War amounted to an unsparing and remorseless civil war in which each side cited the other's crimes in justifying carrying out further ones.

In 1956 the protectorates of Morocco and Tunisia became independent and were able to step up their assistance to the rebels. The western part of Tunisia harbored a number of ALN bases, training camps, refuges, and arms dumps provided by the Egyptian leader Gamal Abdel Nasser. In an attempt to stop infiltration across the long Algerian-Tunisian frontier, the French built a heavily defended fence known as the Ligne Morice. Another line was constructed on the border with Morocco. These barriers proved fairly successful. They succeeded in curtailing rebel movement, supplies and reinforcements, and they contributed to denying the ALN access to the battlefield. The years 1957 and 1958 also coincided with a period of vicious internecine feuds and bloody purges inside the rebel regional command, which, without scruple, was skillfully exploited by the French intelligence service.

General Challe's plan

When de Gaulle appointed General Maurice Challe commander-in-chief in December 1958, the whole rhythm of the war changed in France's favor. The French army was then really able to do something about quelling the Algerian insurrection owing to good intelligence, speed, flexibility and coordination of large ground and air forces. Challe collected together the wastefully dispersed troops and concentrating them with the aim of clearing the rebel-held spots one by one using chasing "hunting commandos" for making contact, parachute regiments carried by helicopters for intervention, a strong force of tactical aircraft to locate and straff, and local sector troops for mopping up. At the same time, the French launched another "hearts-and-minds" program, the carrot accompanying the stick. The inhabitants were removed from certain sectors, which created free-fire zones denying ALN troops of background and support; however, large-scale forced "resettlement" of villagers from combat zones caused great misery.

Due to low morale, defeats and

Harki

Below: *Vertol Model 43 (H-21C) "Flying Banana." The French did much pioneering work with the use of helicopters during the Algerian War. There were comparatively few air drops and most paratroopers' missions were helicopter-borne. Offering tremendous flexibility, speed and mobility, helicopters were particularly useful in low-intensity operations in difficult terrain for observation, ground attack, landing troops and supplies and evacuating casualties. The twin-rotor Vertol-Piasecki H-21, nicknamed "the Flying Banana," was operated by a crew of three, powered by a 1,425 hp Wright engine, had a speed of 163 km/h and a range of 584 kilometers, and could transport a load of 2,565 kg or 12 fully armed soldiers. Other helicopters used by the French included the U.S.-made Sikorsky H-19 and H-34, Bell 47G, Westland-Sikorsky S-51, and the small French-made Alouette II (lark).*

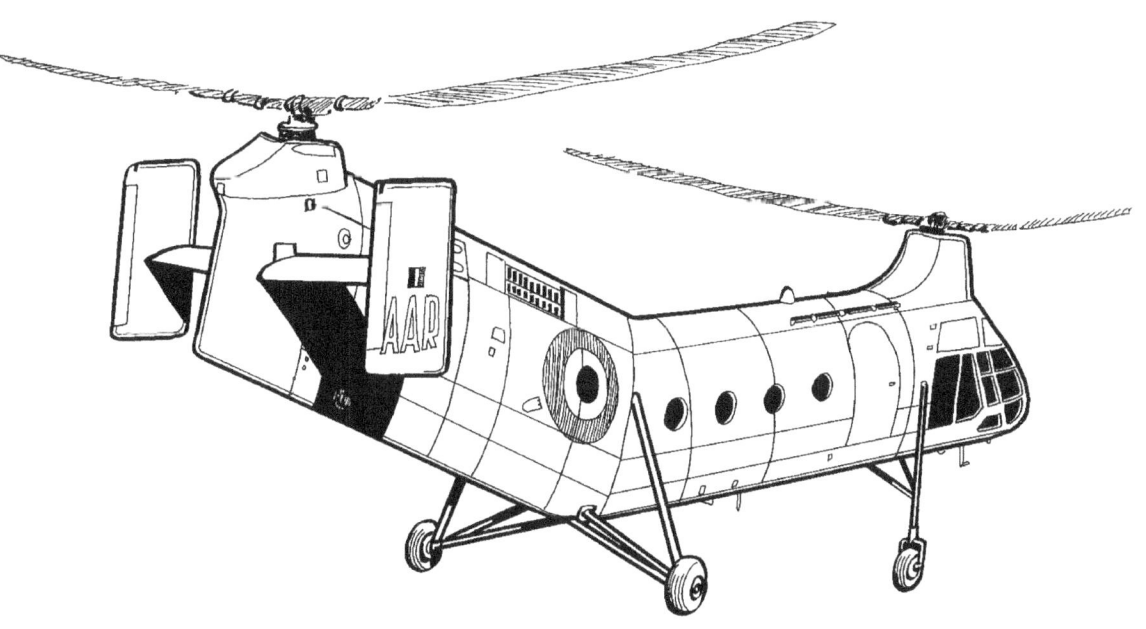

internal feudings, defections mounted appreciably and turned-coat disheartened fellaghas and *harkis* (loyal local Muslim auxiliaries under the direction of French veteran professionals) were used to locate and fight the nationalists; in 1959 there were some 30,000 *harkis* in service with the French army, and, worthy of mention, this represented about twice the active strength of the ALN inside Algeria.

By 1960, the "Challe Steamroller" was highly successful and the French army and the civilian *Pieds-Noirs* population felt confident and thought they could envisage the future of *Algérie française* with optimism. Thousands of rebels were killed, weapons captured, the chain of command disrupted and survivors became isolated fugitives, deprived of support and constantly pressed by French mobile columns that forced them to disperse in small units to evade the hunters. Although urban terrorism was never completely stamped out, the war on the ground had been undeniably won.

Although effective in the short term, French military victory was unable to provide a satisfactory long-term political solution. The conflict, indeed, ended bitterly for the French army and the *Pieds-Noirs*. General de Gaulle, under growing pressure from the international community and because the war had become highly unpopular at home, accepted participation in negotiations which led to Algerian independence on July 3, 1962, with Ahmed Ben Bella as premier. Some among the *Pieds-Noirs* and some French officers felt betrayed and launched a revolt, as described further below.

The Legion in Algeria

The Legion saw heavy fighting in the Algerian War, the whole corps being committed to the conflict. After a period of reduced strength, mainly induced through the discharge of legionaries whose terms of service had expired, the Legion began to build itself up again. In keeping with the antiguerrilla military tactics then prevailing, the Legion was dispersed far and wide into the danger spots where legionnaires spent their time patrolling and searching both by day and night, in an effort to bring the ALN to battle. Skirmishes and bloody contacts with the elusive enemy were many, and not always successful. In 1956 and 1957 particularly the Legion suffered from rebel enemy guerrilla tactics and its casualty list grew long. In 1959 and 1960 they were heavily committed in General Challe's Plan and regrouped, helping to produce the victorious results previously described.

- The Premier Régiment étranger (1st RE), based at Sidi-Bel-Abbès, was a training and depot regiment pure and simple, but it provided several units used in a combat role and security operations in the immediate vicinity of the Legion's home, and elsewhere in Algeria. In all, the 1st RE lost 53 dead and 97 wounded.
- The Deuxième Régiment étranger d'Infanterie (2nd REI) was reduced to single battalion size from 1957 on. The number of companies varied, depending on how many support and specialist companies were attached at any one time. The 2nd REI, as a motorized infantry battalion, mostly patrolled the southern part of Oran Province from Ain Sefra to Géryville. In five years of continuous operations the 2nd REI lost 266 dead and about 600 wounded.
- The Troisième Régiment étranger d'Infanterie (3rd REI) mostly operated in the mountains of Kabylia, always one of the hot spots of Algerian sedition. The 3rd REI also saw combat along the Tunisian border, around Bône, and took part in General Challe's plan, with total losses of 197 dead and 390 wounded.
- The Quatrième Régiment étranger d'Infanterie (4th REI) came back to Algeria from Morocco in 1958, and was deployed

Left: *Legionary, 1st CSPL, c. 1960. This man of the desert patrol company wears the Legion képi, goggles, the traditional* **chèche** *(desert scarf), a sandy yellow* **gandourah** *(smock), baggy spahis trousers, and local sandals. He is armed with a MAS 36 rifle.* **Right:** *Sergeant, 1st RE, c. 1956. The sergeant wears the Legion white képi, a desert scarf, the Model 1947 fatigues, leggings and boots. He is armed with the MAT 49* **pistolet-mitrailleur** *(PM submachine gun) with leather pouches fixed on waist belt.*

in southeast Algeria from Tebessa with the task of guarding the Tunisian border. The 4th REI also saw combat in the Aures and Nementcheta mountains with a total of about 73 casualties.

- The Cinquième Régiment étranger d'Infanterie (5th REI) was used in numerous missions all over Algeria. By the end of the war the 5th REI had lost 146 dead and 353 wounded.
- The Sixième Régiment étranger d'Infanterie (6th REI), posted in Syria, had been disbanded in 1941. It was re-formed in Tunisia in 1947 as reception and transit

pool for Indochina drafts. In 1954, reduced to one battalion, it saw combat against Tunisian insurgents before being disbanded in June 1955.
- The legendary World War II "Bir Hakeim" Treizième Demi-Brigade de la Légion étrangère (13th DBLE) fought in numerous engagements all over Algeria from 1955 to 1962 with 159 legionnaires killed.
- The Premier Régiment étranger de Cavalerie (1st REC), split up to provide armored car support for various operations, was used in numerous missions all over Algeria. In 1962, total casualties amounted to 45 dead and about 150 wounded.
- The Second Régiment étranger de Cavalerie (2nd REC), took part to numerous operations all over Algeria. In 1962, casualties totalled 56 dead and about 98 wounded.
- The four Compagnies Sahariennes portées de la Légion (CSPL), progressively raised between 1946 and 1949, were colorful deep-desert patrol companies. Descendants of the legendary "Mounted Companies," highly mobile and self-sufficient, they fought in the Sahara but also took part in combined operations with the intervention formations in the north of the country.
- The Premier Régiment étranger Parachutiste (1st REP, descendants of the martyred Indochina 1st BEP Foreign Para Battalion, which had been re-formed and expanded to regiment size in 1955) was based at Zeralda near Algiers, and formed part of the French *réserve générale* (mobile striking force). A controversial and "scandalous" unit, the 1st REP took part to the April 1961 putsch.
- The Second Régiment étranger Parachutiste (2nd REP), descendants of the Indochina 2nd BEP, was based at Philippeville, and formed part of the French mobile striking force.

There is no space here, and little point in attempting to narrate a description of each and every combat activity fought by the French Foreign Legion in the Algerian War. The following sections will deal with only a few important events of the war and representative engagements in which the Legion played a central role.

The Suez Crisis, 1956

Political background

Following Egyptian president Gamal Abdel Nasser's nationalization of the Suez Canal in July 1956 the British moved to reassert their power in the eastern Mediterranean Sea. The French had three main goals in joining them: first, the assurance of

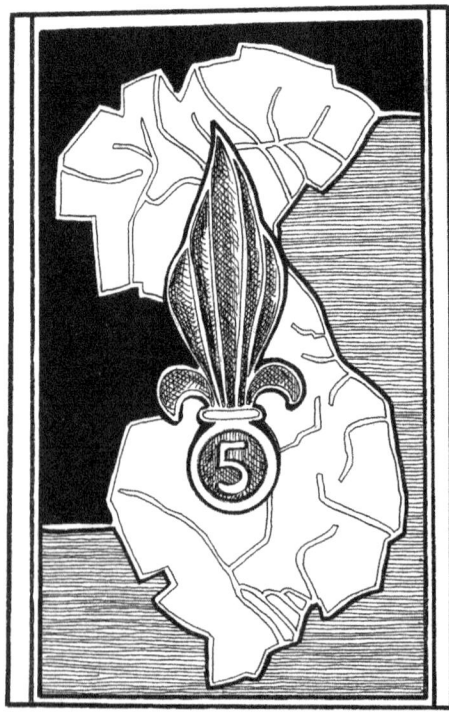

Badge of the 5th REI, 1955–1963. Worn on the right breast, hanging from a fob attached to the pocket button, the badge had a black and white map of Indochina as background, a red flame, a green bomb carrying the figure 5, and a golden rim.

regular sources of petroleum; second, the protection of the friendly state of Israel; and third, the opportunity to strike at Egypt, the heart of the Algerian rebellion's major supply base. Indeed overthrowing Nasser's regime would mean the elimination of a strong support to the Algerian nationalist rebels and, it was hoped, the end of the guerrilla war in Algeria. France and Britain, allied with Israel, launched an attack on the canal zone in late October 1956. Militarily, the operation was reckless and ill-conceived, but, owing to Egyptian weakness, it was a complete success.

The campaign

For this expedition, the French military authorities created a special elite airborne task force, known as 10ème Division parachutiste (10th DP, Paratrooper Division) placed under the leadership of General Jacques Massu. This included the 1st REP—Foreign Paratrooper Regiment headed by Colonel Brothier and his assistant Colonel Jeanpierre. In the night of November 5 and 6, Operation Amilcar and Operation Musqueteer were launched by the 10th DP and British troops in coordination with Israel. The French legionaries of the 1st REP landed at Port-Fouad without resistance and

Legionary with AAT 52. The MAS AAT 52 caliber 7.5 mm (0.295 in.) general-purpose machine gun was designed from the outset for ease of production. Operated by delayed blowback, it weighed 9.97 kg (21.98 lbs.), had an overall length of 1.150 m (45.08 in.) and a cyclic rate of fire of 700 rpm, and was fed by a 50-round metal-link belt.

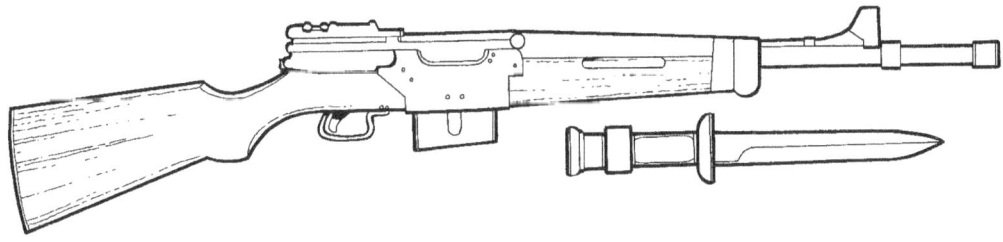

MAS 49/56 Rifle. The MAS 49 was originally designed for French paratroopers in Indochina. It resembled the preceding MAS 36 because it used a similar two-piece wooden stock, but in fact it embodied a completely different design. The MAS 49 was a solid—if uninspiring—semi-automatic, gas-operated rifle, firing the obsolete prewar French 7.5 mm × 54 cartridge, held in a 10-shot detachable box magazine. Its weight (loaded) was 4.34 kg (9.52 lbs.) and overall length was 1,010 mm (39.8 in.). It was fitted with a bayonet and an integral grenade launcher. Modifications in the mid–1950s gave rise to the improved MAS 49/56, which served in the French army until the mid–1980s. There was a version, known as MAS 49/56 MSE, with a pistol grip and telescopic sight for target shooting and sniping.

suffered only one wounded. At noon they obtained their objectives. Port Fouad and El-Cap were occupied without a fight. Elsewhere the Israeli, British, and French troops achieved a quick victory too. This was, however, only a Pyrrhic victory.

Condemned by international opinion, without the support of the United States and strongly opposed by the Soviet Union, the expedition ended in humiliation; the victorious but totally isolated French, British and Israeli governments were forced to accept a cease-fire. In December 1956, the 10th Division parachutiste and the 1st Régiment étranger parachutiste—their officers greatly frustrated by their military victory turned into a diplomatic defeat—came back to Algiers for a new mission.

The Battle of Algiers, 1957

FLN terror in Algiers

The FLN always lacked means, weapons and men to wage Viet Minh–like guerrilla warfare in the countryside but the Liberation Front was perfectly aware of the critical importance of sowing terror, panic and disorder at the very nerve center of the French military and administrative network. To this end the Zone Autonome d'Alger (ZAA, autonomous zone of Algiers) was created and carved out of the Wilaya 4, corresponding to the metropolitan district of Greater Algiers, with its impregnable base, the Casbah (old Arabian part of the city) populated with approximately 100,000 Muslims. The ZAA was handed over in mid-1955 to a young militant named Yacef Saadi who, by the spring of 1956, set in motion a powerful and concentrated terrorist organization. Bombing actions began in the following autumn and winter, and almost everyday bombs exploded in cafés, dance halls, cinemas and on buses and trolley buses, leading to about 200 civilian victims among the white *Pieds-Noirs* population, and causing panic in the city of 700,000. The attitudes of both communities remained tensely inimical, and the French police proved helpless. The danger existed that the European civilians, blind with fear and fury, might take matters into their own hands, and there was an equal possibility that the Casbah might explode in a large-scale insurrection. This was actually the ultimate goal of the FLN: to incite an unrestricted civil war between the European and Muslim communities, causing the French to lose heart and grant Algeria her independence. In this atmosphere of blind violence, fear and mounting hatred, the civil authorities were paralyzed with powerlessness. In desperation, they demanded the intervention of the army to take over the task of the police. The government, overwhelmed by the crisis in Paris, agreed. For this high-risk mission, it was decided to use General Massu's 10th Airborne Division just returning from the aborted Suez campaign. As can be imagined, the soldiers were not particularly happy about the police role. The elite 10th DP arrived at Algiers on January 27, 1957, and the grim urban battle began.

French antiterror campaign

The French responded to blind terror by organized terror. On January 28, 1957, as a protest and a show of strength, the FLN announced a general strike in the Casbah, but General Jacques Massu, desperately anxious to make a powerful impression, was quick to react. With harsh and spectacular methods including merchants compelled to open their shops, people "encouraged" by threat and force to go to work as they normally did, housewives firmly pushed into the streets, and striking teachers and pupils transported by army trucks to their schools, Massu frustrated the strike attempt. Now the 10th DP started its campaign against the bombing terrorists. To find the hard-core rebels, the paratroopers first had to gather

*Legion headgear worn in the Algerian War. Depending upon the type of duty, the Legion wore various headgear. Along with the Legion white képi, legionaries wore either the M1951 steel helmet (1) with or without net, or a green beret with the Legion flame (2), or the para badge (3), or a **calot**, a standard forage cap (4), or less frequently, the camouflage "leopard" soft-peaked cap (5), which was popularized by Colonel Bigeard's 3rd RPC (Régiment de Parachutistes coloniaux), or a bush hat (6).*

intelligence. It was obviously known that Yacef Saadi's bombing commandos were supported, more or less willingly, by the Muslim population in the Casbah. But finding them among many tens of thousands of Muslims living in a labyrinthine maze of interconnecting houses, narrow streets, stairways, courtyards, alleys and rooftops was not an easy task. The old Arabian city was completely blockaded and checkpoints were established at its entrances. Control was tightened and everyone leaving the neighborhood was searched, ID checked, and suspects arrested. Curfews were imposed and military patrols roamed the streets at night. Quick raids and sudden arrests were made at random by day and night, and masked informers helped screen FLN supporters picked up in the mass sweeps and round-ups. Suspects were interrogated with vigorous brutality, routinely involving torture by electrodes by a special secret army branch known as Dispositif opérationel de Protection (DOP). As soon as someone had "talked" and had given a hint, a name or an address, a team of paratroopers was quickly rushed to the suspected place, resulting in further arrests. Targeted raids went on and on netting further prisoners for "special interrogation" by DOP teams. Progressively the 10th DP, working as a ruthless battering ram, broke up the insurrectional apparatus and choked off the rebel leadership. Using these hard, illegal and morally indefensible methods of inquiry, the paratroopers soon destroyed the FLN terrorist cells, seized documents, discovered hideouts and weapon caches, identified and arrested sympathizers and funds collectors, and, most important, captured clandestine stocks of bombs and arrested active terrorists. On September 24, 1957, after an operation honeycombing the Casbah and a series of events too strange for fiction, the bombing networks were dismantled and Yacef Saadi was arrested. He was replaced by his lieutenant, Ali La Pointe ("The Knife"), who kept the bombing campaign going for a while. Ali's hiding place was discovered, and the building in which he had taken refuge was blown up by the Legion paratroopers of the 1st REP. With the death of the last ZAA leader by mid–October 1957, the triumph of Massu's paratroopers was total, the ZAA was destroyed and the FLN terror bombing campaign was stopped. The 10th DP paratroopers and the men of the 1st REP, as can be imagined, were immensely popular with the *Pieds-Noirs* community and immensely hated by the Muslim population.

Operations in the Sahara

Operations in the wide southern desert were mainly made by the 1st and 2nd REC (cavalry regiments) and more particularly by four Compagnies Sahariennes Portées de la Légion (CSPL). Equipped with 4 × 4 trucks, scout cars, and light armored cars (occasionally mounted on camels and very often proceeding on foot), their mission was to protect the transcontinental road, tracks and railways in the Sahara, the oases along them, the pipeline Bougie-Touggourt-Hassi Messahoud, the oilfields in the far south of the desert, and the huge southern region at the Algerian-Libyan border. The mobile desert patrol units were engaged in the war as early as July 1955. In the blazing sun and the choking dust, with the horizon dancing in the heat, and during the freezing nights, in a landscape not meant for human beings, the CSPLs performed very well. Although the rebels avoided at all costs large-scale confrontations, there were a number of unpleasant clashes.

The 1st CSPL, created in March 1946, was based at Ain-Sefra in 1956 and at Fort Flatters in 1958. It saw combat at Amoura among many other locales; in January 1962 the company was expanded, redesignated 1st Escadron Saharien Porté de la Légion (ESPL), and deployed to protect the test site of Reggane where the first French

AML Panhard. The Automitrailleuse Légère (AML) built by the Panhard Company constituted the motorized equipment of the Legion Cavalry RECs and CSPLs. Operated by a crew of three (commander, driver and gunner) it was a small 4 × 4 lightly armored vehicle with a height of 1.86 m, a length of 3.75 m, and a weight of 4.5 metric tons. Powered by a 90 hp Panhard 4 HD engine it had a range of 600 kilometers and used 25 liters of gasoline fuel per 100 km. It was usually armed with one 60 mm breech-loading CS mortar and two 7.5 cm model 52 machine guns. The heavier U.S.–made six-wheel M-8 armored car, and the 8-wheel Panhard Engin Blindé de Reconnaissance (EBR) were also widely used, as well as modernized versions of the U.S. M-2 halftrack, and various Renault 4 × 4 and Dodge 6 × 6 trucks.

nuclear bomb (four times the power of the 1945 Hiroshima bomb) was exploded on February 13, 1960.

The 2nd CSPL, based at Lagouhat and Ouragla, fought at Messad, Djebel Amour, Kef Mimouna, Bou-Guerfour and in other places.

The 3rd CSPL, formed in February 1949, was based in the Fezzan region, later at Issendjel and Fort Leclerc; it fought at Kef-Nasseur, Oued N'tila, Djebel Bou-Kahil and Lagouhat as well as elsewhere.

The 4th CSPL, created in 1956, was based at Colomb-Bechar, later in the southern part of Oran Province; it was engaged at Oued Guettara, Djebel Mizeb and Timimoun. By 1961, the Sahara was practically cleared of rebel activities, and the CSPLs totaled 64 killed, including five officers.

The Battle of the Frontier, 1957–1958

By September 1957 the Morice Line (320 kilometers [200 miles] along the border with Tunisia) was completed. Defended by a total of some 80,000 French troops, it consisted of a lethal 5,000-volt electrified high fence, extensive barbed wire networks, and highly dangerous antipersonnel minefields; it was electronically monitored with searchlights, with radar sensors and with artillery batteries that could fire with pinpoint accuracy at the spot where a breach was made.

The line was constantly observed from the air by spotter aircraft, and it was protected day and night by local patrols. As soon as a breach was made, the "general reserve" (motorized, infantry and helicopter-borne units) rushed to the scene of the crossing and quickly intervened for search-and-destroy sweeps. The Morice Line (and its extension at the border with Morocco) had cost a fortune, and taken a great deal of manpower, but it proved a very successful enterprise cutting off the infiltration of insurgents from Tunisia to a trickle.

It became vital for the ALN, massed and trained in Tunisia, to breach the barrier to join and supply the *fellaghas* inside Algeria, and this led to the fiercest battles of the war. The rebels tried every means and tactic to cut their way through the line (mainly by explosives but also by digging tunnels under it), after which they had to force-march quickly away from the breach dispersing into cover before the fast helicopter-borne intervention units, armored troops, artillery and fighter bombers could locate, attack and destroy them. From October 1957 to April 1958, almost every day and every night, the so-called Battle of the Frontier raged, to which the Foreign Legion committed crack units of 3rd and 4th REI, 13th DBLE, both RECs and 1st REP. During this period, as expected, the Legion performed with distinction. The defense of the barrier worked well, and ALN casualties grew still higher. For instance, in March 1958 the rebels lost 3,132 dead and 714 captured, and in April 3,728 killed and 756 captured.

Between April 28 and May 3, 1958, a major battle took place near Souk-Ahras during which a force of 1,300 rebels tried to force the line. Some 800 succeeded in crossing; of these 436 were killed, 100 captured in the first two days and another 93 killed later; only 160 escaped into the interior. Some 412 individual weapons, 46 machine guns, one mortar and four bazookas were captured. French casualties in the same period were 38 killed and 35 wounded.

Legionary with quilted jacket, c. 1958. Winter could be freezing cold in the mountains of Algeria so soldiers were issued various pieces of uniform including warm coats, anoraks, woollen jumpers, quilted jackets and toques.

On May 29, 1958, at Guelma, near the Tunisian border, Lieutenant-Colonel Jeanpierre, the legendary commander of 1st REP, was killed when his command helicopter was shot down. A highly regarded soldier, Jeanpierre had worked his way up through the ranks by merit. Graduated from officer school in 1936, he served his entire career in the Legion, except from a period in 1943–1944, when he served with the French Resistance. Captured by the Nazis, he was sent to Mauthausen concentration camp. In Indochina he served as second-in-command with the 1st BEP, and he took much of the weight of command off the severely wounded Major Segretain during the ill-fated RC4 fighting in October 1950. He led the re-formed 1st BEP after his second destruction at Dien Bien Phu. Back in Algeria, Jeanpierre took over command of the enlarged 1st REP in March 1957. He was a hard and earthy soldier driven to perfection, mercilessly demanding of himself and of his foreign paratroopers. Under his inspired leadership, his men achieved extraordinary results, and officers, NCOs and legionaries regarded him with awed admiration.

By 1959, both barriers along the Moroccan and Tunisian borders blocked 95 percent of the rebel infiltration, leaving the ALN fighters inside Algeria deprived of major sources of supply and reinforcement.

Challe's Plan

As already said the central elements of Challe's plan were concentration of forces, rapid and flexible intervention of "hunting commandos" and parachute regiments carried by helicopters and supported by tactical aircraft, including T-6 Texans, P-47 Thunderbolts, B-26 Invaders, A-1 Skyraiders and T-28 Troyans. The Legion played a central role in Challe's plan, which aimed at destroying the ALN. Hardly an action was fought or an operation of any magnitude carried on without elements of the Legion being included. At one stage there were no less than units of six Legion regiments engaged in action at the same time.

The ALN faced greater difficulties than had the Viet Minh in Indochina. It was not wholly unified, it was weakly equipped, and the civilian population was far less automatically supportive. The rugged Algerian hinterland provided much less overhead cover than did the Indochinese jungle, so when a *katiba* was forced to move it was much more vulnerable to air attack. The reconquests of previous "no go" areas was, however, a hard task, which kept troops out in harsh terrain for weeks, under canvas in extremes of heat and cold, marching, searching and fighting violent and bitter skirmishes.

Operation Couronne

Started in early February 1959, Operation Couronne was launched in the region of Frenda, Dahra and the western part of the Ouarsenis Mountains. The 5th REI operated in the sector Orléansville-Inkermann where it destroyed Chief Menouar's *katiba*. The 1st REP was deployed around Tenes. The 3rd REI, engaged in the Saida and Dahra Mountains, destroyed ALN chief Hamdania's *katiba*.

Operations Courroie and Etincelles

Operation Courroie was launched in the eastern Ouarsenis Mountains and in the hills around the city of Algiers. The Legion 1st and 2nd REP took part, and were engaged at Cherchell and Molière where they destroyed 40 percent of the ALN troops. Courroie was followed by Operation Etincelles in the Hodna Mountains where the Legion 1st REP, 3rd and 5th REI and two squadrons of 2nd REC were engaged. Within a week the region was cleared of half the rebels it contained, the survivors being totally isolated and disheartened.

Operation Jumelles

Started on July 22, 1959, and directed by General Challe himself, Operation Jumelles was launched in the Kabylia Mountains, which had always been a hard-core region of resistance owing both to the nature of the terrain and the warlike, hostile attitude of the Berber inhabitants. The Legion deployed four regiments. The 1st REP operated in the northern pass of Tidourna, Boubehir and Iffira; The 13th DBLE, engaged in the Djurdjura mountains. The 3rd REI and the 5th REI, deployed around Drar-Chek-Bout, fought a difficult battle against rebels entrenched in grottoes; they killed 462 of the enemy, took 684 prisoners, and captured 320 weapons and 12 light machine guns.

Left: *Legionary, 3rd REI, c. 1959. The man wears the French M1951 steel helmet, and the M1947/52 fatigues; he is armed with a MAT 49 submachine gun.* **Right:** *Captain, 2nd REP, walking-out dress, c. 1960. The walking-out dress consisted of a képi or a green para beret, white shirt and green tie, officer's khaki service tunic (with collar badges, shoulder boards, para badge,* **médaille militaire** *and* **fouragère** *= lanyard indicating that the regiment has been awarded a decoration as a whole), ornate black belt with gilt medallion-and-snake clasp, white gloves, officer's khaki service trousers (with double dark brown side stripe 50 mm broad), and black-laced shoes.*

Operation Pierres Précieuses

This operation involved a series of four actions, code-named Rubis, Saphir, Emeraude and Turquoise, launched in September and November 1959 in the region of Philippeville. The 2nd REP was engaged in the sector of Djidjelli and Oued Askeur, the 3rd REI in the Djebel Taya, and the 5th REI in the peninsula of Collo. In a difficult mountainous and forested terrain the legionnaires managed to kill and capture about 2,000 *fellaghas* and seized some 1,400 weapons.

Operations Cigale and Ariège

On April 23, 1960, for political reasons, the much too popular General Challe was replaced by General Crespin. The new commander-in-chief in Algeria continued the offensive actions.

Operation Cigale, started at the end of July 1960, was a repetition of Couronne, to make sure that the ALN did not resume its activities in the Ouarsenis Mountains. This was followed in September by Operation Ariège, in the Aures Mountains, in which the 2nd REP killed 95 rebels at Ain Taga, the 3rd REI killed 200 and the 5th 124. In January and February 1961 Operation Dordogne was launched followed by Operation Isère. These were the last French military offensives in an Algeria that was on the point of becoming independent. By that time, Colonel Houari Boumedienne, commander-in-chief of the ALN in Tunisia, had lost interest in supporting the forces fighting inside Algeria. They were lost anyway, and the ambitious colonel preferred to spare his own loyal troops for his future political career. Boumedienne supported Ben Bella, who seized power in September 1962, but overthrew and imprisoned him in June 1965. He became leader/dictator of the Algerian Republic from 1965 until his death in 1978.

The Putsch of April 1961

Malaise and crisis in the Army

The Army's general reaction to de Gaulle was, at first, supportive in expecting his backing as the army had been instrumental in bringing him back to power in May 1958. Within a year and a half the army was harshly disabused of this notion. It never criticized de Gaulle for his lack of strength; rather, the army challenged the president for using this strength in what it claimed to be an arbitrary, duplicitous, and ultimately unsound manner. In the past the army (called *la grande muette*, "the great silent one") had abstained from involvement in politics, contemptuous of the governing class, but unprepared and unwilling to move against it. The ideological conflicts of the 20th century had changed this oversimplified, apolitical and "neutral" position, and increasingly the army became involved in politics and in choosing ideological sides. In 1940 and 1942 militaries had to choose their camps (de Gaulle or Pétain) and the Indochina War had been both a French colonial conflict and a struggle against international communism. The complex Algerian War was to see a dramatic tightening of links with the politic civilian world and the apogee of the French army's involvement in political matters.

When de Gaulle in his speech of November 1960 referred for the first time to a possible future "Algerian Algeria," a wave of indignation broke out among both civilian European extremists and the professional French army. When the brilliant operations launched by General Challe and his successor General Crespin almost led to victory in the field, these men did not understand and could not accept that the militarily defeated "bandits" should win through political means. At the same time, FLN terrorism continued, particularly targeting Muslim Algerians supportive of de Gaulle's offers. The French electorate became increasing war-weary, the use of draftees was highly unpopular, and foreign criticism and international pressure weighed more and more on the development of events. In December 1960, at a time when the ALN suffered heavy blows on the field, the FLN won an important diplomatic success: the United Nations recognized the Algerian right to self-determination.

When it became clear that de Gaulle's policy inevitably would lead to Algerian independence, some Army seniors officers felt themselves betrayed, particularly since the successful General Challe had been dismissed from his command in Algeria. De Gaulle had also concluded a truce and ordered to cease offensive operations, but the FLN did not reciprocate and the defeated ALN infrastructure was quietly rebuilt. Many army officers felt that a military victory had been deliberately sacrificed to political expediency. In early 1961, the idea of a rebellion against de Gaulle began to gain ground in the professional French army. A plot was organized by determined professional ultra officers, Legion and paratrooper leaders, most of them veterans of Indochina who stubbornly refused to lose another war. These lieutenants, captains and colonels, needed a general as a figurehead. At first, Challe—a Republican military legalist to the marrow—was reluctant to rise against the state, but the plotters succeeded in convincing him to take the daring step of crossing the Rubicon. Challe rallied three other retired generals who shared the conspirators' views: Edmond Jouhaut, André Zeller, and Raoul Salan.

The controversial and rebellious ex-general Salan (once commander-in-chief in Indochina and now head of the extreme right anti–Gaullist terrorist OAS) soon proved a cumbersome and embarrassing ally as he introduced a neo–Fascist dimension into plans for a putsch that Challe, Jouhaut and Zeller had intended to be a purely apolitical military affair. The generals' aims were, however, vague and hazy. What Challe wanted was the means to definitively defeat the ALN, and, once having done that, to offer his victory to France, which would keep Algeria. Salan and the activists of the OAS, on the other hand, had more ambitious plans. According to the historian Yves Courrière, it seems that their goal was no longer to secure a French Algeria but rather to make a clean break with France, eradicate the FLN, and establish an independent, racist state more or less similar to South Africa in Algeria, with a firm authoritarian structure and a society based on white domination and apartheid (racial segregation).

Major secret preparations were made to rally units, and some senior officers promised to help the highly popular General Challe. Soon the number of regiments supporting the plotters grew, and Challe came to think that the scheme designed by Colonel Yves Godard had a good likelihood of success. It was anticipated that the French Foreign Legion, headed by Colonel Brothier would rally as soon as the putsch started; at least that was the hope of the plotter and former inspector-general of the Legion Gardy. Already the 1st REP (1st Foreign Paratrooper Regiment), temporarily headed by Major Elie Denoix de Saint Marc was totally committed and would act as the spearhead of the coup. No attention was paid at all to the conscripted *contingent*, the approximately 400,000 drafted soldiers who constituted the static sector troops. They were totally ignored and it was strongly believed that they would obey their officers and would be glad only to be sent back home. The Muslim population, too, was totally ignored. For Challe and his henchmen they were a vague and colorless crowd of sheep who would follow the strongest party. As for the white *Pied-Noir* population, the conspirators were certain of their total and unconditional support.

Given the scale of the plot and the number of people involved, the secret leaked out, and the French Intelligence Service knew that something was going on. But there had been so many plots and clashes in the past in the Algerian volcano that the civil authorities in Paris did not actually take the threat of a real putsch seriously. When informed of the preparation for a coup, de Gaulle is said to have replied: "Come on now! If for a few malcontents, the army is faithful to me!"

On April 11, 1961, General de Gaulle held a press conference in which he reaffirmed his intention to negotiate with the FLN and grant Algeria its independence. This declaration, interpreted by the plotters as a betrayal of trust, worked as a detonator and the conspirators decided to strike before negotiations could be resumed.

Algiers taken by 1st REP

The putsch began rather well and the operation was carried out smoothly by the 2,000 legionaries of the 1st Foreign Legion Parachute Regiment under the command of Denoix de Saint Marc together with the two para regiments (14th and 18th RCP), highly popular since the Battle of Algiers. At first Challe objected to use of a foreign unit for an operation pitting Frenchmen against Frenchmen, but General Gardy swept his scruples aside: the leadership of the regiment was wholly French and the legionaries were potentially French too by the traditional principle of *sang versé* ("shed blood"). Besides, Challe was not in a position to quibble as the 1st REP was the only unit he could rely upon for the putsch; all other units commanders had only *promised to follow*. None of them wished to be at the spearhead, and Commandant Elie Denoix de Saint Marc was the only officer ready to take the lead. A highly regarded figure of the French Foreign Legion and the French army, Saint Marc was the epitome of the steely, devoted Legion para officer. Originating from a well-educated family from Bordeaux, the young Elie had been a member of the Resistance in World War II. Like Lieutenant-Colonel Jeanpierre, he had been captured by the Gestapo, tortured and sent to the Buchenwald concentration camp — aged 19 — and had miraculously survived Nazi inhumane brutality. After the war Denoix de Saint Marc enlisted in the army, volunteered for the Legion, and fought with distinction in Indochina and Algeria. He had taken part in the Battle of Algiers, in the events of May 13, 1958, which had brought de Gaulle back to power, and to Challe's successful operations in the field. Like many of his comrades, Denoix de Saint Marc had truly believed in the realization of the dreams of *Algérie française* with social justice, political and racial equality, and territorial integrity which successive French governments had always promised but had never been able to carry out. Deeply disillusioned and embittered, he had developed a profound disgust for politicians and felt an affectionate admiration for General Challe in whom he saw the last rampart against both Salan's neo-fascism and de Gaulle's policy of abandonment.

During the night of April 21-22, the 1st REP left its base at Zeralda and drove to Algiers at about 2:00 A.M. Colonel Godard and his assistant, Captain Bayt, had selected a number of central objectives including the *Délégation Générale* (siege of government), the Interarmy Head-Quarter, the Military Head-Quarters of Algiers, the command headquarters of the military region of Algiers, military barracks, the radio and television broadcast buildings, public power plants, telephone exchanges, post offices, civilian and military airports, the central police station and several other key targets, as well as residences of important political leaders, administrative personnel and top civil servants who were to be arrested. Owing to good coordination, perfect timing, clear itineraries and the use of civilian guides recruited by Captain Bayt from among reliable right-wing activists, the operation went swiftly and proved almost bloodless. There was only one fatality:

Maréchal des Logis (Sergeant) Pierre Brillant who tried to defend the radio broadcast station of Ouled-Fayet and who was shot by the legionaries.

In the early morning of Saturday April 22, 1961, all objectives were taken, and vital centers occupied by legionaries and paratroopers. All significant personnel loyal to the government were sequestered at the prison of In Salah, notably General Gambiez (the new, Gaullist commander-in-chief of the army in Algeria) and Jacques Morin (minister delegate). Algiers was conquered and the conspirators were exultant. Early in the morning the putschists' staff drew up a proclamation in which it was solemnly announced that reserve Generals Challe, Jouhaut and Zeller in liaison with ex-general Raoul Salan—a last-minute gesture of appeasement directed toward the OAS and the civilian extreme activists—had taken over power in order to hold the French army's oath to keep the Algerian *départements* an integral part of France. Martial law was declared, and all power temporarily exercised by the Army.

The seizure of Algiers was, however, only the first step. The most difficult task remained to be achieved, namely, rallying the French army, conquering the rest of Algeria, and—most difficult of all—forcing President Charles de Gaulle to accede to the putschists' demands.

De Gaulle's reaction

From the start de Gaulle was convinced that the putsch would lead to nothing, but obviously, the president—who was also a general—was deeply shocked by the military insurrection and deeply disappointed by the generals' lack of political foresight. At first de Gaulle decided to play a waiting game and allowed pressure to build up and confusion to grow, convinced that time was on his side and that the chaotic situation in Algeria would inevitably turn in his favor. On Sunday, April 23, 1961, in the evening, de Gaulle made a famous television and radio address. The president, in a grave and firm voice, declared: "An insurrectional quartet of retired generals and a group of fanatical officers have illegally taken power in Algeria, exploiting the passion and fear of a number of Army cadres and European civilian population. The State is scoffed, the Nation defied, our strength jeered, our international prestige lowered, our place and our role in Africa jeopardized. And by whom? Helas! Helas! By men whose duty, honor and reason to be were to serve and obey. In the Name of France." The general continued, in an extremely tense tone: "I order that all means, I say all means, be employed to stop them. I expressly forbid all Frenchmen both civilian and military, to obey the usurpators' orders." After having affirmed his Republican legitimacy and personal determination, de Gaulle concluded with an emotional call: "Françaises, Français! Aidez-moi! (Help me!)." De Gaulle's speech was widely heard both in Algeria and in France owing to the recent development of transistor portable radio sets. His address proved a formidable psychological shock, to the military rebels that carried immediate and significant consequences.

The failure of the putsch

The evidence uncovered in the wake of the putsch suggests strongly that the coup was hasty and ill-conceived. The whole affair was designed by Colonel Yves Godard, the ringleader of the attempt and the former head of the Algiers Sûreté, who this time did not produce a masterpiece. The conspiracy was rudimentary and feeble, and if the hard core of "Ultras" was determined, the followers had made only promises. Challe had hoped to carry with him the quasi unity of the French army; instead, he rallied only the frustrated minority and a handful of fanatical fire-eaters. Almost all those who had expressed their sympathy, and had promised to follow him, were now para-

Left: *Legionary, 1st REP, Algiers, April 1961. The depicted "putschist" paratrooper wears the para Legion green beret, heavy "rangers" leather jump boots, and the highly typical para model 47/52 camouflage suit, manufactured by the Boyé and Texunion Companies. He is armed with the standard MAT 49 submachine gun. Minimal belt equipment was worn for urban duties.* **Right:** *5th REI caporal-chef in walking-out dress, c. 1960. The summer walking-out dress was composed of the Legion white képi, light khaki/sand yellow drill shirt and slacks worn with a web belt. For daytime the sleeves could be rolled up and the collar open without tie. For evening the sleeves and collar were usually fastened and a green tie added.*

lyzed, faced with an extremely difficult decision to make for men accustomed to obeying orders issued by the legal government. They grew reluctant to proceed, wondered where the putsch would lead, and raised last-minute objections. Most would-be putschists adopted a wait-and-see attitude. The French Foreign Legion, which would have acted as the leading force, did not join the putsch. Colonel Brothier, in spite of for-

mer inspector-general of the Legion Gardy's repeated efforts, did not rally. On the contrary, Brothier forbid the Legion units to take any part. The 1st Foreign Regiment was ordered to stay at Sidi-Bel-Abbes. The 5th Foreign Infantry Regiment and the 2nd Foreign Infantry Regiment were consigned to their barracks. The leadership of the historical "Bir Hakeim" 13th Foreign Legion Half-Brigade was taken over by the pro-

Challe major Gendron, who overthrew the staunchly Gaullist Colonel Vaillant, but this "palace revolution" led to nothing; the 13th DBLE, did not join. Brothier also firmly ordered the subversive 1st REP to return to Zeralda, but this was not obeyed.

After de Gaulle's April 23 speech, those military commanders who still wavered turned coat. Defection, desertion and active opposition to the putsch increased. The ignored conscripted *contingent* woke up and rose spontaneously. The *bidasses* (Army slang for draftees) played an important role in defeating the putsch attempt mostly by passive opposition and technical sabotage, but also by a few acts of active resistance.

The ill-fated putsch lingered on in confusion for another two days until Challe perceived that his supporters constituted a wavering fraction rather than the vanguard of a growing movement of solidarity. Totally isolated, General Challe, exhausted from sleepless nights, embittered by defections, thwarted by a general opposition, and heavily criticized by his own supporters, decided to surrender on Tuesday, April 25, 1961. Challe, Denoix de Saint-Marc and the legionaries of the 1st REP left Algiers, a city now in a total state of anarchy. They drove back to Zeralda to prepare to capitulate, which happened the following morning. The "Putsch of the Generals," which sought to change the fate of France and Algeria, was over. It had lasted for four days and five nights.

The End of the Algerian War

De Gaulle's government had known how to defend itself and disaster had been averted, but the country had teetered close to civil war and the price paid was high. The victorious French army in Algeria was broken, disheartened and divided, and its reputation stained. The "putschist" 1st Legion Parachute Regiment was dissolved, its leadership arrested and NCOs and men dispatched to other Legion units. The men who had brought France to the brink of civil war were tried in June–July 1961. The fugitive Reserve generals Raoul Salan, Edmond Jouhaut and Paul Gardy as well as Colonels Antoine Argoud, Joseph Broizat, Jean Gardes, Yves Godard and Charles Lacheroy were condemned to death in absentia. Reserve generals Maurice Challe and André Zeller were condemned to 15 years criminal detention. Commandant Elie Denoix de Saint Marc (1st REP), and several para colonels were condemned to 10 years criminal detention. Every officer in command in Algeria and in France was interrogated and had to make a detailed report on his personal activities during the four days of the April putsch. The army was subsequently purged and penalties were imposed on peripheral accomplices who had flirted with sedition. A painful silence fell over the French army, but it was not over.

General Salan, the most distinguished activator of anti–de Gaulle agitation, gathered the ruins of the putsch into his arms and, making cause with neo–Fascist activists, decided to continue the hopeless struggle with the OAS and the camarilla of fugitive "ultra" officers. Salan sought to catalyze the anti–Gaullist opposition of all sorts. By using terror and ruthless methods including kidnapping, hold-ups, blind bombings, destruction of property and assassination, the OAS was determined not to give up Algeria or at least to destabilize preparations for independence by carrying out pointless scorched-earth tactics. The putsch was followed by a desperate and terribly bloody terrorist campaign. This did not prevent Algerian independence from being proclaimed on July 3, 1962.

The failed putsch and murderous gangsterism of the OAS had tremendous consequences. By their actions, they destroyed France's negotiating position with the FLN, and they raised such hatred among the now independent Muslim Algerians that, for fear of retaliation, the Christian and Jewish *Pieds-Noirs* population, totaling about 1,000,000 people, were forced to leave in a massive exodus. Most emigrated to southern France while an important part of the Jewish community went to Israel. Only a few *harkis* left with the French (about 15,000) and they escaped an atrocious fate; most of the rest, as well as those who had served the French (c. 100,000), were butchered in revenge attacks immediately after independence. Interestingly all protagonists of the April 1961 failed putsch and most OAS activists were pardoned and given amnesty by General de Gaulle in 1968 when his regime was threatened by a large-scale popular revolt.

The last notable battle of the Legion in North Africa was fought at Bizerte in Tunisia. When this French-held base was invested by the Tunisian army in early July 1961, the French reacted by sending an intervention force composed of the 2nd and 3rd Régiments Parachutistes d'Infanterie de Marine (RPIMa), 8th Hussard Régiment and the Legion 3rd REI. On July 19, the paratroopers were dropped above the base and recaptured it after fierce fighting with the Tunisians. On July 21, the Legion 3rd REI retook the barracks, installations and positions dominating the base. The day after the 8th Hussard landed the whole area was secured. The "operations to maintain order in Algeria" cost the Legion 65 officers, 278 NCOs and 1,633 legionnaires killed.

9

The French Foreign Legion from 1962 until Today

The Legion After the War in Algeria

The period following the end of the Algerian War was a very unhappy time for the Legion. Only one regiment, the 1st REP, had actively participated in Challe's putsch. The subversive OAS had counted in its ranks a number of Legion deserters, it is true, notably the ex-lieutenant Roger Degueldre and ex-sergeant Albert "Bobby" Dovecar both from the 1st REP. For having led the OAS murder squads (commando Delta), Degueldre and Dovecar were condemned to death and executed by firing squad in 1962. Guilt by association meant that the honor of the whole Legion was stained, and, although the bulk of the Corps had remained loyal, its reliability was put in question. Besides, France had lost her colonial empire: Indochina since 1954, Tunisia and Morocco in 1956, and all African possessions, which had been granted independence without bloodshed by de Gaulle, in 1960. With the grant of independence to Algeria, many politicians, a part of public opinion and even some military authorities held that the Foreign Legion had lost its raison d'être and that there was no longer a place for mercenaries in the French postcolonial armed forces. To many, empire and Legion had become discarded notions of the past.

If France had lost her empire, she still had small territories and islands all over the world. In addition, the agreement of Evian (signed on March 18, 1962) stipulated that France was allowed to maintain a number of army units in Algerian bases (Colomb-Bechar, Reggane, Mers-el-Kebir and Bou-Sfer) for a transitory period. France thus still needed a determined striking force available immediately to protect these bases and assure her presence in overseas territories. The Legion still represented a convenient pool of professional fighters, most of whom embodied the advantage of providing a supplementary source of manpower from outside France. The Legion remained a useful force and was thus maintained, but it was reduced in size and reorganized. When the residual Algerian bases were given up the French Foreign Legion was dispersed elsewhere.

- In October 1962, after 122 years in the country, the 1st RE left Algeria for good.

9. The French Foreign Legion from 1962 until Today

Left: *Legion captain, late 1960s. The man wears a M46 képi and green M47 fatigues.* **Right:** *Sergeant, 2nd REP, in walking-out dress, c. 1970. The képi, fitted with a black leather chin-strap, is midnight blue with a red top and gold Legion grenade at the front. The shirt is pale khaki and the tie dark green. Tunic and trousers are khaki and the laced shoes black. The double gold chevron of rank are worn on both arms and the crimson* **fourragère** *of the Regiment's Légion d'honneur is worn on the left arm.*

In an emotional farewell, the historic base at Sidi-Bel-Abbes and all establishments, camps, homes and barracks the Legion had known for generations in a country they had done so much to create were abandoned. The 1st RE established itself in a new home at Aubagne near Marseilles in southern France, and it continued its task as central headquarters.

- The 2nd REI Infantry Regiment was regrouped at Colomb-Bechar in October 1962 as a garrison for the southern Sahara concession areas and the French nuclear

Paratrooper, 2nd REP, c. 1979. The typical Algeria para camouflage dress, considered a provocative symbol of rebellion after the failed 1961 putsch, was withdrawn from use in January 1963. It was replaced by the green treillis satin 300 M1964 fatigues, which became standard and remained in service for some 25 years. Our man, armed with a MAT 49, is equipped with conventional webbing with drinking bottle and two magazine pouches.

test center. The regiment absorbed the 1st and 4th CSPLs and remnants of the 4th REI. In late 1957, it was posted at the base of Mers-el-Kebir, near Oran. The 2nd REI was disbanded in January 1968 except for a single company, which in August 1968 was the last Foreign Legion unit to leave Algeria.

- The 3rd REI Infantry Regiment was sent to Diego-Suarez on the island of Madagascar where it stayed until September 1973.
- The 4th REI Infantry Regiment was posted in July 1962 to southern Sahara in the sector Colomb-Bechar-Reggane to protect the oilfields and the nuclear test center. The regiment absorbed the 2nd and 3rd CSPL in April 1963. A year later it was disbanded, and remnants were transferred to the 2nd REI.
- The 5th REI Infantry Regiment was based at Colomb-Bechar and Ain-Sefra after the cease-fire of 1962. The regiment was disbanded and remnants were incorporated into a newly formed 5th Régiment Mixte du Pacifique (RMP). This unit, comprising both army and Legion engineering personnel, was shipped to Tahiti in French Polynesia (Pacific Ocean) in June 1963.
- The 13th DBLE Infantry Regiment was shipped in October 1962 to the French-held strategic base of Djibouti in the then-called Territory of Affairs and Issas (French Somaliland, an enclave adjacent to Ethiopia).
- The 2nd REC Cavalry Regiment was disbanded in July 1962 and remnants were transferred to the 1st REC. The 1st REC was based at Mecheria from March 1962 to January 1964. After a period of garrison at Mers-el-Kebir, the regiment

left Algeria and was established in October 1967 at Orange near Avignon in southern France.
- The rebellious 1st REP Airborne Regiment had been disbanded right after the April 1961 putsch and remaining effectives had been transferred to its sister unit, the 2nd REP. In September 1962 the 2nd REP was posted at the Mers-el-Kebir base, and helped build the new military camp of Bou-Sfer, before being transferred to Calvi, Corsica.

The post–Algerian War period was thus a time of grim hardship in an atmosphere of distrust when the life of the Legion seemed to hang by a thread. It took some time before the French authorities felt they could trust the Foreign Legion again. Gradually a section of the French public, and indeed of military opinion, was no longer of the mind that the Legion was something that one did not speak about, like a less reputable relation. Things were forgiven—if not forgotten—and the Corps was brought back to its rightful place as one of France's elite combat formations.

Legion Interventions

Throughout its history, the Foreign Legion had provided a force of good heavy infantry and served as a powerful combat machine to conquer and defend colonies. In the late 1960s, it was decided to give the Corps a new style. Pioneered by the paratroopers of the 2nd REP, the emphasis was now on flexibility, fast mobility, multiple combat techniques, modern equipment and updated tactics. Large regiments were dissolved and the Legion was soon composed of small but hard-hitting detachments placed at strategic points, ready for any kind of mission, at any time and anywhere in the world. Officers and legionnaires came to master a broad range of military skills such as mountain warfare; antitank fighting; parachute, helicopter and amphibious operations; sabotage; mining; advanced reconnaissance work, etc. To achieve these goals, the Legion became extremely selective and accepted in its ranks only the best and fittest young men. Individual physical training, collective field training and the ability to master a wide range of modern weapons became paramount. The core units of the Legion, the 2nd REI and 1st REC, were

2nd REP captain, c. 1978. The depicted captain wears the green para beret and olive green combat dress model 1964 Satin 300. The short jacket is tightly tailored and elasticated with two vertically zipped chest pockets. On the belt are a bayonet/fighting knife and a MAC 50 pistol.

Legion sniper, c. 1987. This mountain training sniper is armed with an FR-F2 rifle. Issued in 1984, the manual bolt action rifle uses a 7.62 × 51 mm NATO cartridge fed in a 10-round box magazine, with a maximum effective range of 800 m. It is fitted with a padded cheek rest, an adjustable buttstock, folding bipod legs, and a 6x power sniping scope. Loaded, the weapon weighs 12.75 lbs., its total length is 120 cm (47.21 in.).

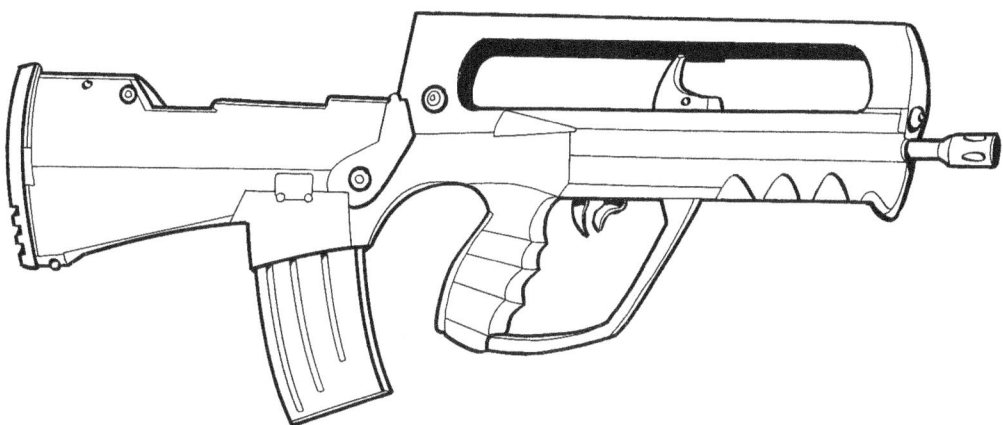

FA MAS. The Fusil d'Assault de la Manufacture d'Armes de Saint-Etienne (FA MAS), often nicknamed "clairon" (bugle) because of its unusual appearance, was accepted in 1978 as the standard service assault rifle for the French army replacing the aging MAT 49. A short, handy, accurate, effective, compact and easy to maintain weapon, it is operated on the delayed blowback principle, and has three firing options: single-shot, three-round burst, and automatic (with a cyclic rate of fire of 1,000 rpm). Caliber is 5.56 mm, length is 757 mm (29.8 in.), and weight (loaded) is 4.59 kg (10.12 lbs.). The straight box magazine holds 25 rounds, and there is provision for a small bayonet, folding bipod legs, infrared night sighting, and grenade launcher.

fully integrated into the French line of battle; other Legion units were supplemented by formations rotating from France. In short, by the late 1960s and 1970s the Legion was transformed from a conventional army into a uniquely skilled intervention force, and it remains so today. France retains various commitments to her former colonies, particularly in black Africa, and France's international role requires peacekeeping duties for the UN and NATO, and thus the Foreign Legion, reinstated as one of France's elite combat and most prestigious units, stands ready for active service again.

French interests in Africa are still widespread, and in the recent past France made several military interventions in that volatile continent. In 1969 in Chad elements of the 2nd REP fought against rebel groups who wanted to overthrow President Ngarta Tombalbaye. Actions took place along the Sudanese border and in the Sahara Desert. In the 1970s and 1980s other expeditions saw the dispatch of the Legion again to Chad, a chronically ill-governed but strategic land

Overseas Medal. The old Médaille coloniale (Colonial Medal) was renamed Médaille d'Outremer (Overseas Medal) in June 1962. The medal (here shown commemorating a tour of duty in Chad) is silver with a light blue and white ribbon.

Legion headgear. (1) Model 1978 F1 helmet with cloth cover, rubber retaining band and chin cup; (2) chèche *scarf worn in desert and African posting; (3) green beret with Legion flamed-grenade badge; (4) traditional white képi.*

south of President Muammar al-Quaddafi's Libya. In May 1978 elements of the 1st REC fought against Libyan-backed rebels at Salal, Ati and Djedda. In the period 1983–1987, a large French force, including Legion units, took part to several operations intended to control the unruly Chad-Libyan border.

In February 1976, at Djibouti, Legion paratroopers of the 2nd REP and elements of the 13th DBLE took part in the rescue of civilians and children hijacked by Somalian terrorists.

In May 1978 in Zaïre (Congo), a force of Congolese nationalists seize the mining town of Kolwezi in Shaba Province; when they started to maltreat civilian white hostages, French Legion paras of the 2nd REP together with Belgian troops were dropped in to rescue them. The audacious operation was a success in showing the world that France had a quick intervention force which could strike with might over enormous distances at great speed.

At Beirut (Lebanon) in August–September 1982, elements of the 2nd REP, 2nd REI and 1st REC (alongside an international force) helped supervise the agreed withdrawal of Yassir Arafat's defeated PLO. The highly sensitive mission was carried out by the French legionaries without serious incident.

In May–June 1990, two companies of the 2nd REI and 2nd REP were engaged in Port Gentil, Gabon, to rescue European hostages held by antigovernment rioters.

The first Gulf War in 1990–1991 saw the participation of elements drawn from the Legion 2nd REI, 1st REC, 6th REG, 1st RE, 2nd REP and 2nd REI—known as Groupement de marche de la Légion étrangère (GMLE, Foreign Legion Task Force). Deployed on the western flank of coalition forces, they formed a two-pronged motorized column, and attacked the Iraqi 45th Division. In less than 50 hours, the GMLE reached its objectives, the town and airfield of As Salman, taking some 3,000 prisoners, seizing large quantities of material and, most important, suffering no casualties and sustaining no material damage.

In 1994, units of the 2nd REI and 13th DBLE were flown to Rwanda in an attempt to create protected zones during the appalling Hutu and Tutsi tribal massacres.

During the civil war in Bosnia from 1993 to 1996, the French Foreign Legion made a remarkable contribution to the international force IFOR under NATO and UN command by sending elements of the 2nd REI, 1st REC and 6th REG. In this difficult and sensitive mission, the Legion operated with self-discipline and efficiency giving a brilliant account of its professionalism.

The Legion Today

An elite and sophisticated force of motorized and airborne infantry, paratroopers, light armor, combat divers, as well as engineers and support troops, the French Foreign Legion today is a purely volunteer force composed of men (women are still not allowed to join) who want to be soldiers, and who enjoy the life they have chosen to lead. Indeed, the Legion is still composed of volunteers of many nationalities. The men (over 18 but under 40 years of age when they apply) now serve for five years under who-cares-what names, men who are (often) given a second chance in the hard life of the Legion. However, the days of joining "no question asked" are a thing of the past, now the Legion has a unit (ironically called "Gestapo" in slang) concerned with internal security and screening of candidates. A minor criminal background is not necessarily a problem but the Legion is no longer a hiding place for wanted criminals. Extensive checks are made and a confirmed criminal would be rejected and handed over to the appropriate authority.

Thoroughly imbued with its own spirit, the Legion has kept its attachment to the past, it has retained its traditional parade uniforms, its ceremonies and its pride, philosophy, way of life, esprit de corps, and a liking for work well done, but conditions of service have enormously improved since the time when the Legion was a neglected repository for colonial cannonfodder. Officers and NCOs are intelligent, skilled and experienced leaders who care for their men. Corporal punishment is still a factor in the Legion though on a much smaller scale than it used to be. It has, in fact, almost been completely eradicated as an accepted form of discipline, but isolated incidents do occasionally occur.

In the past there had always been a strong criticism that, off-duty, the Legion neglected the man and allowed him to drink, revel and laze about as he wished in his own time. This is no longer true and sport, recreation and entertainment are now organized for free time. In fact the Legion tends to make its members totally dependant on the Corps for everything in an attempt to bond them together as a family. Legionnaires must be prepared to deny wife, children and family for many years until they qualify by rank or service to have the right to get married. Serving in the Legion is not a simple 9 to 5 job, and the Corps deeply intrudes in its members' lives. A typical garrison day in a regiment would be scheduled something like the following.

5:00 Wake up call
5:30 Roll call
5:30–7:00 Breakfast, followed by ablutions and *corvée* (cleaning) duties
7:00–7:30 *Corvée quartier* (garbage sweep of company area)
7:30 *Rassemblement compagnie* (Company assembly)
7:30–9:00 Sport and fitness activities
9:00–9:30 Showers followed by a snack
9:30–12:00 Morning training, work details
12:00–13:30 *Soupe* (lunch) followed by cleaning sweep
13:30–14:00 *Corvée quartier*
14:00 Company assembly
14:00–17:30 Afternoon training, work details
17:30–21:30 End of work day, dinner and free time
21:30–22:00 Cleaning duties
22:00 Roll call
22:30 Lights out

Marche ou Crève ("March or Die") is an ominous motto from the Legion's past, alluding that stragglers on a march either kept up or were left behind to perish. Things are no longer that severe but the spirit of these words lives on, and training for combat units includes long marches in full pack, in all kinds of weather, by day or night in difficult terrain.

With the current emphasis on health and fitness, alcoholism, always a vexing problem, is no longer tolerated and strongly disallowed except on a few holiday occasions such as Camerone Day or Christmas when exceptional drinking bouts are permitted.

Well-fed, properly paid, well-motivated, well-led, intensively trained and well-equipped, the Legion is a modern force in every way that counts. The Corps is one of the toughest and most highly regarded military formations in the world. As France has not been involved in a major war since 1962, the Legion does not need a large pool of manpower, and is able to be extremely selective about recruiting; it is estimated that seven out of every 10 applicants are turned away. Only the youngest, fittest, most intelligent and best-motivated candidates who can meet the most exacting physical standards succeed in finishing out the three months of hard basic training demanded before posting to a unit. The Foreign Legion's well-deserved high reputation also attracts many professional officer applicants from the French army, anxious to add a tour with this unique and prestigious force to their records, and only the best of them are selected. The other side of the coin is that foreign legionnaires tend to live in a world of their own.

Counting some 20,000 men in 1962, the Legion totaled only 8,000 in 1976. Today the French Foreign Legion has some 8,500 men divided into the following units posted both in France and in the *Territoires d'Outremer* (overseas territories).

1st RE/COMLE

The Premier Régiment étranger/Commandement de la Légion étrangère (1st Foreign Regiment/Foreign Legion Command), based at Quartier Viennot Aubagne (near Marseilles in southern France), is the central depot for recruitment, selection, personnel management, administration, and a wide range of services including welfare, rehabilitation, pensions and family allowances for ex-servicemen just to name a few. It also deals with matters pertaining to "rectification" (getting the discharged legionaries their original names when they wish to do so).

Ceremony has always played an important part in the Legion as it is held to be closely connected with identity and morale. Today all Legion units have a Color, some of which are heavily decorated; the Color is the symbol of command and when leaders change over there is a parade and the flag is formally handed over by the old commander to his successor in full sight of the men of the regiment. *Fourragères* (multiple lanyards) are worn on the shoulder as a mark of distinction by some regiments. Bands were an early feature with the Legion and every regiment has one. In addition the 1st RE has a famous pioneer company which displays the most popular and best publicized image of the Legion. Used in parades and commemorations, the pioneer company of the 1st RE is a very impressive ceremonial unit composed of tall, strong, bearded men wearing white képis, red and green epaulettes, green ties, impeccable khaki uniforms, large white gloves, thick leather aprons and white gaiters. The men carry axes on their right shoulders and march at the solemn slow Legion parade tempo (88 paces to the minute only, instead of 120 paces/minute for the French army).

2nd REI

The Deuxième Régiment étranger d'Infanterie (2nd Foreign Infantry Regiment), resuming its title in June 1980, is currently based in Quartier Vallongue at Nîmes (southern France). While retaining a specialist training role, it is an armored infantry and light antitank regiment which is an element of the French FAR (rapid action force). The more than 150-year-old regiment embodies the traditional spirit of the Legion, but it has also adapted to a future in which the potential enemy is longer so clearly designated. The 2nd REI is fully capable of the most varied missions including conventional warfare, keeping order or countering a mechanized adversary in the desert. Equipped with 92 armored vehicles, the 1,200 men of the 2nd REI form a powerful motorized shock infantry unit, men

Pioneer 1st RE in ceremonial dress

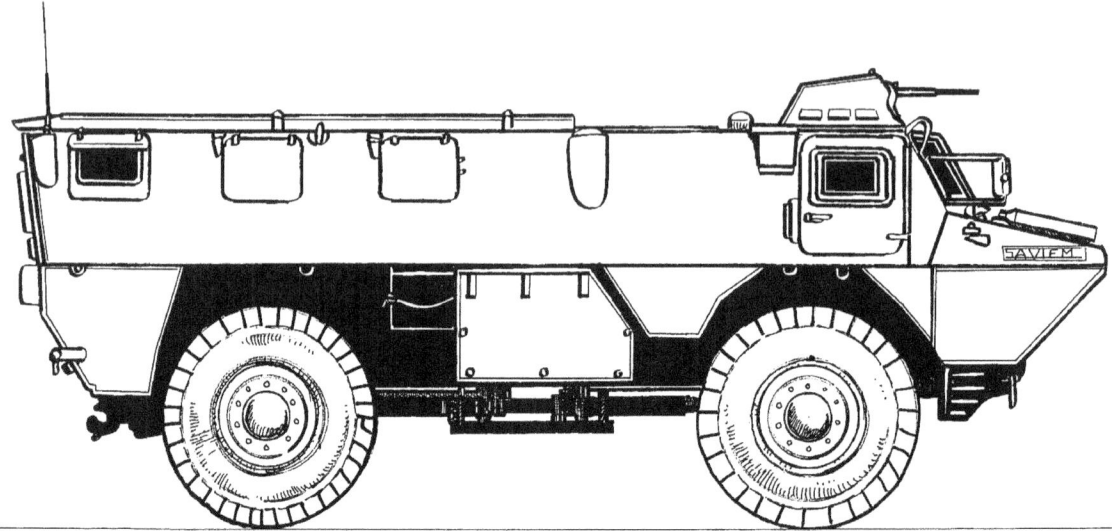

Renault VAB (Armored Personnel Carrier). The Renault-Saviem VAB, **véhicule de l'avant blindé** *(frontline armored vehicle) is a sturdy and reliable APC. It has four driving wheels (six wheels in export versions), is NBC-protected with welded armor, has a capacity of 12 fully equipped infantrymen and can be transported by transport airplane. Amphibious as well, the VAB is powered by a 162 kW diesel engine, and has a length of 5.980 m, a width of 2.490 m, a height of 2.060 m, and a maximum speed of 100 km/h (7.2 km/h on water). It can be fitted with a turret or a ring mounting for 7.62 mm or 12.7 mm (.50 in.) machine gun, ports are provided for individual weapon firing as well as smoke screening dischargers. The basic vehicle has been adapted to a wide range of other roles including as an ambulance, antiriot security, reconnaissance, repair and command vehicle, mortar, antitank missile and anti-aircraft weapon carrier. The VAB was a major export success, over 1,000 having been sold to the forces of at least 15 countries. A new design known a VAB NG (New Generation) has been developed by Renault and Creusot-Loire with many improvements.*

who have proven their professionalism, solid military skill and confident dignity on countless occasions.

3rd REI

After Madagascar, the Troisième Régiment étranger d'Infanterie (3rd Foreign Infantry Regiment) has been posted to French Guiana, a territory on the northeast coast of South America. Currently housed in Quartier Forget at Kuru, it is a motorised light infantry regiment whose mission is to protect the French/European Kuru Space Center. The 3rd REI is the descendant of the prestigious Foreign Legion Task Regiment (RMLE) formed in 1915, heavily mauled in World War I and placed under the leadership of Colonel Rollet, who is regarded as the creator of the modern-day Legion. The 3rd REI, the second most decorated regiment of the French army (after the RICM, Marine Infantry Regiment), now joins its high traditions with the task of guarding France and Europe's precious asset in the outer space race. The regiment is composed of a Headquarters and Services Company; the Second Rifle Company equipped with "ultra-lite" aircraft and a team of sharpshooters tasked with the defense of the Space Center; and the Reconnaissance and Support Company, which includes a scout platoon, a 20 mm anti-aircraft gun platoon and an engineering platoon. During rocket launches extra troops are deployed around the base, but not necessarily provided by the Legion. The regiment is also tasked with missions in remote parts of the country in deep jungle and along the waterways, including land surveying and patrolling or chasing smugglers, illegal immigrants and poachers. During these demanding in-depth patrols, which can last for weeks, supplies are brought in by helicopter, but it can happen that the men must live off the country. The 3rd REI also runs the Regina Jungle Training Center set in scenery of breathtaking beauty high on a hill overlooking the Approuague River. The comprehensive training is intended for French soldiers and Legion members but the center also opens its door to trainees from American, Canadian, Dutch and Brazilian forces.

4th RE

The Quatrième Régiment étranger (4th Foreign Regiment), the descendant of the 4th REI, was re-formed in September 1977 and retitled 4th RE in June 1980. The regiment is currently based in Quartier Danjou at Castelnaudary, about 50 kilometers southeast of Toulouse in southern France. The 4th RE is subordinated to COMLE from Aubagne, and tasked with all Legion training. The very demanding basic training lasts 16 weeks in the Legion "farm," and promising candidates may progress further to NCO training.

5th RE

The Cinquième Régiment étranger (5th Foreign Regiment), known as 5th Régiment mixte du Pacifique (RMP) from 1963 to 1984, was established in the Centre d'Expérimentation du Pacifique (CEP) at Mururoa Atoll in French Polynesia, with a transit camp at Arue, Tahiti. The 5th RMP included Legion and Army engineers and their first task in the 1960s was to be built the Experimentation Center itself, where French nuclear weapons were to be tested. In particularly difficult conditions, everything had to be constructed from scratch on the small remote coral atoll (Mururoa is 19,000 kilometers from France and 1,200 kilometers from Tahiti). Drawing upon their reputation as builders ("legionnaires can build anything anywhere"), the Legion engineers constructed most of the CEP installations. When this work was completed the regiment was tasked with maintenance, and provision of local and regional security to the French military nuclear test center. Before being officially dissolved in June 2000, the 5th RE included a Headquarters and Services Company; an Engineer Company tasked with public works; a Rifle and Heavy Works Company tasked with engineering work and defense on the atoll and throughout the Polynesian archipelago; and a Transport and Maintenance Company tasked with transport, shipping and equipment maintenance and repair.

1st REC

The Premier Régiment de Cavalerie (1st Foreign Cavalry Regiment) was created in 1921 and, following in the hoofprints of their forebears who fought in Syria and Morocco in the 1920s and 1930s, is one of the oldest and most endearing units of the Foreign Legion. It absorbed its sister unit, the 2nd REC, when this was disbanded in July 1962. Both legionnaires and cavalrymen, blending traditions in a modern context of efficiency, the members of the "Royal" regiment are often regarded as the "iron fist" of the Legion. Currently based in Quartier Labouche at Orange (near Avignon in southern France) the 1st REC is equipped with modern vehicles including 4 × 4 Peugeot P-4 light field cars, and 6 × 6 AMX-10 RC wheeled heavy armored vehicles armed with 105 mm guns. The regiment is composed of a headquarter's squadron, three armored squadrons, and one antitank squadron equipped with VAB-HOT (armored vehicles armed with HOT-2 antitank guided missiles).

6th REG

The Sixième Régiment étranger de Génie (6th Foreign Engineer Regiment), created on July 1, 1984, is the heir to the traditions of the 6th REI infantry regiment that won fame in Syria in 1941. Also a worthy heir to the traditions inherited from the "foreign builder legionnaires," the 6th REG is a dynamic and modern motorized assault unit whose tasks include providing assistance during difficult crossings, clearing the way, light bridging, assaulting fortified positions, demolition, blowing up or placing barbed wire and erecting, breaching and removing obstacles and mines, to name a few. For these dangerous and various tasks, the regiment is equipped with highly sophisticated equipment and specialist vehicles (e.g., bulldozers). Currently based in Quartier General Rollet at Laudun (southern France), the 6th REG is organized into one headquarter's company, three assault engineer/sapper companies, one support company, and a service company.

The Regiment has also developed DINOPS (para-combat divers comparable to the U.S. Navy SEALs) used in a wide variety of missions including rescuing, reconnaissance, sea mine clearing, infiltration and sabotage. These highly selected specialists may arrive on location by means of air drops or by submarines, helicopters, landing boats, Zodiac or kayaks. A high level of professionalism is maintained through intensive training.

2nd REG

The Second Régiment de Génie (2nd Foreign Engineer Regiment), created in July 1999, is currently based in Quartier Maréchal Koenig at the air force base of Saint-Christol d'Albion in southern France. It is an assault engineer unit specialized in mountain warfare. It counts 920 men divided into six companies, including one command and logistics company, three combat companies, one support company and one training company. Its device is : "Rien n'empêche!" (Nothing can hinder!). These unsung heroes tirelessly carry out their obscure but vital missions.

2nd REP

The Deuxième Régiment étranger Parachutiste (2nd Parachute Foreign Regiment), successor to the Indochina 2nd BEP and Algeria 2nd REP, is currently based at Camp Raffali at Calvi, Corsica. The Legion paratroopers, together with their comrades of the 3rd RPIMa and 8th RPIMa (Marine paras) form the spearhead of the Force d'Action rapide (FAR, France's immediate intervention force). The 2nd REP is structured like all French airborne regiments. Light, flexible, quick, intensively trained to operate in all climates and terrains, it can be used for missions ranging from maintaining order to conventional infantry or light antitank combat. The First Company (Green) is tasked with urban and night fighting. The Second Company (Red) is specialized in mountain warfare and often trains in the Alps. The Third Company (Black) is entrusted with amphibious operations. The Fourth Company (Grey) specializes in sabotage and sniping. One particularity of the regiment includes a firefighting unit for coping with the forest fires which frequently occur in Corsica in summer.

13th DBLE

The Treisième Demi-Brigade de la Légion étrangère (13th Foreign Legion Half-Brigade)—heir to the legendary Narvik, Bir-Hakeim and Dien Bien Phu Legion 13th DBLE—is now posted in Quartier Montclar at Djibouti. Located in the "Horn of Africa," Djibouti is a strategic French military base at the crossroads between Africa, the Middle East and the Far East, allowing control on the outlet to the Red Sea. As a result of defense agreements with

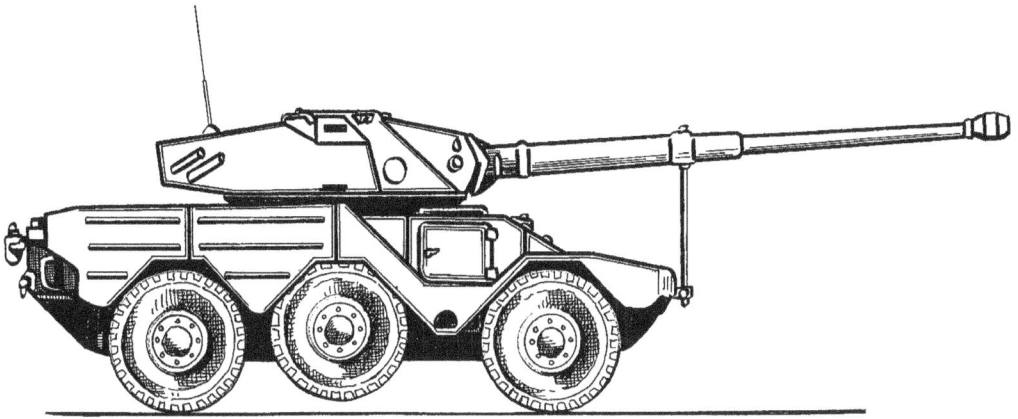

Panhard ERC Sagaie. The **Engin de Reconnaissance Canon** *(ERC, cannon-armed reconnaissance vehicle), specially developed by the Panhard Company for desert operations, is powered by one 2,800 cubic cm Peugeot V6 PRV petrol engine developing 106 kW with a speed of 95 km/h on road (7.2 km/h in water) and a range of 700 kg. Length is 7.68 m, width is 2.50 m, and height is 2.32 m. In combat order the armored amphibious machine weighs 8,300 kg. It is operated by a crew of three (commander, gunner and driver). It is armed with one long-barrelled 90 mm F4 gun, one coaxially-mounted 7.62 mm machine gun, one close-defense 7.62 mm machine gun, and smoke dischargers mounted on each side of the GIAT TS-90 turret. Equipment includes air-conditioning, laser rangefinder, night vision system and NBC protection. All six wheels are powered and the center pair can be raised off the ground for road travel and lowered for cross-country travel.*

the Republic of Djibouti, France maintains a body of troops code-named Forces françaises à Djibouti (FFDj), of which the 13th DBLE is one of the pillars of the garrison. To fulfill its mission in an arid, desert land, the 13th is an all-arms regiment composed of: Headquarters, services and support company, including an antitank Milan missile platoon and a 120-mm mortar platoon; Second Engineer Company; Third Rifle Company adapted to motorized infantry combat and specialized skill including divers, demolition experts, and snipers; and Reconnaissance Squadron, based at Oueah, about 40 kilometers from Djibouti

Caporal-chef, 13th DBLE, c. 1980. This lance-sergeant, posted at Djibouti, wears the summer tropical walking-out and parade uniform including white képi, sand yellow sleeveless shirt with traditional green/gold/red épaulettes, black sash under waist belt with combat knife, shorts, and dark green socks turned down over polished black "rangers" (boots).

equipped with ERC-90 Sagaie armored vehicles. In addition the 13th DBLE is reinforced by a rotating parachute company from the 2nd REP based at Arta. The 13th DBLE also runs the Arta Beach Training Center used by both Djiboutian and French troops.

DLEM

The Détachement de la Légion étrangère à Mayotte (Foreign Legion Detachment at Mayotte), established in 1967, is now based at Dzaoudzi, Mayotte, Comoro Islands. Subordinate to Forces Armées Zone Sud de l'Ocean Indien (FAZSOI, South Indian Ocean Command), the detachment constitutes the French presence in the strategic Mozambique Channel, a zone of great importance halfway between Africa and Madagascar, where giant tankers carrying crude oil from the Middle East pass by every day. In 1974, when the Comore archipelago became independent, the population opted to maintain links with France, and by a referendum held in 1976, the residents of Mayotte voted to remain part of France. The DLEM is composed of a headquarters and services element, a rotating company provided either by the Legion or by another regiment from the 11th Parachute Division. Since 1984, the DLEM has been entrusted with the standard of the 2nd REC, the Legion Cavalry Regiment disbanded in 1962.

The last survivor in a long and glittering line of units of mercenary troops fighting for a country other than their own, the French Foreign Legion is a relic of the legionnaires of ancient Rome, the bands of armed knights of the Middle Ages and 16th-century Swiss mercenary pikemen, of the old days when Europe swarmed with Condottieri and *Grandes Compagnies* led by swashbuckling captains who sold their swords to the highest bidder.

The ambiguous relationship between the Legion and France in the early 1960s is now long forgotten. Since October 1997 France has abandoned the system of national conscription and has moved toward creation of a wholly professional army, of which the Legion is one of the key units. In spite of her love-hate/contempt-admiration relationship

Legionary, Iraq, 1991. The 6th REG legionary depicted here wears the M1978 helmet with desert camouflage cloth cover and goggles, and a camouflage body armor covers the temperate climate fatigues in a yellow/light brown desert camouflage pattern. He is equipped with the standard M1974/79 webbing in synthetic material, and is armed with a FAMAS assault rifle.

9. *The French Foreign Legion from 1962 until Today* 233

Spectra helmet. Based on the U.S. Kevlar-PASGT, the Spectra helmet was introduced in 1992 during the war in Bosnia to replace the older 1978 model. Manufactured by the CGE Gallet Company, the helmet is made of dyneema fibers, weighs 1.300 kg and is available in two sizes. It is generally worn with a removable camouflage cover with various patterns, and for UN peacekeeping missions is painted in light blue.

with the Foreign Legion, France possesses in the Legion an extraordinary force. In today's world there quickly arises some dirty thankless fighting as well as humanitarian and peacekeeping job to be done, efficiently, without delay and without complaint. In this volatile environment the future of the Legion seems assured, and there can be no doubt that the foreign legionnaires, drawing from century-old traditions and paying for their loyalty to France in blood, are serving and will continue to serve with *Honneur, Valeur, Discipline et Fidélité*.

Legion 2nd REP paratrooper, c. 1992. This legionary, about to emplane for a jump, wears camouflage fatigues and is equipped with a 696-26 parachute and FAMAS assault rifle hitched in a canvas cover.

Appendix 1
Ranks and Units

Concise listing of French army ranks most commonly encountered and corresponding British ranks

Hommes de troupe — *Privates*
Legionnaire — Legionary
Grenadier — Grenadier
Voltigeur — Skirmisher
Tirailleur — Rifleman
Fusilier — Rifleman
Chasseur — Rifleman
Fusilier-Marin — Marine
Artilleur — Artilleryman
Canonier — Gunner
Cavalier — Horseman
Infirmier — Medical Orderly
Sapeur — Sapper
Chauffeur — Driver
Parachutiste — Paratrooper
Chasseur-Parachutiste — Paratrooper
Radio — Signalman
Soldat de deuxième classe — Private
Soldat de première classe — Senior Private

Petits gradés — *NCOs*
Caporal — Corporal
Caporal-Chef — Lance-Sergeant
Sergent — Sergeant

Maréchal des Logis	Sergeant
Sergent-Chef	Company Sergeant-Major
Maréchal des Logis-Chef	Company Sergeant-Major
Adjudant	Sergeant-Major
Adjudant-Chef	Staff-Sergeant
Aspirant	Officer cadet

Officiers subalternes	*Junior Officers*
Sous-Lieutenant	Second Lieutenant
Lieutenant	Lieutenant
Capitaine	Captain
Chef de Bataillon	Major
Commandant	Major

Officiers supérieurs	*Senior Officers*
Lieutenant-Colonel	Lieutenant-Colonel
Colonel	Colonel or Brigadier
Général de Brigade	Lieutenant-General
Général	General
Maréchal	Field-Marshal

Units

Section	Squad
Peloton	Platoon
Compagnie	Company
Bataillon	Battalion
Régiment	Regiment
Regiment de Marche	Task Regiment (for a special mission)
Demi-brigade	Half-Brigade (Regiment)
Brigade	Brigade (two regiments)
Groupement	Group of units (for a special mission)
Division	Division
Armée	Army
Corps d'Armée	Army Corps

Appendix 2
The Legion's Song: "Le Boudin"

It is hard to find an exact origin for this song. The origins of the title, as well as the origins of this famous chorus, are not known. Some Legion historians believe the title has gastronomic origins. *Boudin* actually means blood sausage (for the Americans) or black pudding (for the British). Others think the title derives from the cloth roll which was carried on the backpack that legionnaires would call "boudin." Another origin of the "Boudin" goes back to 1860, when the king of the Belgians sent men to France for enlistment in the French Foreign Legion. For unknown reasons, the Belgians were treated as "lazy bastards" by the German legionaries, who at this time represented the major nationality in the French Foreign Legion. The expression *tirer au cul* in Parisian slang means to "laze about," so *un tireur au cul* can be freely translated as "lazy bastard" or "lazy son of a bitch."

It seems that a lot of alternative lyrics have been sung due to the fertile imagination of the legionnaires. The current lyrics were probably adopted about 1870, at a time when the king of the Belgians had requested that his subjects not join the French Foreign Legion while many volunteers from the provinces of Alsace and Lorraine did. This might explain why the meritful volunteers from Alsace, Lorraine and also Switzerland "may have black pudding" and why "none is left for the Belgian lazy sons of bitches."

In fact, it will undoubtedly never be known if the lyrics are due to the shoulders of the legionaries or their stomachs, but it is undeniable that the "Boudin" is a song whose lyrics exalte glorious death, major love of the legionnaire for his flag and for his fatherland of adoption.

As for the tune, it is sometimes said to be inspired by a Rameau's writing, a remake of the 67th Regiment Infantrie chorus in 1862. Another source mentions that a short time before the departure of the Foreign Regiment for Mexico in January 1863, Mr. Wilhelm, who directed the brass band of the 2nd Régiment étranger, might have composed the first 16 measurements of the Legion's famous marching song.

One salutes during the playing of "Boudin," unless one is a member of the band and one sings it when standing at attention.

Le Boudin
Marche de la Légion Etrangère

Music of the "Boudin." (Typographic layout by Eltjo de Lang and Ben Marcato)

Refrain

Tiens, voilà du boudin, (*Here have some boudin*)
Voilà du boudin, (*Have some boudin*)
Voilà du boudin, (*Have some boudin*)
Pour les Alsaciens, les Suisses et les Lorrains, (*For the Alsacians, the Swiss and the Lorrainners*)
Pour les Belges, y en a plus, (*For the Belgians none is left*)
Pour les Belges, y en a plus, (*For the Belgians none is left*)
Ce sont des tireurs au cul. (*They are lazy bastards*)

Verse I

Au Tonkin, la Légion immortelle (*In Tonkin the immortal Legion*)
A Tuyen-Quang illustra notre drapeau, (*At Tuyen Quang illustrated our flag*)
Héros de Camerone et frères modèles (*Heroes of Camerone and exemplary brothers*)
Dormez en paix dans vos tombeaux. *(Sleep in peace in your graves)*

Verse II

Au cours de nos campagnes lointaines, (*During our remote campaigns*)
Affrontant la fièvre et le feu, (*Facing fever and fire*)
Oublions avec nos peines, (*Let us forget with our suffering*)
La mort qui nous oublie si peu, (*Death which never forgets us*)
Nous, la Légion. (*We, the Legion*)

Sonnerie A

Nous sommes des dégourdis (*We are clever guys*),
Nous sommes des lascars (*We are sharp fellows*),
Des types pas ordinaires (*We are no ordinary chaps*),
Nous avons souvent notre cafard, (*We often have the blues*)
Nous sommes des Légionnaires. (*We are legionaries*)

Sonnerie B

Nos anciens ont su mourir, (*Our veterans knew how to die*)
Pour la gloire de la Légion, (*For the glory of the Legion*)
Nous saurons bien tous périr, (*We shall know how to perish*)
Suivant la tradition. (*Following the tradition*)

Appendix 3
The Code of Honor

The Code of Honor must be memorized and recited in French flawlessly in a ceremony during which newly graduated legionnaires receive their white képi.

1. Légionnaire, tu es un volontaire servant la France avec honneur et fidélité.

2. Chaque légionnaire est ton frère d'arme quelle que soit sa nationalité, sa race, sa religion. Tu lui manifestes toujours la solidarité étroite qui doit unir les membres d'une même famille.

3. Respectueux des traditions, attaché à tes chefs, la discipline et la camaraderie sont ta force, le courage et la loyauté tes vertus.

4. Fier de ton état de légionnaire, tu le montres dans ta tenue toujours impeccable, ton comportement toujours digne mais modeste, ton casernement toujours net.

5. Soldat d'élite, tu t'entraînes avec rigueur, tu entretiens ton arme comme ton bien le plus précieux, tu as le souci constant de ta forme physique.

6. [La mission est sacrée, tu l'exécutes jusqu'au bout et si besoin, en opérations, au péril de ta vie.] *Nouvelle version (depuis novembre 2000):* La mission est sacrée, tu l'exécutes jusqu'au bout en respectant les lois, les usages de la guerre, les conventions internationales et, au besoin, au péril de ta vie.

7. Au combat, tu agis sans passion et sans haine, tu respectes les ennemis vaincus, tu n'abandonnes jamais ni tes morts, ni tes blessés, ni tes armes.

Here is a translation in English.

1. Legionnaire, you are a volunteer serving France with honor and fidelity.

2. Every legionnaire is your brother-in-arms regardless of his nationality, race or religion. You demonstrate this by the strict solidarity which must always unite members of the same family.

3. Respectful of traditions, devoted to your leaders, discipline and comradeship are your strength, courage and loyalty your virtues.

4. Proud of your status as legionnaire, you show this in your uniform which is always impeccable, your behavior always dignified but modest, and your living quarters always clean.

5. An elite soldier, you will train rigorously, you will maintain your weapon as your most precious possession, you are constantly concerned with your physical form.

6. [A mission is sacred, you will carry it out until the end at all cost.] *Updated version (since November 2000):* A mission is sacred, you will carry it out until the end respecting laws, customs of war, international convention and, if necessary, at the risk of your life.

7. In combat, you will act without passion and without hate, you will respect the vanquished enemy, you will never abandon your dead or wounded, nor surrender your weapon.

Appendix 4
If You Want to Join the French Foreign Legion

Joining the Legion today is not recommended for anyone. It is a serious matter which demands serious thought. It is not something to be entered into lightly. It is a way of life like no other, and—if you are accepted—there are many sacrifices to be made. Indeed not everybody can become a legionnaire, the selection process is very hard. Outside of operations, most of the time is devoted to drill, training and maintaining equipment. Spare time is available but scarce. The Legion does everything in its power to avoid low morale and constantly reminds its members that respecting the traditions and the esprit de corps (by ceremonies, parades and celebrations) of the Legion should contribute to making every legionnaire feel at home. Like everything in life, being a legionnaire is only as good as one makes it. It is not an easy way out of one's problems, but if one can adapt to it and if one is determined to make it work, it can be a life-changing experience.

The main enlistment requirements, the list of recruitment offices with address and telephone number, enlistment procedures, contract and length of service, posting position, training, specialties and qualifications, pay, promotion and career prospects, social advantages, acquisition of French nationality and resident permit, help in returning to civilian life, and many other aspects of the Foreign Legion are covered by several Internet websites. Candidates can get useful information by visiting the following Internet sites (notably that of the Foreign Legion and that of the embassy of France in the United States):

http://www.foreignlegionlife.com   www.7flammes.com
http://www.ambafrance-us.org   www.monsieur-legionnaire.com
www.samle.fr   www.jlplib.com

Bibliography

Amen, Patrice, ed. *Magazine Histoire et Patrimoine No. 3. France Coloniale.* Toulouse: Milan Presse, May 2005.

Armes-Militaria. Magazine published by Librairie Histoire et Collections Paris.

Augusta, Pavel. *Encyclopédie de l'art militaire.* Paris: Ars Mundi Editions, 1991.

Bail, René, and Jean-Pierre Bernier. *Indochine 1945–1954.* 3 vol. Bayeux: Editions Heimdal, 1988.

Baron, Etienne. *La France et ses régions, L'Union française, classe de troisième, cours complémentaire.* Editions Magnard, 1947.

Bergot, Erwan. *Bataillon Bigeard.* Paris: Presses de la Cité, 1977.

———. *Dien Bien Phu.* Paris: Presses de la Cité, 1989.

Bertin, François. *Les Véhicules alliés de la liberation.* Rennes: Editions Ouest-France, Edilarge SA, 2004.

Blond, Georges. *Histoire de la Légion étrangère 1831–1981.* Paris: Editions Plon, 1981.

Bonnecarrère, Paul. *Par le sang verse.* Paris: Fayard, 1968.

Bornert, Lucien. *Dien Bien Phu.* Paris: Nouvelles Presses Mondiales, 1954.

Bromberger Merry, and Serge Bromberger. *Les treize complots du 13 Mai.* Paris: Editions Fayard, 1959.

Brunon, Jean, Manue Georges, and Pierre Carles. *Le Livre d'Or de la Légion étrangère: Edition du cent-cinquantième anniversaire 1831–1981.* Paris: Charles-Lavauzelle, 1981.

Castellan, Georges. *Histoire de l'Armée.* Paris: Presses Universitaires de France, 1948.

Courrière, Yves. *La guerre d'Algérie.* 4 vol. Paris: Editions Fayard, 1970.

———. *La guerre d'Algérie en images.* Paris: Editions Fayard, 1972.

Fouquet-Lapar, Philippe. *Histoire de l'Armée française.* Paris: Presses Universitaires de France, 1986.

Gazette des uniformes. Paris: Editions Regi-Arm.

Grauwin, Paul. *J'étais médecin à Dien Bien Phu.* Paris: Editions France-Empire, 1954.

Guerrilla. Magazine published by Etat-Major 2ème Bureau of Commandement supérieur des Troupes françaises d'Extrême-Orient, CSTFEO.

Hartink, A. E. *Geïllustreede antieke Wapens Encyclopedie.* Lisse, Belgium: Rebo Productions, 2002.

Historia Special No. 414 bis *150e Anniversaire Légion étrangère.* Paris: Jules Tallandier, 1981.

Hornung, Peter. *Die Legion: Europas letzte Söldner.* Munich: Meyster Verlag, 1981.

Hougron, Jean. *Soleil au ventre.* Paris: Editions Domat, 1952.

Képi Blanc. Official magazine of the French Foreign Legion.

Kilian, Robert. *Les Fusiliers marins en Indochine.* Paris: Editions Berger-Levrault, 1950.

Lartéguy, Jean. *Les Centurions.* Paris: Presses Pocket, 1961.

———. *Les Prétoriens.* Paris: Presses Pocket, 1961.

Lebrun, François, and Jean Carpentier. *Histoire de France.* Paris: Seuil Editions, 1987.

Magazine l'Illustration. *Album de la Guerre* (2 volumes) Paris 1926.

Ministère des Armées (Section Technique). *Guide technique sommaire du pistolet-mitrailleur*

de 9 mm modèle 1949. Paris: Ministère des Armées, 1964.
Miquel, Pierre. *Histoire de la France*. Collection Marabout Histoire. Paris: Anthème Fayard, 1976.
O'Ballance, Edgar. *The Story of the French Foreign Legion*. London: Faber & Faber, 1961.
Pouget, Jean. *Le Manifeste du Camp No.1*. Paris: Editions Fayard, 1969.
Ripert, Pierre. *Histoire de la guerre d'Indochine*. Paris: Editions Maxi-Livre, 2004.
Robinet de Cléry, Adrien. *Histoire de France 1789–1963*. Munich: Max Hueber Verlag, 1965.
Sergent, Pierre. *Je ne regrette rien*. Paris: Fayard, 1972.
Summer, Ian, François Vauvillier, and Mike Chappell. *The French Army 1939–45* (1). Oxford: Osprey Publishing, 1998.
_____. *The French Army 1939–45* (2). Oxford: Osprey Publishing, 2001.
Volkmann, Jean-Charles. *La Chronologie de l'Histoire de France*. Paris: Editions Jean-Paul Gisserot, 1997.
Windrow, Martin. *The French Foreign Legion*. London: Patrick Stephens Airfix Products, 1976.
_____, and Mike Chappell. *French Foreign Legion 1914–45*. Oxford: Osprey Publishing, 1999.
_____, and _____. *The Algerian War 1954–62*. Oxford: Osprey Publishing, 2000.
_____, and _____. *The French Indochina War 1946–54*. Oxford: Osprey Publishing, 1998.
Windrow, Martin, Wayne Braby, and Kevin Lyles. *French Foreign Legion Paratroops*. Oxford: Osprey Publishing, 2002.

Index

Aage (prince of Denmark) 121, 122
Abd-El-Kader (emir) 5, 16, 21, 25, 27
Abd-El-Krim (Algerian leader) 125, 126, 127, 129
Adrian helmet 92
Alessandri, Colonel 163
Ali la Pointe 206
Amazons 78, 79
Amilakvari, Lt.-Col. Dimitri 147, 149, 154
Ananas grenade 129
Arago, Commandant Victor-Joseph 57
Aumoitte, Lieutenant-Colonel 143

Bao Dai (emperor) 193
Baraka 107
Barda 66, 118
Barre, Commandant 82
Batallions d'Afrique 55, 87, 119, 135
Bayt, Captain 213
Bazaine, Col. Achille 33, 45
Behanzin, King of Dahomey 77, 78, 80
Ben Bella, Pres. Ahmed 200, 211
Berber 30, 38, 197, 210
Berg, Corporal 51
Berliet VUDB 124
Bernelle, Colonel 14, 17
Berthier carbine 92
Berthier model 1907/15 rifle 91
Besson, Colonel 142

Bir Hakeim, siege of 147–153
Biscuitville 27
Bismarck, Chancellor Otto von 57
Bordel Militaire de Campagne 120
Borelli, Captain 70
Bou Ziane 28, 29
"Le Boudin" (song) 56, 104, 238, 239
Bouilloux, Legionary 104
Boumedienne, Pres. Houari 211
Breguet Br.19 airplane 124
Bren LMG 152
Brillant, Sergeant 214
Brothier, Colonel 203, 212, 215, 216
Bugeaud, Gen. Thomas 23, 25, 26

Cafard 87, 121
Camerone, battle of 45–53
Canrobert, Colonel 28, 33, 34
Casmene, Georges 100
Cendrars, Blaise 101
Chabrière, Colonel 41
Challe, Gen. Maurice 198, 211, 212, 213, 214, 216
Charles X (king of France) 5
Charton, Colonel 183, 184
Chassepot rifle 55
Chauchat LMG 97, 106
Colombat, Colonel 120
Colonial Army 9
Colonnes volantes 23
Combe, Colonel 21
Commune of Paris 59, 60

Compagnie montée 66
Conrad, Col. Fritz 18
Cot, Lieutenant-Colonel 104
Courbet, Adm. Amédée 67, 68
Crapouillot 99

Danjou, Capt. Jean 47, 48, 49, 51, 53
Debuissy, Lieutenant-Colonel 142
De Cadoudal, Colonel 163
De Caprez, Colonel 33, 34
De Gaulle, Pres. Charles 140, 144, 145, 154, 155, 164, 196, 200, 211, 212, 213, 214, 217
De la Croix de Castries, Gen. Christian 188, 192
De Lamaze, Captain 140, 151
De Lattre de Tassigny, Gen. Jean-Marie 162, 185, 186
Denoix de Saint-Marc, Maj. Elie 212, 213, 216
De Sairigné, Colonel 159
Desertion 55
Dodds, General 77, 80
Dodge truck 153, 159
Dominé, Commandant 70
Druses 130, 131, 132
Dunant, Henri 43
Duriez, Lieutenant-Colonel 106, 108

FAMAS rifle 223
Faurax, Major 77, 78
Ferry, Jules 61
Flying banana helicopter 199

Franz-Ferdinand (archduke of Austria) 89
FR-F2 rifle 222
Fusil Mitrailleur Model 24/29 123, 154

Gambetta, Léon (politician) 57
Garand M1 rifle 161
Gardy, General-Inspector 213, 215
Garibaldi, Giuseppe 101
Gas mask 98, 105
Genet, Jean 122
Gestapo 225
Giap, Gen. Vo Nguyen 165, 166, 182, 183, 185, 186, 187, 188
Glockner, legionary 23
Godard, Col. Yves 212, 213, 214
Gueules Cassées 109

Harki 200, 217
Hindenburg line 110, 111
Ho Chi Minh 164, 165, 166, 167, 186, 187, 193
Hoberg 121
Honneur et Fidélité 18, 136
Hotchkiss FM 123
Hotchkiss machine gun 97

Jeanningros, Colonel 45, 47, 51, 53, 54
Jeanpierre, Captain and Lieutenant-Colonel 184, 203, 209, 213
Jouhaut, Gen. Edmont 212, 214
Juarez, Garcia Benito 44, 54
Junger, Ernst 101

Karageorgevitch 57
Klems, Joseph 125
Koenig, Gen. Pierre 149, 150, 151

Lamoricière, Gen. Christophe Louis 6
Landriau, Captain 131
La Rafale 175, 176
Lebel model 1886 rifle 79
Lee Enfield rifle 152
Legio Patria Nostra 87
Le Mat model 1856 revolver 33
Lemeunier, Lieutenant-Colonel 192
Léon, Adjudant-Chef 112
Lepage, Commandant 183, 184
Lightning war 142
Louis II Grimaldi 101
Louis XVIII (king of France) 9

Louis-Philippe (king of France) 5, 6, 20
Lun-Vinh-Phuoc 67, 71
Lyautey, Marshal Louis 115, 116, 117, 118, 125

MacMahon, General 29, 39, 40
Mader, Adjudant-Chef 106
Magrin-Verneret, Lt.-Col. Raoul 140, 146, 147
Maire, Colonel 122
Mallaret, Colonel 63
Mangin, General 90
Maoist guerrilla warfare 174, 175
Marche ou crève 84, 226
Martinez, Major and Colonel 41, 43
MAS AAT 52 machine gun 203
MAS 49 rifle 203
MAS M 1850 pistol 30
MAS model 1874 Gras rifle 64, 66
MAS 36 rifle 169
MAS T40 rifle 26
Massu, Gen. Jacques 203, 204
MAT 49 submachine gun 174
Maudet, Second-Lieutenant 47, 51, 53
Maximilian, Archduke 44, 45
Mendès-France, Pierre (politician) 193
Metropolitan Army 9
Milan, Col. Francesco 47, 48, 50, 51
Minnaert, Sergeant 68, 69
Monclar, Gen. Ralph see Magrin-Verneret
More Majorem 140
Morin, Lt. Jacques 173
Mortar 99
Mouliney, Captain 70, 71
Murette 129
Musket model 1816/1822 15
Mutiny 107

Napoléon III 31–60
Nasser, Pres. Gamal Abdel 198, 202
Négrier, Col. François 65, 66, 67, 72, 108
Nieger, Lieutenant-Colonel 112
Nom de guerre 13

Panhard AML car 207
Panhard ERC Sagaie 231
Pavillons Noirs 67, 74
Percussion model 1857 rifle 43
Pétain, Marshal Philippe 107, 109, 126, 127, 144, 146, 155
Peter I of Serbia 57
Pieds-Noirs 194, 196, 200, 204, 212, 217
Pieron, Colonel 115
Piroth, Colonel 190
Porter, Cole 101
Pourquet, Charles (sculptor) 136

Ranavalona (queen of Hovas) 80
Raphanaud, Captain 176
Renault FT 17 tank 99
Renault VAB 228
Revolutionary warfare 167
Rollet, Legion Inspector Paul 107, 108, 109, 110, 111, 134, 135, 136, 158
Rommel, Lt.-Gen. Erwin 147, 150, 151
Royal étranger 120

Saadi, Yacef 204, 206
Saint-Arnaud, Marshal 33
Salan, Gen. Raoul 186, 187, 212, 214, 216
Salaud 122
Seeger, Alan 101, 105
Segretain, Capt. Pierre 173, 209
Seven-flamed grenade 37
Shaffee M24 tank 191
Soult, Marshal Nicolas 11
Stoffel, Col. Christoph Anton von 13, 14
Stoßtruppen 110

Tanezrouft 85
Thiers, Pres. Adolphe 60
Thompson submachine gun 160
Travers, Susan 150
Trench warfare 93, 94, 95
TRP light mountain gun 123
Tuyen Quang, siege of 69–72

Viénot, Colonel 35
Vilain, Second-Lieutenant 47, 50, 51, 53
Villiers-Mor, Lieutenant-Colonel 143

Weasel M29 C amphibious vehicle 177
Wilaya 195
Wilhelm II (emperor of Germany) 92
Winchester M1 carbine 169

Zeller, Gen. André 212, 214

www.ingramcontent.com/pod-product-compliance
Lightning Source LLC
Chambersburg PA
CBHW081550300426
44116CB00015B/2825